RELIGION, IDENTITY AND POWER

Edinburgh Studies on Modern Turkey

Series General Editors: **Alpaslan Özerdem**, Dean of the School for Conflict Analysis and Resolution and Professor of Peace and Conflict Studies at George Mason University, and **Ahmet Erdi Öztürk**, Lecturer in International Relations and Politics at London Metropolitan University and a Marie Sklodowska-Curie Fellow at Coventry University in the UK and GIGA in Germany.

Series Advisory Board: Ayşe Kadıoğlu (Sabancı University), Hakan Yavuz (University of Utah), Samim Akgönül (University of Strasbourg), Rebecca Bryant (Utrecht University), Nukhet Ahu Sandal (Ohio University), Mehmet Gurses (Florida Atlantic University), Paul Kubicek (Oakland University), Sinem Akgul Acıkmeşe (Kadir Has University), Gareth Jenkins (Institute for Security and Development Policy), Stephen Karam (World Bank), Peter Mandaville (George Mason University).

Edinburgh Studies on Modern Turkey is an outlet for academic works that examine the domestic and international issues of the Turkish republic from its establishment in the 1920s until the present. This broadly defined frame allows the series to adopt both interdisciplinary and trans-disciplinary approaches, covering research on the country's history and culture as well as political, religious and socio-economic developments.

Published and Forthcoming Titles
Policing Slums in Turkey: Crime, Resistance and the Republic on the Margin
Çağlar Dölek

Islamic Theology in the Turkish Republic
Philip Dorroll

The Kurds in Erdoğan's Turkey: Balancing Identity, Resistance and Citizenship
William Gourlay

Peace Processes in Northern Ireland and Turkey: Rethinking Conflict Resolution
İ. Aytaç Kadioğlu

The Decline of the Ottoman Empire and the Rise of the Turkish Republic: Observations of an American Diplomat, 1919–1927
Hakan Özoğlu

Religion, Identity and Power: Turkey and the Balkans in the Twenty-first Century
Ahmet Erdi Öztürk

Electoral Integrity in Turkey
Emre Toros

Erdoğan: The Making of an Autocrat
M. Hakan Yavuz
edinburghuniversitypress.com/series/esmt

RELIGION, IDENTITY AND POWER

Turkey and the Balkans in the Twenty-first Century

Ahmet Erdi Öztürk

EDINBURGH
University Press

To my wife Bahar and our gorgeous daughter Isabella Perin

Edinburgh University Press is one of the leading university presses in the UK. We publish academic books and journals in our selected subject areas across the humanities and social sciences, combining cutting-edge scholarship with high editorial and production values to produce academic works of lasting importance. For more information visit our website: edinburghuniversitypress.com

Edinburgh University Press Ltd
The Tun – Holyrood Road
12(2f) Jackson's Entry
Edinburgh EH8 8PJ

Typeset in 11/15 Adobe Garamond by
IDSUK (DataConnection) Ltd, and
printed and bound by CPI Group (UK) Ltd,
Croydon, CR0 4YY

A CIP record for this book is available from the British Library

ISBN 978 1 4744 7468 9 (hardback)
ISBN 978 1 4744 7471 9 (webready PDF)
ISBN 978 1 4744 7470 2 (epub)

CONTENTS

FIGURES AND TABLES

Figures

Tables

ABBREVIATIONS

AKP	Adalet ve Kalkınma Partisi (Justice and Development Party)
ALSAR	Alternativa e së Ardhmes (Alternative for the Future)
ANAP	Anavatan Partisi (Motherland Party)
AP	Adalet Partisi (Justice Party)
BESA	Lëvizja Besa (BESA Movement)
CHP	Cumhuriyet Halk Partisi (Republican People's Party)
CIDA	Canadian International Development Agency
CKPM	Cumhuriyetçi Köylü Millet Partisi (Republican Villagers Nation Party)
CUP	İttihat ve Terakki Cemiyeti (Committee of Union and Progress)
DOST	Демократи за отговорност, свобода и толерантност (Democrats for Responsibility, Solidarity and Tolerance)
DP	Demokrat Parti (Democrat Party)
DYP	Doğru Yol Partisi (True Path Party)
EEC	European Economic Community
EU	European Union
GTZ	Deutsche Gesellschaft für Technische Zusammenarbeit (German Society for International Cooperation)
HDP	Halkların Demokratik Partisi (People's Democratic Party)

HÖH   Движение за права и свободи (Movement for Rights and
         Freedoms)
HSYK   Hakimler ve Savcılar Yüksek Kurulu (Council of Judges and
         Prosecutors)
IMF   International Monetary Fund
IRC   Исламската Верска Заедница во Македонија (Islamic
         Religious Community of North Macedonia)
İHH   İnsani Yardım Vakfı (Foundation for Human Rights and
         Freedoms and Humanitarian Relief)
JICA   日本国際協力機構 (Japan International Cooperation
         Agency)
KAICIID King Abdullah bin Abdulaziz International Centre for
         Interreligious and Intercultural Dialogue
KCK   Koma Civakên Kurdistan (Kurdistan Communities Union)
MC   Milliyetçi Cephe (National Front)
MHP   Milliyetçi Hareket Partisi (National Action Party)
MİT   Milli İstihbarat Teşkilatı (National Intelligence Agency)
MNP   Milli Nizam Partisi (National Order Party)
MSP   Milli Selamet Partisi (National Salvation Party)
NATO   North Atlantic Treaty Organization
OECD   The Organisation for Economic Co-operation and
         Development
PDIU   Partia Drejtësi, Integrim dhe Unitet (Party for Justice
         Integration and Unity)
PKK   Partiya Karkerên Kurdistanê (Kurdistan Workers' Party)
RP   Refah Partisi (Welfare Party)
TBMM   Türkiye Büyük Millet Meclisi (Grand National Assembly
         of Turkey)
TDP   Демократска партија на Турците (Turkish Democratic
         Party)
TDV   Türkiye Diyanet Vakfı (Turkish Diyanet Foundation)
THP   Движење на националните единици (Turkish National
         Unity Movement)
TİKA   Türk İşbirliği ve Koordinasyon Ajansı Başkanlığı (Turkish
         Cooperation and Coordination Agency)

TİP   Türkiye İşçi Partisi (Workers' Party of Turkey)
TİS   Türk İslam Sentezi (Turkish-Islamic Synthesis)
UETD   Avrupalı Türk Demokratlar Birliği (Union of European
           Turkish Democrats)
UNESCO   United Nations Educational, Scientific and Cultural
           Organization
USAID   United States Agency for International Development
YEE   Yunus Emre Enstitüsü (Yunus Emre Institution)
YTB   Yurtdışı Türkler ve Akraba Topluluklar Başkanlığı (Presidency
           for Turks Abroad and Related Communities)

ACKNOWLEDGEMENTS

Around ten years ago, when I completed my first master's degree at Hacettepe University in Ankara, I never would have guessed that my academic life would have brought – or, perhaps, dragged – me to where I am today. At the time, my goal was to finish my doctorate in Turkey and work as an academic at a Turkish university. But life truly is what happens to you while you're busy making other plans; as I look back now, I might suggest that this phrase precisely describes the life of an academic. If somebody were to tell me, a young graduate student awaiting nothing more than a future in Turkey, that one day I would write the acknowledgements for my book as its sole author in an office in Rugby after putting my daughter to sleep with my beloved partner, I would have probably said, after a fit of laughs, that I had no time to waste with such dreams and changed the subject. But this is exactly how my situation played out, though I supposed differently than intended or imagined.

But if someone were to tell that same graduate student that the academic life was challenging and entailed more than just reading, writing, thinking and researching, I would never have believed them. I can say, after ten years have passed, that the academic life has two completely distinct yet intertwined facets. One of the coin's two sides is challenging, truly arduous. It demands resistance and struggling against loneliness, silence, hopelessness and always different things. The prevailing conditions for academics around the world are quite gruelling; finding jobs, obtaining scholarships and producing articles is both onerous and contentious. You must turn inward, into a profound silence, to accomplish these. But if you're lucky and gain a little visibility, you have many 'professors' who, rather than view you as someone struggling to work, position you as a challenger and seek to stunt your personal growth. This accompanies a constant battle, a practice of resistance. But, if you come from a place – like Turkey – in which instability has recently been repositioned as stability, and where everything begins to crumble with political intoxication, and if you essentially study that area, struggling with and resisting political pressures that target you, your friends and your colleagues just become part of the job. The first side of the coin compels us to turn the struggle into a daily practice, to rebel against arrogance, inferiority complexes, jealousy, slander, and gossip. In doing all this, it demands that we produce quality work, without pause, just to keep our heads above water.

The second side of the coin, in my opinion, is to see its first side and realise, while holding our heads high, the products of our labour. Because whatever happens, nobody can cope with the coin's first side alone, and solidarity is essential in myriad forms. I define myself as an individual who experiences the first side of the coin each day but who is always aware of its second side. I would thus like to thank the people who contributed to this book you hold in your hands, whose help ultimately has allowed me to write these words after these past ten difficult years. Because if they had not been on the second side of the coin, I surely would have been lost in the darkness of the first, and you wouldn't be reading these words.

I want to primarily thank people here. If today, I am a scholar who has laid the scholarly foundation for modern Turkey and, moreover, the convoluted relationship between religion, society and politics, İştar Gözaydın would certainly come to mind first. This foundation no doubt reveals itself both in this book and in every word of my other studies. Second, from what I can gather, it is either a responsibility or a tradition to start here with one's PhD advisor, but these acknowledgements are neither a responsibility nor an obligation. They are purely the product of my own appreciation. I would like to stress my gratitude to Samim Akgönül, my advisor, mentor and senior fellow. The smile spreading across my face as I write this accompanies my heartfelt appreciation. He took me under his wing at a difficult time and helped me become the person I have always wanted to be. He has been at times an uncompromising advisor and at other times an older brother, contributing not only to my thesis but also to my overall thinking. He did a truly great thing for me. He patiently guided me and walked me through the issues, asking much more than just the questions I had. That, I will never forget.

Since so many people contributed to my work on this book, I would like to mention them briefly. Without being too much of a bore, I ask that you at least read some of the book in order to understand who these people are. Although I had to chase Fatih Ceran even more than I chased my interview subjects, without his 'third eye' and persistent nagging, it would have been impossible for me to be where I am today. Standing by my side and all the while pushing me, as true friends do, Salih Doğan and Taptuk Emre Erkoç will always hold a distinguished place in the formation of this book and in my life. Yasemin Aydın helped me with crucial issues in my field-work. The process of writing this book introduced me to countless friends who have helped me as mentors, teachers, co-authors or confidantes. Their company will remain with me forever. Among them are Bülent Somay, Ezgi Keskinsoy, Karabekir Akkoyunlu, Senem Aydın-Düzgit, Chiara Maritato, Ayşe Kadıoğlu, Levent Köker, Ioannis Armakolas, Nil Mutluer, Eda Ayaydın, Tuba Çandar, Cengiz Çandar, Ömer Tekdemir, Ayşe Betül Çelik, Pinar Dinc, Ömer Turan, Semiha Sözeri, Begüm Zorlu, Emre İşeri, Onur Bakıner, Vera Eccarius-Kelly, Dilek Çınar and Ibrahim Sirkeci.

It is an unspoken requirement of international academia to produce work over and above a dissertation, so I have tried to follow suit like a tidy nerd, as much as I could. I must mention Jonathan Fox, Daniel Philpott, Nukhet Ahu Sandal, Guy Ben-Porat, Jocelyne Cesari, Mehmet Gurses, Hakan Yavuz, Peter Mandeville, and Luca Ozzano, as they read my op-ed pieces, articles, reports and other writing and, from their positions as prominent scholars of religion, politics and Turkish studies, provided valuable insight and criticism. More importantly, they never turned me down as the rookie that I was. I would like to thank all these distinguished scholars, and I hope one day for the opportunity to collaborate more deeply and intellectually with them. If I were to highlight one person in particular among these names, it would be Jeffrey Haynes, an exemplary mentor, colleague, intellectual and friend through his writing, working discipline and behaviour towards less experienced academics such as myself. Without his contributions, it is likely that I would have been unable to write much of what I did, and I would not be where I am today. I hope I have the opportunity to work with him for many years to come.

I spent periods of my research time in Slovenia, France, the United Kingdom, the United States and Sweden. If I have learned anything at all about the Balkans, it is thanks to Mitja Velikonja from Ljubljana University and Florian Bieber from the University of Graz. Vincente Fortier, Stéphane de Tapia and Anne-Laure Zwilling provided the perfect academic atmosphere for me at the University of Strasbourg and supported me whenever I needed it. Marianne Erhart and Stephane Coly also helped me significantly during my days at Strasbourg. Furthermore, I twice received scholarship support from the Swedish Research Institute during my last year of study and had the chance to meet great colleagues, such as Branka Likic-Brboris, Carl Ulrik Schierup, Aleksandra Alund, Anders Neergaard and Charles Woolfson at REMESO at Linköping University. During my tenure as a post-doctoral visiting scholar at the University of Notre Dame's Kroc Institute, Perin Gurel, Elena Stavrevska, Marcos Scauso, Caroline Wilson Scauso and Garrett FitzGerald were like a family to me. And finally, during the final days when I was completing this book, I learned that I had won the prestigious Marie Curie Individual Fellowship, which will help me conduct further research on religion and global politics, and I will always be grateful to Heaven Crawley for her support with my application for this award. My warm and beloved friends in the UK, Cihan Dizdaroglu, Durukan Kuzu, Dzeneta Karabegovic, Jessica Northey and Julie Northey, supported me when I needed it. I would like to thank each of them for everything they did for me.

This entire process was crowned with two beautiful events. First was establishing the Edinburgh University Press Series on Modern Turkey with Alpaslan Özerdem, whom I find great pleasure in working with and who has always guided me in my academic career. I would especially like to thank him along with the whole Edinburgh University Press family, particularly Nicola Ramsey and Emma Rees, with whom we worked. Second, the pages of the book were written at London Metropolitan University, a place that became my home, changing my life since September 2019. I would like to thank all my family members here in this home, especially Jo Skinner, Andrew Moran, Mark Wheeler, Don MacRaild and Wendy Stokes.

When I left my country to conduct academic research, I always felt a sense of trust. My mother and father – Nükhet and Kemal Öztürk – were fixated on my studies and, at times, neglected themselves to do what was best for me. The souls of this happy couple, growing anxious with every imperfection in my voice, are evident in each sentence of this dissertation. If it were not for their ceaseless support, I would never have seen through to the end of this book. Their co-star, my uncle Ertuğrul, is also deserving of an award. I also would like to thank Başers – Nihat, Nursel and Burçe – for their important support.

For some, the academic life is 'cool and prestigious'. But it actually entails a bit of loneliness, a feeling of insecurity, anxiety for the future, economic problems and some unhappiness stemming from all these. However, I was lucky to have met my best friend, my love, my beloved wife Bahar Başer. Without her care, understanding, experience and love, it would all have been in vain. Academic positions, scholarships, articles, books and ideas are all gifts of the academic life, no doubt about that. But the greatest gift of all is my partner in life. I appreciate her very existence more than anything I could ever imagine.

But there's more than that: my darling baby girl Isabella Perin, who slept in her mother's belly during the most complicated phases of this book has turned just one month old – and is in fact sleeping one storey beneath me as I write these words. I can't tell how far she is aware of this process, but my only wish is that she understands how much I love her. With her arrival in our lives, the two-sided academic world I described above transformed into a tool to maintain her happiness and future. I hope that, in the future, she reads these words once again with her mother and understands the riveting emotions I feel as I dedicate this book both to her and her mother Bahar.

Hoping that she grows up with her mother in a more beautiful world, I dedicate this book, with all errors being my own, to Isabella Perin and my wife and colleague who protects her, Bahar Başer. I hope for them always to be with me in life.

Ahmet Erdi Öztürk
Rugby, England
February 2020

FOREWORD

Turkey is a country with an active and wide-ranging foreign policy. Over the last two decades, the country has become a major international actor, and during that time its international influence has grown considerably. For many years, it seemed that Turkey's main foreign policy goal was to join the European Union (EU). When the likelihood of achieving that goal receded almost to the point of invisibility following sustained and vocal hostility from several EU member states, Turkey's government began to look elsewhere for foreign policy wins.

Turkey is one of the few countries with an explicit Islamist orientation but without a stated aim of achieving what Islamists are said to desire: an 'Islamic state'. Quite what such a state is, however, open to question, not least because the number of such states that might be described as 'Islamist' is tiny: Iran, Saudi Arabia and, for a while, Sudan. So, what ideology does the Turkish government exhibit in its foreign policy? How does it express what might be called its 'quiet' Islamism in international relations?

Despite growing interest in Turkey's foreign policy, very few – if any – scholarly studies have sought to answer this question definitively – until now. This book, for which I have the honour to write the foreword, examines Turkey's attempts to wield soft power in international relations through a focus on the country's recent foreign policy in relation to its Balkan neighbours. Dr Ahmet Erdi Öztürk book's main contention is that Turkey has sought to use Islam-oriented religious soft power in the Balkans in order to acquire and retain enhanced standing and prestige with a view to building its power and authority in the region.

This comprehensive and well-written book began life as a PhD thesis. I had the honour of being one of the external examiners of the thesis. In a long academic career, I have examined more than thirty doctoral theses and this was one of the best that I have seen. I am delighted that Dr Öztürk has seen fit to convert the thesis into a book for much wider circulation than most PhDs achieve and I commend Edinburgh University Press for publishing the volume.

Religious Soft Power and International Relations: The Case of Turkey

The book's starting point is that religious soft power is important in international relations, although very little sustained research has as yet been undertaken into the phenomenon. Öztürk's book not only exhaustively delineates Turkey's efforts in this respect but also suggests a potential avenue for future research on this issue. Thus, the main purpose of the book is twofold: (1) to examine and account for Turkey's attempts to use religious soft power among its neighbours in the Balkans, and (2) to suggest ideas for future research on the role of religious soft power in contexts beyond the single, albeit important, case of contemporary Turkey.

The background to the book is that many observers and analysts of international relations agree that it is now impossible to ignore the international influence of religion. Yet while it is widely accepted that there is a widespread international religious resurgence affecting international relations (Fox and Sandler 2004; Haynes 2013), it is far from clear just *how* religion does this. Voll (2008: 262) refers to a useful starting point in this respect, noting the growth in importance of religious soft power consequent to major changes in 'the structure of world affairs and global interactions', following the end of the Cold War and the subsequent implosion of the Soviet Union. Voll also sees its importance '[b]oth in terms of actual operations and the ways that those operations are conceived and understood by analysts'. As a result, 'the old systems of relationships are passing rapidly'. Arquilla and Ronfeldt (1999: ix) emphasise that 'soft power' is notable 'across many political, economic, and military areas . . . taking precedence over traditional, material "hard power"'.

To this list of areas where soft power is influential, we can add religious soft power and its influence on international relations.

Some non-state religious actors seek to enhance their influence via transnational networks. For example, extremist transnational Islamist actors, such as Al-Qaeda and more recently, Islamic State, use soft power to 'enhance' their strength (Voll 2008: 15; also see Haynes 2005). Another way that religion can affect international outcomes is via often 'significant influence on domestic politics. It is a motivating force that guides many policy makers' (Fox and Sandler 2004: 168). Finally, as this book makes abundantly clear, foreign policy too can be affected by religious soft power.

Contemporary examples of religious soft power in international relations often focus on the impact of transnational, non-state religious actors. Öztürk cleverly takes a different approach, focusing on the influence of religious soft power in Turkey's foreign policy. The country's government seeks to influence international outcomes via its foreign policy use of policies informed by religious and cultural tenets and beliefs. Over the last few years, Turkey has encouraged neighbouring countries in the Balkans to respond positively to the former's religious soft-power-based foreign policy, via an ideology based on religious and cultural beliefs, norms and values.

How might such influence be wielded? Why should secular policy-makers in Turkey's neighbouring countries listen to Turkey's religiously and culturally oriented appeals for closer ties and better relations? Katzenstein (1996) suggests a useful starting point when he refers to the general importance of religious and cultural norms and identity in contemporary international relations. Rejecting both neorealism and neoliberalism because of their focus on the physical capabilities of states and institutions, Katzenstein (1996) suggests that explaining apparently inconsistent or irrational foreign and national security policies can depend on factoring in the influential norms, collective identities and cultures of the relevant societies from whence the policies emerge. The often close relation between religion and culture is exploited by the Turkish government in its foreign policies in relation to its Balkan neighbours in order to achieve foreign policy goals designed to improve the country's national status, position and prestige.

Dr Öztürk's meticulously researched, clearly argued and well-structured book breaks new ground in the understanding not only of Turkey's contemporary domestic and foreign policy but also more generally in how religious soft power can be a potent tool to achieve wider foreign policy goals. Anyone with an interest in the role of religion in international relations and global politics, in Turkey's changing foreign policy, and in how countries win, build and embed status and prestige would read this book with great benefit.

Jeffrey Haynes
Emeritus Professor of Politics at
London Metropolitan University

References

Arquilla, John, and David F. Ronfeldt (1999) *The Emergence of Neopolitik: Toward an American Information Strategy* (Santa Monica: RAND).

Fox, Jonathan, and Shmuel Sandler (2004) *Bringing Religion into International Relations* (Basingstoke: Palgrave Macmillan).

Haynes, Jeffrey (2005) 'Al-Qaeda: Ideology and action', *Critical Review of International Social and Political Philosophy*, 8, no. 2, 177–91.

Haynes, Jeffrey (2013) *Religious Transnational Actors and Soft Power* (Aldershot: Ashgate).

Katzenstein, Peter (ed.) (1996) *The Culture of National Security: Norms and Identity in World Politics* (New York: Columbia University Press).

Voll, John (2008) 'Trans-state Muslim movements and militant extremists in an era of soft power', in Thomas Banchoff (ed.), *Religious Pluralism, Globalization and World Politics* (New York: Oxford University Press), pp. 253–74.

INTRODUCTION
TURKEY AND THE BALKANS IN THE NEW MILLENNIUM: RELIGION, IDENTITY AND POWER

'Turkey is back!' Since the beginning of the 2000s, a considerable number of semi-academic and academic productions, echoing popular opinion, have been building around this theme with regard to the role of the Turkish Republic in the Balkan Peninsula and its social, cultural, economic and religious ramifications. Some claim that the policies of the successive AKP (Justice and Development Party – Adalet ve Kalkınma Partisi) governments and the political strategies of President Recep Tayyip Erdoğan concerning the Balkans have long been energised by Turkey's desire to re-establish political, economic, religious and cultural hegemony in the region through various neo-imperialist and neo-colonial projects, and to foresee the revitalisation of the multifaceted Ottoman legacy.[1] Others argue that Turkey and the Balkans have reached the peak of their mutually beneficial relations, economic enlargement and proactive utilisation of the transnational state apparatus on the part of Turkey.[2] Indeed, all of these claims are quite predictable and not very complicated, but some of the issues between Turkey and the Balkans are anything but simple. Some are actually very controversial. For instance, one such assertion has been voiced by Herbert Raymond McMaster, former national security advisor to US president Donald Trump, who accused Turkey of spreading what he called extreme Islamist ideologies around the world. Beyond that, regarding Turkey's Balkan policies, he declared, 'We're seeing great involvement by Turkey from everywhere from West Africa to Southeast Asia . . . particularly the Balkans is an area of grave concern now'.[3] Similar ideas have been expressed by other experts on the Balkans and political actors over the last couple of years, and it is difficult to turn a blind eye to these cumulative claims. In a variety of forms, the significance and controversy of religion in relations between Turkey and the Balkans have become more visible and more determinant since the beginning of the new millennium.

In light of these ideas, in this book I scrutinise Turkey's increasing involvement and activism, seeking to uncover the role of its religion- and power-oriented identity reflections in the Balkans in the 2000s. The book aims to illuminate this aspect of Turkey's relations with its Balkan neighbours, in the context of the broader shift in domestic and foreign policy under the changeable political faces of the AKP regime, from a realist–secular orientation to an adventurist and ambivalent one featuring the coercive, ethno-nationalist Sunnification[4] of the state identity. It endeavours to explain the complex relations between religion, state identity and Sunnification in Turkey as they reflect on state power resources in various and complicated ways. This work also argues that Turkey's increasingly authoritarian-reactive domestic and reactive foreign policy and overtly Islam-based discourse cannot simply be regarded as benign (in this context, religious) soft power, but on the contrary should be defined as ambivalent religious soft power. To analyse how these concepts have been utilised and how their presence has been received locally, the book draws on fieldwork conducted between 2015 and the early months of 2019, including almost 130 semi-structured elite interviews with experts, political actors, diplomats, religious leaders and scholars as well as journalists in the three case countries – the Republic of Bulgaria, the Republic of North Macedonia and the Republic of Albania – as well as in Turkey.

A Researcher's Journey in the Balkans: Why This Topic?

In 2015 and 2016, for more than twenty months I made my home in Ljubljana, the capital of Slovenia, and used it as the main base for direct observatory fieldwork in various parts of the Balkans, ranging from regions where Turkey has a clear influence to those where it is a middle-sized actor at best. Ljubljana itself is an example of the latter category, Turkey being an ineffective actor there. I would argue that Ljubljana is one of the most Europeanised capitals of the Balkans with very limited Turkish influence;

yet even there it is possible to single out cases that are worth mentioning. In the icy winter of 2015, I went to the gym, which is a five-minute walk from the central Prešeren Square. Entering the main door, I was assailed by familiar imagery: the popular Turkish television series *The Magnificent Century*[5] was being broadcast on all screens. With some curiosity, I asked the concierge why this programme was on television instead of the near-ubiquitous music programmes that form the sound- and videoscape of fitness centres worldwide. In her reply, the concierge expressed her infatuation with the Ottoman clothes and courtly love, as well as actual Ottoman culture. She also underlined that the history of the Ottomans is a crowd-puller these days among both the Muslim Slovenian citizens and everyone else in the Balkans.

This short reminiscence reveals many things about the different and increasing types of soft power and cultural influence exerted by Turkey in the Balkans. Turkey's impact is moreover not limited to the popularity of its soap operas and the repackaging of old memories in a fancy new wrapper: some of the pro-AKP media organs are constantly promoting the 'new Turkey' vision in the eyes of the 'others'[6] through heavily indoctrinated broadcasts and publications. Beyond these points, the common elements shared between positive and negative perspectives revealed in my fieldwork were Turkey's economic investments, political influence, activism through various transnational state apparatuses, and the instrumentalisation of Ottoman nostalgia as a policy tool. However, above all, one other issue has been in the limelight: ethno-religious discourses and policies and their instrumentalisation in the Balkans by the AKP's 'new Turkey'.

From the very beginning of my residence in the Balkan region, many of the people I spoke with said I should talk to the *Baklavacı Teyze* (the old woman who has a sweet pastry shop) in the Old Bazaar (Стара чаршија) of the North Macedonian capital Skopje. In March 2017 (and later in January 2019), I had the opportunity to do so. Her tiny shop was full of pictures of Erdoğan as well as a middle-sized Turkish flag and a calendar of Turkey's Presidency of Religious Affairs (Diyanet). After a couple of minutes of warm-up conversation, she learned I am from Turkey and that my name is *Ahmet*. She then asked me two direct questions: 'Are you a Muslim?' and 'Do you like Erdoğan?' Without waiting for the responses, she pointed out that if I am a Turk and love Erdoğan, I must be a good Muslim, and one single baklava was free of charge for me. She made it clear that religion and admiration of Erdoğan are central to everything. She talked about Erdoğan as if he were the world's only religious figurehead and a true leader, referring to him as 'my son' and 'my leader'. She supposed Erdoğan had been praying every Friday in Hagia Sophia[7] in Istanbul, which according to her is the biggest symbol of the salvation of Muslims by Erdoğan. Even though she did not clearly explain from whom Erdoğan would save her, along with the rest of the Muslims, an educated guess would indicate that she meant salvation from *gavur* – the infidel.[8] Although loaded with factual mistakes,[9] her utterances were resourceful in their perceptions about Turkey's religious role and Erdoğan's identity as a Muslim leader. This particular example typifies both the role of religion in the Balkans, where it has gained global prominence especially since the Iranian revolution, and its undeniable influence and motivational power over individuals.[10]

Figure I.1   *Baklavacı Teyze* in Skopje. Photo by the author with the consent of the shopkeeper.

Even though the exact number of Muslims in the Balkans is unknown due to the high level of migration and population change, almost every single Balkan country has a significant Muslim population. In Bulgaria, both Muslims and Turkic-originated Bulgarians historically constitute significant components of the population.[11] After almost five centuries of Ottoman rule, Bulgaria gained independence in 1878, and defined the remaining Muslims and Turks as 'others' in its nation-building process. They were mostly alienated from politics and bureaucracy. Even though some of the legal regulations took religious and national identities under protection during the communist period (1946–90), Bulgarian Muslims suffered due to the prohibitions on mother-tongue education, Turkish names and Islamic practices. After the assimilation campaign led by Todor Zhivkov, the first secretary of the Central Committee of the Bulgarian Communist Party, between 1981 and 1989, reinstating the rights of the Turks and Pomaks was among the first democratic acts of the new regime in Bulgaria.

In April 2017, Mihail Ivanov, one of the chief advisors on minority rights to Zhelyu Zhelev, the first post-communist president of Bulgaria between 1990 and 1997, underlined that their aim at the time was to establish a democratic Bulgaria, and they knew they had to provide religious services for Muslims. However, they did not have enough financial resources and educated staff, and they realised that the Jordanians and the Saudis wanted to create an influence on the Muslims of Bulgaria. This possibility was frightening for the Bulgarian administration, since these actors might radicalise the Muslim population. Therefore, at the beginning of the 1990s they requested the assistance of 'secular', modest Turkey and its Diyanet.[12] However, these days Ivanov and most of his advisors are revisiting the wisdom of their decisions since they do not see the new Turkey as a modest, secular country; they are blaming themselves for having invited in a political and very disputable understanding of politicised Islam. They are also aware that they cannot simply send Turkey away, but its continued presence in their country will be difficult for Bulgarian policy-makers.

That there is an overlap between Ivanov's concerns and McMaster's claims regarding financial support supplied by Turkey to 'radical-extreme' Islamic groups in the Balkans may be debatable, but one point can be conceded: Turkey is no longer defined as an indisputably secular country by many political elites, either local or international. The common point in the otherwise opposing views of the *Baklavacı Teyze* and Ivanov is Turkey's increasing religious impact in the region. The radical changes in Turkey's domestic and foreign policy have the capacity to impact the Balkans very readily due to historical ties, kinship relations and Turkey's influence on the region via various transnational state apparatuses. However, considering Turkey as a non-secular country signifies a historic extreme in the socio-political transformation the country has recently been going through, which is reflected in the Balkans' perceptions of the country. Therefore, the conditions are ripe to ask some broader questions regarding the role of religion in state identity transformations, the impact of these transformations on perceptions of the state, and whether Turkey's multi-layered transformations and different perceptions of the Balkan countries regarding the AKP's Turkey constitute unique examples of these complicated relations.

After some critical socio-political junctions of the power struggle in Turkey, the AKP strengthened its position both politically and within the strong bureaucracy, at least until the very beginning of the 2020s. Since late 2013, having no significant competitor, the party has started implementing more ethno-religious-oriented and reactive policies both at home and abroad. Particularly, Erdoğan has instrumentalised some of the exceptional situations to obtain more power in the state structure and expand his electoral base, and this has led to multi-layered transformations that has affected both the party and the state. Some of the old historical apprehensions, biases and frustrations exhibited by Turkey as a middle power has infected the AKP. Moreover, Erdoğan has seen the party's socio-political fears and ethno-religious desires as inalienably linked to state power. As the dominant political actor, the AKP has begun to transform the state structure and its transnational apparatuses alongside state identity. As a result of this two-pronged transformation, Turkey has become a state with hegemony over its society, yet at the same time it is a weak and fragile state with authoritarian rule.[13] Sunni Islam, ethno-nationalist discourse and authoritarianism, under pragmatic political strategies, has become the focal point for bolstering this new regime, which has marginalised any social and political opposition. The Erdoğan administration has internalised almost all the behavioural patterns of the old Kemalist Turkey and utilised them in its hegemonic project of transformation of the state. It has also added the element of Islam to both domestic and foreign policy in very pragmatic ways. With their appropriation and management via the state structure, Sunni Islam and nationalist discourse have become both instrument and purpose of the new regime. The Turkish secularisation project has been replaced by a pragmatic ethno-nationalist, coercive Sunnification of state identity, and therefore the question remains: Did this pragmatic Sunnification constitute a pro-Sunni sectarian foreign policy? If the answer is yes, then was the Balkan region a suitable and desirable area for the AKP's Turkey to implement this policy?

Whether Turkey has been using pro-Sunni and Turkist-Ottomanist foreign policy in the Balkans remains debated, but it is obvious that domestic coercive Sunnification on an ethno-nationalist basis has brought new discussions on to the agenda of various groups and elites in the Balkans. In our interview in April 2017, Genc Pollo, the former minister of innovation, technology and communication in Albania between 2009 and 2013, underlined a common point of view regarding the AKP's transformation as it appears from the Balkans. According to him, at the very beginning of the AKP's journey, Erdoğan's pro-EU and pro-democratic perspectives were welcomed by the Balkan elites; and the AKP's political strategy, which indicated that Islam was compatible with democracy, was also an antidote for some of the fundamentalist movements in the region. But especially after 2010, with its pro-Islamist ideas, its aggressive tone towards the EU, its reactive political strategies and authoritarianism, the AKP's Turkey started to lose both influence and prestige in the region.

Even though Pollo gives an idea of the general outlook of the AKP's journey and of local actors' perceptions in the Balkans, this does not represent all the views regarding Turkey's transformation of Turkey. Likewise, there are different perspectives in the region about the role of religion in power relations in Turkey and its recent identity transformation. According to these other perspectives, many times in my interview notes I recorded that Erdoğan's Turkey is more aggressive, reactive and somewhat more religious compared to previous days, but this is the correct policy under the contemporary regional and global conditions. This camp also claims that Turkey is a Muslim-majority country, and that there are many Muslims and Turks in the Balkans, Europe and all around the world who support Erdoğan because of his political behaviours and protective policies for his country and religion. These policies have made him a powerful actor in the region. All of these polarised ideas, I believe, make the Balkan image of the AKP's new Turkey a subject that can be scrutinised most fruitfully using an interdisciplinary approach.

The Puzzle and the Scope of This Book

Even though religious identity remains significant for many people – as do other 'old' identities[14] – and even though religion has long been a salient force in world politics, scholarly interest in the role of religion in international relations and foreign policy remained quite limited until the last quarter of the twentieth century.[15] With events such as the rise of Al-Qaeda and the so-called Islamic State, the terrorist acts against *Charlie Hebdo* and ethno-religious conflicts all around the world, however, scholars have started to focus on the role of religion in global politics.[16] The role of state identities provides a natural entry point for research on the role of ethno-religious dynamics in global politics[17] since many states have used these particular communalities to define their collective state identity. Despite the emerging critique of secularisation over the past two decades, most countries still define themselves either as constitutionally secular or as endorsing no official religion.[18] Nevertheless, religion and its subsidiary components, such as ethnicity, remain a key source of national identity for many states, laying the ground for their instrumentalisation by political elites in both the domestic and the international arenas.[19] Religion has an ability to shape domestic and foreign policy even if actors and decision-makers are themselves secular. Religion is also a focal point in the measurement and analysis of state power and influence in the international system. For instance, the nature of the Republic of Iran and its role in international relations would not be read without reference to its religious structure.[20] Likewise, the dynamics of the Syrian civil war and its reflection in the international environment should also be analysed alongside the conflicts between different sects of Islam.

Apart from these classical explanations, certain studies are scrutinising the various dimensions of the impact of religion in different corners of the world. For instance, while Howell demonstrates the paradoxical viability of new religious groups in Indonesian politics,[21] Ellis and Ter Haar display the slender line between religion and politics in sub-Saharan Africa.[22] What is still lacking, however, is a clear theoretical account of precisely how and to what extent religion is functional to particular domestic and foreign policy outcomes. The coexistence of religion as an identity norm, and its instrumentalisation via institutions in various ways in domestic and foreign policy-making processes, thus provides an opportunity to ask why and how particular states use their religious norms as a means of establishing power and state identity.

Regarding the role of religion in state identity and power resources, Turkey holds a unique position that needs to be more closely examined. Even though Turkey was not constitutionally a secular state in its formative years, it came to display the cumulative result of a long process of modernisation and secularisation at the state level. The official constitutional article defining Turkey as a *laik*[23] state was added in 1937, yet since the very beginning of the early Republican period the state has tried to control and regulate religion in its assigned boundaries and under state surveillance. Turkey, as a Sunni Muslim-majority country, was intended as an established as a *laik* entity, which gave it a particular attraction among some other Muslim-majority countries. The main reason for this attraction was that because of its *laik* state structure, Turkey managed to pacify most of the fundamentalist Islamist components within the country. Yet the other side of the coin was not so bright. Turkey's repressive policy preferences regarding its Muslim communities have created division among its citizens.[24] The interpretation of Islam preferred by the regime was promoted by the state apparatuses while popular interpretations of Islam were practised by Sufi traditions. Popular Islam found its venue in conservative right-wing and Islamist parties. However, the overall relations between the repressive policies of the state and manifestations of Islam outside the boundaries that it designated were fundamentally problematic.

In the context of such complicated and multi-sided relations, Turkey's November 2002 elections formed a watershed that elicited intense reaction across the political divide regarding the role of religion in both state and society. The AKP won a sizeable proportion of the popular vote and secured a majority of seats in the parliament. Having suffered weak, ineffective and unstable coalition governments for more than a decade, many appreciated the formation of a single-party government and a unified direction for the country. Nevertheless, responses to the AKP's landslide election victory were mixed. On the one hand, many observers expressed scepticism about the prospects for Turkey's *laik*, but relatively weak or semi-established democracy,[25] given the pro-Islamist roots of AKP members.[26] On the other hand, the party's victory was greeted both at home and abroad with a high degree of cautious optimism, not only because of the prospect of stable one-party government, but also because of the AKP's publicly declared commitments to EU reforms and economic stability.[27] With its well-articulated and moderate agenda on political liberalisation and democratic reforms, the AKP had created significant credibility from the outset. By this means, through almost two decades of the 2000s, the AKP established itself as the dominant electoral force in Turkey, becoming the first party in Turkey since 1957 to win more than four successive general elections. Early on, the party won kudos for its explicit public commitment to *laiklik* and its cautious approach in confronting the Kemalist bureaucratic establishment, particularly the military.

In the first two terms of AKP power, the party devoted itself to the struggle with Turkey's classical guardianship mechanism[28] by means of an unofficial and unconventional coalition with the controversial Sunni-Islamic Gülen Movement. The AKP, through its popular power, and members of the Movement in critical positions of the state bureaucracy, tried to suppress and pacify the *laikçi*-Kemalist guardianship mechanisms via legal investigations and cases.[29] This instrumentalisation of the law and judicial processes established a fear among opposition socio-political groups. Furthermore, the unconventional coalition of the AKP with the Gülen Movement engendered a new ruling cadre from a power- and interest-based collaboration, rather than establishing the elements of a more liberal democratic ideology for Turkey.[30] Yet this power- and interest-based marriage of convenience did not last long, and the Gülen Movement and the party fell out with each other in fatal ways. Although the Gülen Movement tried to downscale the power of Erdoğan and the AKP by using the media and the bureaucracy, both the man and his party survived in a stronger position, sometimes in less-than-lawful ways.[31] This fatal conflict also accelerated the transformation of Turkey that has been going on since the beginning of the second decade of the 2000s. The mutual transformations of the state bureaucracy and the AKP have created an authoritarian, ethno-nationalist and Sunni-oriented pragmatic power structure that has gained popular support, via exploitation of states of exception.[32]

According to Agamben, in a state of exception, logic and praxis become blurry and a different type of violence, without *logos*, dominates politics without any theoretical or ideological reference. In the absence of judicial autonomy, the law is exploited by powerful politicians who evolve into exceptional leaders by seizing exceptional authority in times of crisis.[33] In a similar vein, Erdoğan exploited political crises to establish himself further in powerful positions and this paved the way for exceptional leadership mechanisms.

Turkey's rapid political transformation has thus been formative in multiple dimensions. Nowhere is this truer than in the domain of foreign policy, which used to manifest in a realist orientation centred on three enduring principles: Westernisation, commitment to a stable international order and strict adherence to law. After 2002, however, scholars noted Turkey's more active culturally and ideologically driven foreign policy, primarily in its immediate region but also globally.[34] The instrumentalisation of history, culture and ethno-religious components under the influence of the former prime minister and foreign minister Ahmet Davutoğlu, and his foreign policy doctrine of strategic depth,[35] have been the motivating force behind this shift. The novelty of Davutoğlu's perspective lies its definition of Turkey as a state neither at the periphery of Europe nor at the periphery of the Middle East. Rather, Turkey sits prominently at the crossroads of the two continents and is thus a pivotal country due to its unique geographical, historical and cultural links with both regions. With such a mindset, the AKP has shifted Turkey's foreign policy by defining itself as the inheritor of long-standing Ottoman cultural tradition, alongside its Sunni and Turkic priorities and its attempts to influence the former Ottoman territories more assertively.[36] This mindset is one of the elements forming the backbone of the pragmatic, coercive, ethno-nationalist Sunnification of the state of Turkey.

Although Erdoğan dismissed Davutoğlu as prime minister in 2016 due to domestic political struggles, the major elements of foreign policy that he built, and the reactive ethno-religious orientation of foreign policy, still remain. Erdoğan seems to be repositioning the country from a Western orientation to a vague and constantly changing Eurasian one. This reorientation has created an ambivalent identity and power formation in Turkey. The new Turkey has started to demonstrate a new state identity and policy choices wherever it is economically, strategically, culturally and religiously suitable.

The Balkans has become an important area within which to monitor this more reactive and ambivalent foreign policy of Turkey.

The Main Argument and Questions

This book has one major argument, which is that the religion–state relationship forms an important dimension of official state ideology, identity and power resources. Domestic transformations in the position of religion *vis-à-vis* state identity could alter the state's power implementations and resources in foreign policy. In short, religion (with its subsidiary elements) is a factor with the capacity to exert profound changes on the official ideology and identity of states. Changes in state identity through the device of religion transform the existing power dynamics both domestically and internationally. Therefore, in the case of Turkey, I claim that its increasingly authoritarian and overtly ethno-religious pragmatic foreign policies cannot simply be regarded as benign soft power or public diplomacy. Rather, the current shift creates varying effects on different actors in the Balkans: some groups are rather pleased with Turkey's religiously fuelled approach, while others are seriously concerned. This is why the shift is best characterised in terms of *ambivalence*. With this in mind, the primary questions that this book seeks to answer are as follows: What is the role of religion in the power structure and identity of the state in general? And how do these changes manifest themselves in various areas such as utilisation of state apparatuses, foreign policy orientations and preferences of home and host countries?

I take Turkey as testing ground to scrutinise the answers to these questions because of the transformation of its unique *laik* structure under the AKP governments, and the reflection of this transformation abroad. I decided to work on the Balkans as the case study for this research. Bulgaria, North Macedonia and Albania are a fertile control ground for the arguments of the study because of the aforementioned ties and commonalities. These three Balkan countries also invited in Turkey's transnational state apparatuses because of its *laik* state identity at the beginning of the 1990s. Thus, even though Turkey has embassies in all the Balkan countries, only three of them saw Turkey as a totally *laik* and modest state and accepted its presence internally via Turkey's primarily religious state apparatus: the Diyanet.[37] Therefore, the major questions break down into this minor one: What factors determine Turkey's scope of activity in the case of each country?

Indeed, Turkey's activities occur at the intersection of its neo-Ottoman ambitions,[38] its newly emerged kinship and diaspora policy[39] and its commitment to faith-based transnational solidarity. Therefore, while analysing the scope of Turkey's outreach in the Balkans, this book also takes into account the Turkish government-sponsored transnational state apparatuses of cultural diplomacy and cooperation, such as the Diyanet, the Turkish Cooperation and Coordination Agency (Türk İşbirliği ve Koordinasyon Ajansı Başkanlığı, TİKA),[40] the Yunus Emre Institute (Yunus Emre Enstitüsü, YEE),[41] Presidency for Turks Abroad and Related Communities (Yurtdışı Türkler ve Akraba Topluluklar Başkanlığı, YTB)[42] and the Maarif Foundation.[43]

Views from the Balkan Capitals: Division or Diversity?

A road trip from Granishar, one of the most northern settlements of Bulgaria, to Durrës on the seacoast of Albania, via the North Macedonian capital Skopje, involves a journey of just over a thousand kilometres. The total geographic area of these three countries is indeed tiny compared to certain other areas of the world. Yet apart from some similar issues and their approaches to the *laik* Turkey since the beginning of the 1990s, these three countries could be from different planets. Indeed, their diverging historical backgrounds form the main reason for their differences in socio-political and economic aspects, but the capital cities reveal much more in regard to the differences in their current states of mind. The case selection of this book seeks to present the diverse structure of the Balkans.

A photo taken in the Bulgarian capital Sofia from a vantage point below the Serdika underground station, where two lines meet at a major junction, would offer an illustration of the primary economic, cultural and religious structure of the country. On the south side of the photo would be the well-tended and state-funded St Nedelya Church of Eastern Orthodox Christianity. Running just behind the church, the prestigious Aleksandar Stamboliyski Boulevard, with its glamorous architecture, would show the Orthodox domination of the country. Around 200 metres north, Serdika Square hosts the Banya Bashi Mosque. One of the oldest buildings constructed by the Ottomans, the mosque is currently in a state of relative neglect, usually without significant numbers of visitors. Inside the mosque are religious books that were sent by the Diyanet or published by the office of the Bulgarian Grand Mufti with Turkey's financial support.

Its imam was also educated in Turkey on a scholarship given by the Turkish Diyanet Foundation. On the western side of Serdika Square is located the Soviet-style constitutional court building. It is a cold but elegant structure. On the eastern side of the centre of Sofia, a new Roman Catholic cathedral presents itself. The Cathedral of St Joseph was rebuilt at its original location after it was destroyed during the Second World War. It was reconstructed with EU funds and its foundation was laid personally by Pope John Paul II during his visit to Bulgaria in 2002. Among these symbolic places of worship, one stands quite outside the general frame: the Sofia Synagogue, which is located on the north-western side of the square. Even though it has magnificent architecture, one needs to use a map or ask assistance to find it. Taken together, the Soviet-style state building, the visible and sumptuous Orthodox church, the EU-supported Catholic church, the old and ramshackle mosque funded by Turkey and the relatively smaller synagogue exhibit the diverse religious structure of the city.

The North Macedonian capital city, Skopje, is divided by the River Vardar (Axios), but this division means much more when compared to other cities divided by a waterway, such as London or Istanbul. The Vardar divides Skopje in economic, cultural, political and religious terms, in quite visible ways, creating a gap between the two sides that far surpasses the width of the river. The northern side of the river is the Muslim (mostly Albanian and Turkic) majority area, called Old Bazaar and resembling a small Anatolian village with only a few two-storey houses, late Ottoman-style architecture and narrow stony streets. In this part of the city, you may easily communicate in Turkish and be welcomed as a Turkish speaker by most of the residents. Except for a couple of tourist souvenir shops, a dozen meatball restaurants and coffee shops, which also serve the Balkan-style *burek*, it is hard to see anything that can drive the city economically. It is also difficult to find non-*halal* food in this part of the city, and after 9 pm almost all the restaurants and coffee shops lower their shutters. Geographically, this part is a hill with nineteen different mosques, most of which have been renovated or constructed by TİKA, the Turkish Diyanet Foundation or the Islamic Religious Community of North Macedonia (Исламската Верска Заедница во Македонија – IRC), which gets its financial support mostly from Turkey. On the top of the hill and in the midst of all these mosques, the new building of the Turkish embassy is located. This part of Skopje hosts only the embassies of the United State of

America and Turkey. The rest are located on the other side of the city. Here in northern Skopje one may also see the religious foundations supported by Turkey, such as the Ensar Foundation, the Mustafa Pasha Foundation and the Turkish Diyanet Foundation, one on almost every corner.

The southern part of Skopje looks as if it comes from another country, with modern coffee shops, wine houses and pubs on the bank of the river. The architecture is totally different on this side of the city, which is filled with sculpture and newly constructed historical-style buildings under the project Skopje 2014. Furthermore, at the tip of the south part stands a huge Christian cross called the Millennium Cross (Миленниумски крст, Mileniumski krst). This sixty-six-metre cross is situated on the top of Skopje's Vodno Mountain. It was constructed to serve as a memorial of two thousand years of Christianity in North Macedonia and in the world. As an Orthodox Christian symbol, the cross is dominant all across North Macedonia.

In relation to these cities, the Albanian capital, Tirana, is harder to describe from one square in terms of its socio-political and economic issues. Even though almost 60 per cent of the country is Muslim (including Bektashi) and 25 per cent is Christian, it is nearly impossible to feel any single religious domination in the city. Indeed, some parts of the city exemplify the text-book definition of the concept of compossibility. One of the best examples of this compossibility would be Kavaja Street, which runs west from the central Skanderbeg Square for several kilometres and then continues further west to the Adriatic Sea. It is known for its prime real estate and some of the most expensive apartments in Tirana. The street is packed with grill restaurants (*Zgara*), which serve pork and are liberal with the region's wines, Albanian *rakija* and Korça beer (*Birra* Korça), and are mostly full after 6 pm all days of the week. Yet in the midst of these restaurants is located Xhamia Dine Hoxha, one of the best-known Salafist mosques in Tirana. A Catholic church and an Orthodox church are situated nearby and worshippers at all three institutions live, work and socialise together.

For an overview of the entire city, the panoramic view from the Sky Tower Bar would be the best option. From the turntable area it is possible to see more than twenty mosques, but one among them manifests itself exceptionally: The Great Mosque of Tirana (Xhamia e Madhe e Tiranës), which will be the largest mosque in the Balkans when construction is completed. After the fall of communism in Albania in 1991, Albanian Muslims often complained about being discriminated against. While two cathedrals for Catholics and an Eastern Orthodox church were built, as of 2016 the Muslim Albanians still had no great central mosque. The Albanian government and the Muslim community of Albania and Turkey signed an agreement to build such a mosque in Tirana. The financing for the mosque's construction comes from the Turkish Diyanet,[44] and Erdoğan personally attended the inauguration ceremony. Another example of compossibility could be the historic Et'hem Bey Mosque, which is an eighteenth-century building in central Tirana. Located at the back of the state and government buildings where the Christian majority are working for the state, it can be considered one of the symbols of Albanian religious and cultural tolerance, which is also addressed in the constitution of the country.

Tirana is also the centre for Bektashis all around the world. The Bektashi World Centre is in the north-east suburbs of Tirana and features an impressive *tekke* with a fascinating museum in its basement and a small gift shop where visitors can buy various Bektashi-related souvenirs. The Centre is hidden in a network of small streets and is difficult to find. One has to wander through very poor neighbourhoods and follow the 'Kryegjyshata Botërore Bektashiane Selia e Shenjtë' (Bektashi World Headquarters Holy See) sign. The stone entrance will welcome you and it is possible to see and talk with Edmond Brahimaj, also known as Grandfather Hajji Baba Mondi (Haxhi Baba Edmond Brahimaj), the world leader of the Bektashi Order.

These three countries also have many other differences regarding their economic capacity, demographics and role in the international system, which contribute to the already substantial depth of diversity for a comparative study. While the Muslim-majority provinces of Bulgaria, such as Rhodopes, Pazardzhik and Blagoevgard, are economically weak, the Christian-majority provinces, such as Ruse, Dobrich and Pernik, are relatively more developed. In the Albanian case, welfare, economic development and socio-political power are not directly based on religion. For instance, the city of Durrës, which is the second largest in Albania, consists of Muslims (both Sunni and Bektashi) alongside Christians (Catholic and Orthodox) who form a significant part of the urban population, and is the country's most important economic link to Western Europe due to its port. In North Macedonia there are only five cities with populations of over fifty thousand: Skopje, Bitola, Kumanovo, Prilep and Tetovo, and they are the most developed areas of the country. Tetovo is the only Muslim-majority city among them.

Being 'Ahmet Öztürk' in the Balkans

Despite the diverse nature of the Balkans, the region's citizens have complex and interesting categorisations regarding the researcher's positionality. Qualitative research has exposed a range of methodological and practical issues that arise in fieldwork. Some of these fundamental issues concern the relationship between the researcher and the researched in various locations and research sites, and the position of the researcher, which involves some 'uncontrollable points' such as the researcher's name, nationality, skin colour and mother tongue. To minimise some of the issues in the field regarding these uncontrollable points, it is important that the researcher be aware of his/her subject position and consider how this position affects both the conditions in the field and the relationships between the researcher and the interviewee. Baser and Toivanen suggest that scholars need to develop a reflexive approach to various positionalities in the field and should use their insider and outsider positions in smart ways.[45]

In the Balkans it did not matter that I was using my second name 'Erdi' rather than my first name Ahmet, and that I had an affiliation with a 'foreign' or 'Western' university. As a Turkish citizen with the surname Öztürk ('real Turk') and the name Ahmet (one of the names of the Prophet Mohammad), almost all of my interviewees categorised me as a devoted Muslim and a Turkish citizen loyal to the AKP at the very beginning of the interview process. I was repeatedly greeted with phrases such as 'we Turks', 'Muslims like you and me', 'your government' and 'your leader Erdoğan'. Being a 'Turkish citizen' and a 'Muslim' in the eyes of some of the interviewees put me in the position of an insider. In many other cases, I was rendered an outsider since the interviewees had a historical bias against Turks.

It would be most accurate to define my researcher positionality as 'hybrid insider and outsider', which means that the researcher shares characteristics with both majority and minority groups and therefore can contribute to striking a balance between proximity[46] and distance in the relationship between interviewee and researcher.[47] At times I attributed these labels to myself, and at times they were attributed to me by the individuals I worked with in the field. This hybrid positionality gave me wider opportunities, employing the different positionalities. In order to get rich information and data, I tried to develop friendly relationships as a window to dig deeper, and used the insider role with some interviewees, but also tried to scrutinise the issues with my outsider face by appearing as a total stranger.

> Actually, I did not want to talk with you, because I really get bored with the subject of Turkey, but I realised that your name is Ahmet, I would like to talk with you, since I could not say no to this name. You know it is the name of our beloved Prophet.

These were the sentiments expressed by a devoted Muslim interviewee from North Macedonia at the beginning of our conversation on 14 April 2017. It can be said that this was not a unique example of how the name Ahmet helped me during the fieldwork. For instance, in Tirana in the second half of April 2017, some of my interviewees suggested that we go to the Xhamia Dine Hoxha, the Salafist mosque. It would be very hard for a non-Muslim to go to this mosque and conduct an interview with some of the leading persons of the mosque community, but they talked very openly and welcomed me in. All of these positive aspects gave me an opportunity to socialise with Muslim groups all around the Balkans, which was essential to understanding their daily practices. There was also a necessity to work with Muslim groups, since Islam is a religion that covers and penetrates all dimensions of daily life.

Relative insider positionality, within the hybrid structure of researcher positionality, also offered me different experiences with groups and individuals within Turkey and case countries in the Balkans. It is essential to highlight two aspects of interviewee and researcher reflection on certain attitudes. The first attitude was fear and dread of members of the Gülen Movement located in the three case countries. As mentioned previously, the conflict between the Gülen Movement and the AKP is not limited to Turkish territories. It has a transnational face, since both parties have transnational structures. For the people in every single case country, the Gülen Movement is a fundamental actor in Turkey and therefore impossible to exclude from the main research. It was difficult to conduct an interview with these people because they were wary of these Turkish-origin actors. In this regard, they asked for a strong commitment to confidentiality regarding their names and preferred to talk with me in relatively quiet places. The hardest case was North Macedonia, where it was very difficult to meet the interviewees because they did not want to appear in public spaces. In this regard, I was obliged to do meet them in uncharted restaurants or their meeting houses in Skopje. Only one time they accepted me their main management offices which are officially known as the headquarters of Jahja/Yahya Kemal private elementary and high schools.

The second attitude was the hierarchical approach taken by Turkish officials in the case country. Many of them started as follows: 'Your kind of young researcher who comes from another foreign university can't understand the feelings of the Balkans . . . you have to live here like us'. After that they tried to intrude in the research with many sentences that started, 'I know what you heard from the others, but most of them are wrong, you should write this . . .' Beyond this, most of the representatives of Turkey's transnational state apparatuses in the case countries tried to 'correct' certain points of the study with the official Turkish state discourse. This case typifies the classical argument that some interviewees focus on what they could gain from the research.[48]

Structure of the Book

The book is divided into three main parts, each of which contains two to four different chapters that are strongly interrelated. Following this quite comprehensive introduction the 'Theory and History' part begins. The theory chapter forms the skeleton of the book, explaining how religion can be a part of the state's identity and how religion-oriented state identity affects the power resources and notions of the state in foreign policy. In the history chapters, I discuss power relations over the last two centuries, covering the Ottoman state and the Turkish republic since the Özal period.

The second part, 'Turkey's Intense Transformation under AKP Rule', is divided into two chapters outlining the AKP regime's policy-making approaches both at home and abroad, which aim to read Turkey's AKP period in light of a combination of domestic and foreign policies, with religion at the forefront. In these two chapters, the concept of 'state of exception' is employed to understand Turkey's authoritarian ethno-nationalist pragmatic

Sunnification under AKP rule. Indeed, throughout the two chapters the new positions of state institutions such as the Diyanet, the role of the GM, the role of Davutoğlu in the new Turkish foreign policy and the leadership of Erdoğan constitute the priorities, since these have been the main determinants in understanding relations between the Balkans and Turkey since the early 2000s.

The third part, 'AKP's New Turkey and Its Reflections in the Balkans', comprises four chapters. The main discussion and the principal role of the fieldwork start in these four chapters, which talk mainly about how the AKP's Turkey started to serve the Balkans in different ways via its transnational state apparatuses. Each of the chapters scrutinises an important issue: economic investment in Muslims of the Balkans, how the Gülen–AKP conflict has changed the nature of the Balkans, Turkey's interference in the internal affairs of host countries or its negative role in these countries' secular environment.

Finally, the conclusion states the general findings of the three case countries, reviewing how the main contributions have contributed to the theoretical argument, the history of the Balkans and the political discussions on contemporary Turkey. Each of these components of the book draws salient information from the current fieldwork and from relevant new literature on Turkish socio-political history, contemporary Balkan politics, and the role of religion, power and identity in global politics.

Notes

1. Tanasković, *Neoosmanizam-Povratak Turske na Balkan.*
2. Petrovic and Reljic, 'Turkish interests and involvement in the Western Balkans'.
3. Seldin, 'US official accuses Turkey'. For the full explanation please see https://www.voanews.com/usa/us-official-accuses-turkey-pushing-extreme-islamist-ideology, accessed 29 September 2019.
4. Note that the Muslim presence and Islamisation of the public sphere and the Sunnification of state identity are quite different issues, but very much interrelated. 'Ethno-religious coercive Sunnification' is the main term the author has adapted for the purpose of this book and it is this Sunnification, rather than social situations, that defines state identity. In subsequent parts of the book, some of the religious expressions of the political elites of Turkey are emphasised and the numbers of new mosques and Quran courses delivered are presented to readers, but these are quite different issues that relate to social Islamisation

or de-secularisation. The daily life practices of Turkish citizens are not the main subjects of this book, only their experience of national identity politics.

5. *Muhteşem Yüzyıl* is a Turkish historical fiction television series based on the life of the longest reigning Ottoman Sultan, Suleyman the First, who conquered most of the Balkan region.

6. Karanfil and Burcu, 'Politics, culture and media'.

7. On 10 July 2020 the Council of State removed the obstruction preventing the Hagia Sophia – which had been converted into a museum in 1934 during the Ataturk era, and which had long been on the list of World Heritage Sites – from being given the status of mosque.

8. *Gavur* simply means 'infidel'. It is an offensive term and a slur that was used in the Ottoman times mostly for Christians, including Orthodox Christians in the Balkans.

9. For instance, Hagia Sophia has not been suitable for prayer during my fieldwork time.

10. Kubálková, 'Towards an international political theology'.

11. Muslims are the largest religious minority group in Bulgaria and according to the latest census, which was conducted in 2011, constitute 7.8 per cent of the overall population. See Shakir, 'Bulgaria'.

12. Öztürk and Sozeri, 'Diyanet as a Turkish foreign policy tool'.

13. Baser and Öztürk (eds), *Authoritarian Politics in Turkey*.

14. Ben-Porat, *Between State and Synagogue*.

15. Hatzopoulos and Petito, *Religion in International Relations*.

16. Sandal and Fox, *Religion and International Relations Theory*.

17. Philpott, 'Explaining the political ambivalence of religion'.

18. Fox, *Political Secularism, Religion and the State*.

19. Cesari and Fox, 'Institutional relations rather than clashes of civilizations'.

20. Rakel, 'Iranian foreign policy since the Iranian Islamic Revolution'.

21. Howell, 'Muslims, the new age and marginal religions in Indonesia'.

22. Ellis and Ter Haar, 'Religion and politics in sub-Saharan Africa'.

23. The Turkish understanding of 'secularism' has quite a different meaning. The historical establishment of Turkish secularism/*laïcité* (*laiklik* in Turkish) implies that the state should not be blind to religious issues, with religion implicitly referring to Sunni Islam. For details please see Kuru, *Secularism and State Policies toward Religion*.

24. Mardin, *Religion, Society and Modernity in Turkey*.

25. Modood, 'Moderate secularism, religion as identity and respect for religion'.

26. Haynes, 'Politics, identity and religious nationalism in Turkey'.
27. Insel, 'The AKP and normalizing democracy in Turkey'.
28. The guardianship mechanisms of Turkey are the institutions that were established by the Kemalist and other ruling elites of Turkey before the AKP. They aim to protect the Kemalist and *laik* structure of Turkey. The military is one example of such mechanisms. For detailed explanation please see Akkoyunlu, *The Rise and Fall of the Hybrid Regime*.
29. Watmough and Öztürk, 'The future of the Gulen Movement in transnational political exile'.
30. Öztürk, 'An alternative reading of religion and authoritarianism'.
31. Watmough and Öztürk, 'From "diaspora by design" to transnational political exile'.
32. Yavuz and Öztürk, 'Turkish secularism and Islam under the reign of Erdoğan'.
33. Agamben, *State of Exception*.
34. Aras, 'The Davutoğlu era in Turkish foreign policy'.
35. *Strategic Depth* (*Stratejik derinlik*) is a book published by Davutoğlu in 2001 that outlines the central elements of the foreign policy doctrine of the same name. It argues that a nation's value in world politics is predicated on its geostrategic location and historical depth. Davutoğlu, *Stratejik derinlik*.
36. Danforth, 'Ideology and pragmatism in Turkish foreign policy'.
37. Öztürk, 'Transformation of the Turkish Diyanet'.
38. Hoffmann, 'Neo-Ottomanism, Eurasianism or securing the region?'.
39. Mencutek and Baser, 'Mobilising diasporas'.
40. TİKA was established in 1992 as a statutory technical aid organisation under the Turkish Ministry of Foreign Affairs. Its remit was to provide assistance to the Turkic (Turkish-speaking) Republics of Central Asia as they transitioned after the disintegration of the Soviet Union.
41. The Yunus Emre Foundation is a public body established in 2007 to encourage friendly knowledge and understanding between the people of Turkey and the wider world by promoting Turkish language, history and culture abroad.
42. The YTB, established as a transnational state apparatus at the level of Under-secretariat of the Prime Minister on 6 April 2010, has the task of coordinating activities for Turks living abroad as diaspora communities, related kinship communities and international scholarship students studying in Turkey, and developing the services and activities it has undertaken in these fields. This Turkish-originated transnational state apparatus does not have direct offices in

the Balkans but maintains a slight presence, such as scholarships to students, in particular areas.

43. The Maarif Foundation was established in late 2016. Although its stated mission is to serve as a gateway for Turkey to the international educational arena in order to contribute to enhancing cultural and civilisational interaction and pave the way for achieving the common well-being, its ultimate and clear mission is to take over the educational institutions run by the Gülen Movement.

44. Öztürk and Gozaydin, 'A frame for Turkey's foreign policy'.

45. Baser and Toivanen, 'Politicized and depoliticized ethnicities'.

46. Paechter, 'Researching sensitive issues online'.

47. Carling *et al.*, 'Beyond the insider–outsider divide'.

48. Denzin, 'The reflexive interview'.

Part I

THEORY AND HISTORY

1

MULTI-SIDED ROLES OF RELIGION, IDENTITY AND POWER IN POLITICS

The Republic of Turkey is a democratic, secular and social state governed by rule of law, within the notions of public peace, national solidarity and justice, respecting human rights, loyal to the nationalism of Atatürk, and based on the fundamental tenets set forth in the preamble.

> Article 2 of the Constitution of the Republic of Turkey

[T]he characteristics of the Republic in Article 2 . . . shall not be amended, nor shall their amendment be proposed.

> Article 4 of the Constitution of the Republic of Turkey

The second article of the current Turkish constitution enshrines the fundamental nature of the Turkish state, including its *laik* identity. What is more, that *laik* character is immutable: the fourth article of the constitution renders the second unalterable. While the present constitution dates from 1982, *laiklik* has always been at the heart of the identity of modern Turkey. Within the current order, the role of the president of the Republic is equally specified in constitutional terms, as laid out in Article 104 as follows:

> The President of the Republic is the head of the State. In this capacity, he/she shall represent the Republic of Turkey and the unity of the Turkish Nation; he/she shall ensure the provisions of the Constitution are enforced, and the regular and harmonious functioning of the organs of the State is maintained.

What is significant about this rather abstract formulation is what is not stated. The norms and unwritten rules that emerge from Turkey's distinct political culture – and that provide the context in which the constitution's provisions must be read – mean that Turkish presidents in practice have exercised the duty to ensure the provisions of the constitution are enforced in a very specific way.[1] As the main guardianship mechanism of the constitutionally mandated character of the Turkish state, the president's main duty is to represent those qualities when necessary. Central to this mission is the unwritten rule that beyond his or her personal religious perspective, Turkey's president should be neutral in public questions of religion, as the representative of the *laik* state.

While related, the concepts of *laik* state, *laik* society and *laik* political leaders are not identical, and they need not overlap perfectly in practice. Indeed, throughout the 2000s under the rule of the AKP, the *laik* Turkish state has for the first time been led by a highly religious leader. Indeed, this does not mean that Turkish society in the same period has become self-evidently less *laik* by the day, yet, it does raise the question of a changing state identity. Over these years, Erdoğan has increasingly used his bullying pulpit to bring questions of religion to the fore in public policy debates not only at home, but also abroad. In the process, he has marked a decided shift in Turkey's domestic politics, its foreign policy, and its state identity – and the position of religion in all three.

There are obvious examples that one could reference: Erdoğan's public invoking of the Quran at the opening ceremony of a new mosque complex sponsored by the Diyanet in Maryland in the USA in 2016 comes to mind. A handful of less well-known examples, however, serve to illustrate most effectively the general themes that form the core of this chapter, and indeed the book more generally. The first of these is Erdoğan's reaction to German Chancellor Angela Merkel's use of the term 'Islamist terrorism' at a press conference on her visit to Turkey in February 2017, while she was answering a question about the fight against the terror organisation ISIS. Speaking right after Merkel, Erdoğan declared that the expression 'Islamist terror' seriously saddens 'us as Muslims'. He also underlined that such an expression is not correct because Islam and terror cannot be associated. The meaning of Islam is peace. After these sentences Erdoğan gently warned Merkel not to use the expression 'Islamic terror', and added, 'As long as it is used, we need to stand against it. As a Muslim president personally, I cannot accept it.'

What is both unprecedented and crucial here to the present study is Erdoğan's reference to himself as 'a Muslim president'. While his long career of public piety is undisputable – he is a son, after all, of one of the oldest political Islamist traditions in modern Turkey, the Milli Görüş (National Outlook) – such a statement is extraordinary. The president of *laik* Turkey must always remain 'neutral' on questions of religion as per the constitutional norm discussed above.

Moreover, Erdoğan's purpose in responding as 'a Muslim president' was certainly deliberate and most probably speaking to two audiences simultaneously. In the first instance, he was simply speaking to his political base, reinforcing his support among the AKP's largely pious Muslim electorate. His second audience was other Muslim societies and the people leading them, among whom he sought to burnish his credentials as a defender of Islam on the global stage. At the same time, the president was signalling broadly to people at home and abroad that a new dispensation had come to pass in the Turkish order: that religion was no longer a neutral topic within the state structure and that political leaders would make no distinction between their religious identity and their function as representatives of the state.

A second example occurred in early 2018 at the reopening of the centuries-old Bulgarian Orthodox Iron Church (Demir Kilise), also known as St Stephen's, in the historic Balat neighbourhood of Istanbul after a seven-year restoration project. In the presence of Bulgarian prime minister Boyko Borissov, at the 7 January ceremony, Erdoğan spoke to the significance of the renovated church thus:

> An opening like this carries a significant message for the international audience on my behalf. Istanbul has once again shown the world that it is a city where different religions and cultures coexist in peace . . . It is the responsibility of the state to ensure everyone can worship freely.

It is no coincidence that Erdoğan's remarks came in the same month that his guest, prime minister Boyko Borissov, had assumed the six-month rotating presidency of the Council of the European Union. Indeed, in his speech Erdoğan referenced the need to 'normalise' relations between Turkey and the

EU. The phrasing is crucial here: to speak of the normalisation of relations between Turkey and the EU was somewhat euphemistic, given the crisis in Turkish–EU relations since roughly 2010. While the authoritarian drift in Turkey, the lack of rule of law and freedom of speech, and the policy preferences of decision-makers have been at the heart of that crisis, it is also true that the question of religion has lurked in the background. Indeed, Erdoğan's instrumentalisation of religion at the 7 January 2018 ceremony underscored this very point. Even though in contrast with the Merkel example, Erdoğan's reaching for religion in this case was far more ecumenical and friendly, it was a political instrumentalisation of religion all the same. Indeed, the contrasting contexts highlight how religion can be used in various ways in both the domestic and foreign policy domains, by the same political actor.

The final example is Erdoğan's response to Donald Trump's December 2017 announcement of the formal recognition of Jerusalem as the capital of Israel and plans to move the US embassy there from Tel Aviv, reversing nearly seven decades of American policy. Erdoğan's reaction was telling. Exactly one week after Trump's decision, Erdoğan called an emergency meeting of the Organisation of Islamic Cooperation (OIC), the world's main pan-Islamic body. Erdoğan's principal aim was to marshal Muslim leaders in a coordinated response to the US recognition of Jerusalem as Israel's capital. During the meeting, Erdoğan labelled Israel a terrorist state and called for a strong reaction. In the final stage of the meeting, the member states said they considered Trump's decision to move the US embassy to Jerusalem to be an indication of the US administration's withdrawal from its role as a sponsor of peace. Right after the meeting, Erdoğan declared Turkey's aim to open an embassy in East Jerusalem (the ostensible capital of an independent Palestinian state).

The organisation of the meeting and Turkey's decision regarding the establishment of an embassy in East Jerusalem can be read concurrently in three different ways. First of all, Turkey's quick reaction to the US decision is a visible indicator of the axial dislocation of Turkish foreign policy and state identity from its classic and long-standing *laik* Western orientation to an uncertain religion-oriented axis. Second, Erdoğan's call and his protectorate role signal the transformation of Turkey's state identity. Despite Turkey's constitutionally *laik* status, under the AKP regime it has aspired to hold a leadership position among Muslim countries, at least on a discursive level.

Finally, one can remark that religion-oriented foreign policy transformations were insufficient for the policy-makers of Turkey, for Erdoğan forwarded the same issue in domestic policy as in foreign policy, both fed from the same source: religion and its relation with state identity and power.

Indeed, these examples do not suffice to explain the multi-layered instrumentalisation of religion by Turkey's Erdoğan administration and its impact on state identity and power. In this regard, I argue that shared history, culture and traditions make the Balkans a key site to explore the dynamics of Turkey's state identity, its foreign policy preferences and the projection of state power resources beyond Turkish borders. Of course, religion-oriented foreign policy can also manifest itself in a range of bilateral and multilateral relationships, not only in the Balkans but in various geographies. In turn, this situation creates an opportune moment to scrutinise the complex relation between religion, state identity and power in general terms. This chapter therefore seeks to present an idiosyncratic model of the relationship between religion on the one hand and state identity and power on the other, and in so doing to advance the core claim of the book.

Revisiting the Concepts: Religion, Secularism, Identity and Power

> Religion . . . means the voluntary subject of oneself to God.
>
> *Catholic Encyclopaedia*, 1913

> Those who say religion has nothing to do with politics do not know what religion is.
>
> Mahatma Gandhi, 1942

The contrasting notions of religion above highlight a key leitmotif in the political sociology of religion: namely, that it is difficult to find a universal – or even commonly accepted – definition of religion. Like so much else, religion is largely in the eye of the beholder, and its definition depends on the objective of the person doing the defining. The encyclopaedia entry presented above views religion as an individual, entirely private, vocation; whereas the second position sees religion and the public sphere as inextricably linked. And yet both catch something very true about religion: the encyclopaedia expresses the common-sense idea that religion is a personal journey of spiritual realisation, while Gandhi draws our attention to the indisputable fact that religion and power have been fellow travellers since the dawn of civilisation. Ultimately, both positions are correct, if partial, approximations of the true nature of religion. On the one hand, religion provides the bridge that allows humans to approach the divine, the universal life force that both encompasses and transcends the corporeal world.[2] On the other hand, most Islamic scholars argue that religion (read: Islam) is not simply a faith system, but rather a living doctrine and a way of life that demands almost total commitment of the individual in every facet of existence.[3] Despite the various attempts to find the 'correct' definition of religion, no scholarly consensus has yet been reached and nor should this be obligatory. However, one point is certain: religion is a socio-political instrument and a resource of power that has been used by socio-political actors for reasons as diverse as unifying individuals under the same umbrella and creating different socio-political poles within societies.

The notion of 'secular' as an individual personality trait, secularism as a concept, secularisation as a process – in which 'becoming secularised' is the end point – have led to an important and determinant discussion of issues in the fields of sociology and political science. Indeed, this discussion has spread to other fields of social science, such as international relations. Within this frame, secularism is intertwined with the concept of sovereignty, both historically and politically. Secularism cannot be fully understood without reference to European history. The historical narrative of secularisation, as a process, 'presents itself as an ideological victory of liberalism that ended in a pluralist public sphere with a shared and neutralized language that secures individual freedom'.[4] Likewise, Philpott points out that the Protestant Reformation, which was one of the fundamental forerunners of the Enlightenment, provided a moral opportunity for the development of the principle of state sovereignty, which was formally enshrined during the Peace of Westphalia.[5] In this change of direction, the norm of sovereignty not only shifted the classical power relations among the 'civil' power holders, but also undermined the authority of the Western churches. Furthermore, Westphalia marked the beginning of a declining public role for religion in general, and the starting point for the regulation of the relationship between spiritual and temporal authority in Europe. The Westphalian system exhausted the classical concept and practice of Christianity among the different societies of Europe, and the concept of secularism aroused increasing support among the people.

This contributed to the normative basis of the modern system of governance. From this time, secularism moved from a philosophical concept to an institutional reality.[6] As Philpott also notes:

> The discipline of political science and the field of international relations in turn become secularized when its scholars describe politics as secularized, that is, as if states, nations, international organisations and the parties, lobbies and businesses which seek to influence them pursue ends that include power, security, wealth, peace, stability, economic development, robust international law, a cleaner environment, and the alleviation of humanitarian disaster, but do not include the spread or promotion of a religion, or any of these other ends out of religious motivation.[7]

Although the scholarly perspective of teleological secularisation had assumed the status of inevitable fact by the middle of the twentieth century, the end of the Cold War saw many scholars challenge this hegemonic truth, speaking to the very apparent continued salience of religion and, indeed, its determinant role in many societies. Berger was one of the leading voices announcing the death of religion in the 1960s. In 1968, he advised the *New York Times* that by 'the twenty-first century, religious believers are likely to be found only in small sects, huddled together to resist a worldwide secular culture'.[8] However, even Berger was compelled to revise his prediction later in life. In the mid-1990s he retracted his earlier claims and admitted that his ideas in the 1960s were essentially mistaken.[9]

What had happened to forestall the death of religion that scholars like Berger had been so sure was upon us? The Iranian revolution in 1979, for one, signalled that religion remained a central leitmotif in politics, as did the rise of faith-based terrorist groups in Afghanistan, the spread of Pentecostalism in South America and parts of Asia and the ascendance of Christian democrats in continental Europe. Moreover, since the late 1980s, many studies have shown that individual religiosity has not disappeared even in secular European states, where more than two-thirds still describe themselves as 'a religious person'.[10] The presence of religion and various faith-based movements in political and social life persists across three different levels: as a form of identity, as an effect on individual lifestyles and as an effect within institutional bodies, which is a subordinate conjunction for politics and the state.

The rise of religion in social and political arenas cannot be discussed without considering religion itself, because of its impact on individuals and societies. In the same vein, the persistence of individual religiosity in itself does not rule out secularisation. Therefore, secularisation and religiosity are not mutually exclusive. Rather, they are always relative to some definition of religion or religiosity. With the bold title of his study, 'Secularization R.I.P.', Stark demonstrates it is impossible to argue that religion has withered away, since it has always been there.[11] Yet Taylor challenges the conclusion that secularisation has failed. Rather, he sees secularism as a development within Western Christianity, stemming from the increasingly anthropocentric versions of religion that arose after the Reformation. For Taylor, the modern age is not an age without religion; instead, secularisation heralds a move from societies where belief in God is unchallenged to one in which religion is but one 'belief system' among many.[12] Modood also claims that even if humankind has been living through an age of secularism, religion remains highly salient. The condition whereby various 'new age secularisms' coexist can be summarised as follows: religion still plays a dominant role but within different perspectives. and these different perspectives reveal different types of secularism, such as 'aggressive' or 'moderate' and so on.[13]

Central here is the instrumentalisation of Islam by various global terror groups, which draw on particular interpretations of Islamic precepts to wreak violence worldwide. To make matters worse, because of historical and structural conflicts of interest among leading countries worldwide, religion-related issues have become ever more complicated instead of reaching a peaceful resolution. A central thematic emerges at this juncture: religion is a form of power resource and an instrument with distinct effects in various fields within the socio-political arena. As an intrinsic part of identity, religion has the power to reconstruct the identity of politics. State interests are neither given nor immutable and are instead a reflection of state identities; identity (be it religious or otherwise) is thus a central explanatory variable in the analysis of both domestic and foreign policy. Religion, to the extent that it forms part of state identity, can thus shape policies even if actors and decision-makers are themselves secular.

A state's relations with religion have a significant impact on its identity as well as on its normative and practical power. For instance, even though the

Vatican is insignificant both economically and militarily, its historical status as the state representing the Catholic church means it has tremendous transnational religious influence and status in international society. On the other hand, contemporary Turkey, as the successor state to the Ottomans – who possessed the flag of the Islamic caliphate for more than four hundred years – has preferred to be a constitutionally *laik* state, albeit with a Sunni Muslim-majority population. While at the very beginning of the AKP period this historically determined situation was locked into a computable structure encompassing both democracy and Islam, increasing political religiosity has carried Turkey's identity, power and image in different directions. Indeed, identity can be seen as the attribute of individuals that serves as the core driver of all their preferences and behaviours. Identity is a long-standing theme in global politics. Nevertheless, there remains sufficient ambiguity in the concept that it bears taking a little time to contextualise the definition employed here, within the broader literatures. Mitzen, for example, expresses the ambiguous core of the concept of identity as both manifested and determined via action. According to him, identity motivates action, and its stability over time depends on its being supported in practice; thus, identity is a dynamic process.[14]

Thus, identity can explain the actions of individuals, communities, institutions and states. Additionally, identities designate action patterns, and changing behaviour can be tracked to shifts in identity. Conversely, the dynamism of identities can influence transformation in action, and the last stage of action could be defined as the last stage of identity. Therefore, identity and action are interconnected concepts, influencing not only individuals but collective actors such as groups (and even states). When behaviour shifts, we are enjoined to look to changing identity codes and preferences as the explanation. Unlike most of the identity categories, state identity is an artificial entity that can be constructed by history, culture, memory, values, experiences, individuals, political actors' guidance and institutional norms of the state. All these structures and concepts can affect each other and reshape both their own identity and state identity as well. In this regard, Lynch underlines that state identity goes beyond the limits of the leaders' actions and discourses. It is also defined as the set of beliefs about the nature and purpose of the state expressed in public articulations of state actions and ideals.[15]

This means that state identity marks the state's perception of what role it should play and what status it should enjoy among other states. As Matsumura notes, political leaders in most states directly shape state identity by touching upon the institutional structure and public opinion of the state's citizens.[16] There is near-consensus on the effect of political elites and influential leaders on state identity, and much of this literature has engaged with the ways in which political elites, parties and groups might transform existing state identities.[17]

Like the notions of religion and state identity, power is a long-established – if essentially contested – concept in social science. Despite its determinant conceptual position, the definition of power arrived quite late to the field of social science. In a systematic way, Dahl defines the concept of power using this explanation: 'A has power over B to the extent that he can get B to do something that B would not otherwise do'.[18] Here, the salience of conflict and struggle is suggested, with the threat of sanction at least potentially implied as well, a point endorsed by Kreisberg: 'Power is a form of influence in which effect on policy is enforced or expected to be enforced by relatively severe sanctions.'[19] Furthermore, power has long been a central concern of international relations theory. Morgenthau concurs in this regard, arguing that 'statesmen think and act in terms of interests defined as power'.[20] Thus, it is possible to categorise the sources and conceptions of power as both material and non-material.

The material sources and conceptions of power might constitute the simplest access to the principles of power, since all many numerical indicators point to the power of groups and states. Economic resources and military force, for example, would count as material sources of power. By contrast, the issue of non-material sources and conceptions of power is much more complicated. Since these mostly concern the impact factor and the core of power, their definitions are of a more tortuous structure. While Arendt focuses on the notion of living together as a core of power,[21] some extend the sources to a much wider range of non-material ideas, including identity, hegemony, control and pressure.[22] Gramsci, for instance, mentions non-material types and sources of power and adds to the discussions the concept of power as a gift, namely; hegemony.[23] Bourdieu brings to the table his concept of symbolic power, which can be basically defined as the power to impose.[24] Thus, ideologies, belief systems and identities are also constructed by power.

As with so many dimensions of world politics, the end of the Cold War let the genie out of the bottle regarding the definition, categorisation and implementation of power in politics and the international arena. The USA and later the other great powers started to achieve less (or nothing) from their military interventions. Beyond that, military interventions and economic and diplomatic sanctions even produced long-term negative impacts for stakeholders. With the limits of hard power exposed, Nye coined the term 'soft power' as an answer. Over the years he has elaborated the term according to changes and developments in world politics. Nye notes that while power is the ability to influence the main behaviour patterns of others and regulate them according to one's own aims, soft power differs from hard power.[25] Soft power is getting others to agree via cooperation rather than coercion.[26]

Governments, semi-governmental and non-governmental organisations can use soft power as a policy approach. The USA,[27] China,[28] Japan[29] and Russia,[30] are typical case countries for scholars studying the causes and consequences of the use of soft power in international relations. Sweden is another case where effective use of soft power through public diplomacy is observed. A wealthy nation, with the largest population among the Nordic countries, it is the third largest country in the EU by surface area. Even though Sweden is not a member of NATO and does not have a significant and a strong diaspora that can lobby abroad, the Swedish state is able to instrumentalise its governmental and non-governmental organisations as soft power tools. For instance, the Swedish Institute is a non-governmental public agency that aims to bolster interest and confidence in Sweden around the world. It operates in the fields of culture, education, science and business in seeking to strengthen ties and promote development. Scholarships are one inducement, as are organised promotion activities that seek to foster pro-Swedish views abroad.

Indeed, the example of Sweden, which combines hard (economic capacity) and soft (instrumentalisation of transnational institutions) power, is also cited as a smart power. A term also coined by Nye, smart power is mainly seen as a strategy to integrate the tools of both hard and soft power.[31] Yet among these discussions of hard, soft, smart and other types of power, one point remains largely neglected: the role of religion as a power source. Even though religion has an impact on changing regimes as well as on established conflicts and negotiations, and certainly qualifies as a norm regulating behaviours, preferences and identities, the discussion on religion and power is still to be taken up.

Religion as a Source of Identity and an Indicator in Politics

After the Cold War the theory of identity gradually regained prominence among international relations scholars, in a move that Lapid and Kratochwil have addressed as the return of culture and identity to international relations theory.[32] This reawakening has also opened a new chapter in elaborating and counter-elaborating the realist and constructivist theories of international relations. Despite the rich diversity of positions within the tradition, it remains the case that classical realists assume a world that is dangerous and conflict-prone insofar as the absence of any overarching authority conditions states to pursue their individual interests in competition with one another. This emphasis on the currency of power and state competition under anarchy remained the dominant paradigm until the end of the Cold War. Since that time, a range of emerging paradigms have subjected realist assumptions – ontological, epistemological and methodological – to sustained critique. Of these, constructivism emerged as the preeminent challenger, and is a paradigm that is arguably uniquely attuned to questions of identity and the state.

In classical constructivist reading, Waltz argues that all political and social systems are composed of a structure and interacting units. Waltz's theory is understood as 'structural' in the sense that it centres on the effects of the structure of the international system when it seeks to explain outcomes in international politics.[33] Although states were arguably the main agents in the early years of mainstream constructivism, the literature has since embraced a wide range of actors, including non-state entities and transnational organisations. What distinguishes constructivism from other theoretical approaches in international relations is its emphasis on how actors' identities and interests come to be formed in social interaction, rather than taking them as given and exogenous to theory.[34] Furthermore, constructivists see international structure as shaped by norms, rules and law, in addition to material factors.[35] Hopf underlines one of the most important differences of constructivist approaches *vis-à-vis* other international relations theories. According to him, actors in international relations establish and develop their relations via interaction with others through the media of norms and practices.[36] Norms are central building blocks that ground actors' political behaviour in the international arena. Through the lens of constructivist theory, agents (states) and structures (global norms) interact and are also mutually constitutive.[37] Constructivists argue that understanding how non-material structures condition actors' identities is important because identities inform interests and, in turn, actions.

Wendt holds that the identity of the state informs its interests and in turn its actions. He brackets the corporate sources of state identity, focusing entirely on the constitutive role of international social interaction. This leads him to adopt a relatively narrow conception of the structuration process, simply contending that international institutional structures constitute states as legitimate international actors and state practices in turn reproduce such structures. This concentration on systemic processes is adequate so long as one is not seeking to explain fundamental changes in the identity of an individual state (or group of states), or of a specific social structure; say, a regional one. He also posits that 'identities may be hard to change, but they are not carved in stone'.[38] The identity of states is theorised as both relational and discursively constructed. Thus, states establish and re-establish their identities before interacting with other states. This means that the construction of state identity starts in the domestic political arena. Political conflict, the establishment of distinct patterns of political culture and critical moments of domestic institutional formation are thus crucial in understanding a given state's identity. Powerful or dominant groups are seminal in the construction of state identity in the domestic arena, afterwards projecting this identity outwards into the international arena.

With the support of this theoretical discussion, I argue that the establishment and transformation processes of state identity start from the domestic level via both leadership and the effects of critical junctures after domestic struggles among different ideological camps. After that, the dominant group starts to reconstruct discourses and ideas at the socio-political level, which then feed into the transformation of state identity. Finally, the state expresses itself with a new state identity in the international arena and redesigns its policy preferences according to this new identity code. Religion is a fundamental resource during both the establishment process of emotions and the process by which they are legitimised. One of the most facile expectations of political actors is that they will make decisions based on their interests and rationality, but this is not possible for all situations and actors. In specific contexts – particularly at moments of heightened fluidity and change – emotions are far more salient. Emotions, the impact of religious belief on them, and the emotional construction of religious stereotypes are all topics of interest to constructivist scholars. Lim and Putnam highlight the point that political actors' religious worldviews influence social and political practices and discourses, and this influences the way a society's policies are structured.[39] Very much relevant to the relationship between worldviews and political aims, religion and religion-based legitimacy within the constructivist framework define which decisions are validated in which communities and through what means.

A little further away from constructivist ideas, but very much related to the role of religion in the foreign policy decision-making process, Philpott argues that under various conditions legislators making foreign policy decisions are particularly influenced by religion.[40] The institutional structures of religious ideas and their influence in both domestic and foreign policy are important focal points regarding religion in foreign policy. Organised religious interests are present in representative institutions in many countries, through which voters or active societal groups attempt to influence foreign policy. They are more likely to succeed where the state in question is relatively unstable and very dependent on societal forces, including organised religion.[41]

Within the borders of constructivist discussions, but beyond the institutional, cultural, idea and identity-based explanations of religion in international relations and foreign policy, agent-based explanations of international relations have sought to explain the role of religion in foreign policy by the leadership effect. That is, a leader's relationship with religion would be an indicator of foreign policy decision-making processes.[42] In this regard, Malici points out that leaders' religious beliefs may influence foreign policy directly.[43] Along similar lines, political actors employ discourses both to shape the worldview of ordinary citizens and to legitimise political decisions. Concerning the role of discourse in constructivist theory, religious discourses are especially important, as they represent the operationalisation of the agent's motives and understandings. Therefore, what actors say is more of interest to constructivists than their underlying motives.

Beyond doubt, religion is a power and also identity indicator that has a huge capacity to affect issues in both positive and negative ways, but it is still difficult to designate the role of religion as a power source. Even though Nye coined the term soft power he does not prefer to propose religion as a soft power. Among his many studies, he only notes that religion is a double-edged sword as an American soft power resource, and that how it cuts depends on who is wielding it.[44] In a very similar vein, Thomas points out that religion could be a resource of soft power 'when it informs the attitudinal capabilities that make up intangible elements of power for states and non-state actors in international relations'.[45]

The subject matter of soft power is not particularly new, and Jeffrey Haynes is one of the first scholars to address it via religion and religious institutions. In other words, he focuses on how religion can become a source of soft power by dealing with non-state religious transnational actors. He makes no bones about telling us that we are living in a 'post-secular' age of international relations, and briefly notes that 'the idea of "religious soft power" involves encouraging both followers and decision-makers to change behaviour because they are convinced of the appropriateness of a religious organisation's goals'.[46] Many religious actors play effective roles in the international system to spread influence in cross-border areas[47] and among different actors, faith-based organisations in particular are very influential because of their high level of ability to wield soft power to solve a variety of issues in the contemporary world.[48] For instance, the King Abdullah bin Abdulaziz International Centre for Interreligious and Intercultural Dialogue (KAICIID), which is sponsored by non-secular Saudi Arabia and is located in Vienna, has been playing an active role via its multi-religious management structure. These attempts again parallel Haynes's argument on Israel, Saudi Arabia and Iran: 'secular security concerns interact with religious issues in ways that are also linked to various expressions of religious soft power'.[49] In a similar context, *laik* Turkey's official Sunni-Islamic transnational state apparatus, the Diyanet, has the ambition of serving Muslims in more than fifty countries spanning the globe.[50] These brief examples nonetheless serve to illustrate how state structures can instrumentalise their religious face in the international arena. In this regard, one may argue that religious actors, whether subnational, transnational, governmental – or intergovernmental – employ a broad range of means to accrue soft power and generate influence.

Addressing the issue of non-state actors, while on the one hand Haynes notes that 'both secular and religious transnational entities reflect the power of soft power in relations to their adherents',[51] the converse is also salient: there exist a variety of channels related to religion through which states can acquire soft power within the secular structure of international relations. Thus, religion – certainly a part of a culture – can be a soft power resource in international relations and therefore can be used by states in many stages: establishing cooperation with religious groups, creating multiple levels of informal coalition with religious leaders and instrumentalisation of their apparatuses as an actor in international relations, under the norms of religious soft power. Mandaville and Hamid have also sought to apply the concept of religious soft power in their analysis of the foreign policy of several governments. They view the transnational deployment of states' religious soft power as both complicated and multidimensional, and address it in three aspects: (1) states' institutional and normative capacity as well as their civilisational affinity, (2) states' socio-political circumstances and the aims of those seeking to wield religious soft power, and (3) the double-edged structure of religious soft power itself.[52] Since states' transnational religious soft power is based on a range of determinants, the transformation of any of these might affect the impact of such enactment.

Religious actors are either state-related or non-state-related, this being determined according to their dependency on the state. State-related religious actors are those that enjoy close linkages to states. Koesel highlights the various levels of cooperation, alliances and mutually beneficial relationships that exist between states and religious bodies.[53] There is self-evidently a mutuality of interest in such relations; beyond that, though, religious groups can influence the foreign policy decisions of states.[54] Moreover, epistemic communities and their instrumentalisation in foreign policy provides a perspective on the role of religious soft power and religion as a soft power resource in international relations. Sandal claims that the role of religious actors in today's political scene qualifies them as an epistemic community, due to their expertise and status, and for that reason religious epistemic communities can influence politics at the global level.[55] She also notes that the religious dimensions of contemporary conflicts and the rise of faith-based movements worldwide require policy-makers to identify the channels through which religious leaders can play a positive and constructive role.[56]

Governments and/or states can also use religion in international relations as a soft power resource via channels such as the instrumentalisation of transnational religious state apparatuses like the Diyanet. The interests of states can be well served by religious attachés; indeed, the establishment of such an office is often vital in constructive state relationships with local religious actors, foreign publics, and others.

Within the frame of these three different stages, contemporary authoritarian regimes – unlike their Cold War forebears – are more pragmatic than ideological and have the capacity to instrumentalise a great many norms, values and agents in order to retain power. Religion has emerged as a tool of authoritarian regimes worldwide. The Hungarian prime minister Victor Orbán, the Dutch politician Geert Wilders, and Turkey's Erdoğan are prominent leaders who have effectively instrumentalised religious discourse and policies to consolidate their repressive political strategies. That instrumentalisation of religion has fed into foreign policy. This, then, has been a key avenue by which religion has returned to prominence in world politics. Under the conditions of the rise of authoritarian influence in the democratic world, in the Turkish case since 2002, a gradual shift in state identity through the instrumentalisation of religion has been underway in both domestic and foreign policy. Therefore, this is an opportune moment to ask: What is the role of religion in Turkey's state identity transformation process? And is there any effect on the perception of Turkey's power in the eyes of 'others'?

The Ambivalence of Religious Soft Power

Despite the critique of secularisation over the past two decades, most countries still either define themselves as constitutionally secular or endorse no official religion.[57] Nevertheless, religion remains a key source of national identity for many states,[58] laying the grounds for its instrumentalisation by political elites in both domestic and international arenas. As an intrinsic part of identity, religion has the power to reconstruct identity politics. Identity is a frame of reference within which the socio-political environment is discernible.[59] State interests are neither given nor immutable and are instead a reflection of state identities; identity (be it religious or otherwise) is thus a central explanatory variable in the analysis of foreign policy. Religion, to the extent that it forms part of state identity, can act to shape foreign policy even if actors and decision-makers are themselves secular. In this regard, it is possible to divide states into three different categories regarding the position of religion in their state identity: (1) strictly secular states, (2) theocratic states, and (3) legally secular states that nevertheless act practically in favour of the majority religion.

The relationship between these three different state categories is quite complicated and cannot be positioned along linear and/or horizontal frames. While members of the first category have strict and unswerving state identities, there are multi-layered transitions within the last two categories. Scandinavian countries could be the best example of the first group, in their preference not to be associated with any particular religion but enjoying impartiality and secularity in terms of state and religious relations. The second category includes countries that have particular religious identities demonstrated both legally and politically in almost every single arena. The Islamic Republic of Iran, for instance, stands out in this category, while also illustrating how richly complex religious identity formation can be. As noted by Nasr, although a surface reading would indicate that Islam is the common religion for most Middle East countries, the ambiguous equilibriums and tensions between Sunni and Shia provide the main determinant.[60] Therefore, Iran seems to be the protective power for all Shia groups because of its clear Shia-oriented Persian identity. At a deeper level, it is obvious that the identity of Shias is bound up with cultural ties and relations of faith, political alliances, and commercial links that cut across the divide between Arab and non-Arab.[61]

The last category is the most changeable and fluid one. The members of this category are mostly the relatively new nation-states that were established just before and after The First World War and are legally secular, with one particular religion dominant in their population. Furthermore, most of these countries have a historical background where monarchism as the ruling structure includes theocratic power. Turkey as the successor to the Islamic Ottoman state, Austria as the inheritor of the Catholic Austrian-Hungarian Empire and Russia, as the descendant of the Orthodox majority Russian Empire, are exemplars in this category. Members of this group have changeable structures – not only or even legally, but in *de facto* ways, because of domestic political dynamics, historical praxis and memory.

States in this third category are particularly likely to transform their identities through religion, without touching legal norms directly. Indeed, such
transformations do not come into existence overnight, depending as they
do on dominant political power, social support, time and a suitable international arena. This religion-oriented transformation could be described as a
reincarnation of historical roles by means of religion. Transformation of this
sort brings certain advantages to both domestic and foreign policy, albeit
limited. A shift to, or of, religion-oriented identity can change the power
balance at various levels. Countries establish their relations to others according to certain identity codes, and new identities could imply entirely new
foreign relations and networks. In this regard, religion-oriented transformation of the state identity and its instrumentalisation in foreign policy would
synthesise a new situation that I characterise as the ambivalence of religious
soft power.

The ambivalence of religious soft power arises as a function of three different processes, each of which has its unique phases. First, domestic politics
transforms state identity in at least two distinct ways. At home, the identity of a given state is a function of a domestic struggle among political and
social groups that have their own and sometimes conflicting ideas about what
constitutes the state's identity. The dominant domestic actor takes the lead
only with a confluence of factors such as hegemonic and long-standing party
positions, influential leadership mechanisms, prevailing discourse and strong
normative components that can be used as both object and instrument, such
as religion. And externally, from the very beginning of the identity transformation process, the main arguments of the new identity are interpreted and
transferred in various ways by a range of actors and state apparatuses in various countries and get various reactions.

In the second process, after the state identity is transformed by domestic
politics, it is naturally employed in foreign policy by mostly the same political groups. It is subsequent to this enactment that dynamic interactions and
reactions start to occur, as the activities and situations in domestic and foreign policy start to feed into each other in different ways and may create crises
in both domestic and foreign political arenas. These new situations can also
be expected to transform the state's powers in foreign relations and establishing new patterns of relations between countries.

As a last claim, and as the third process of ambivalence discussed here, I argue that countries have multifaceted and multi-layered identities, some of which have a direct and/or an indirect relation with religion. These different relations with religion could be seen as among the identity determinants of many states. More clearly, countries' relations with religion would determine their power roles in international relations. In some cases, being secular would become part of a country's identity and instrumentalised as a soft power resource. In other cases, having an official religious identity would be instrumentalised by countries in their foreign policy decisions and interventions. Yet this correlation is not linear. In some cases, a secular country's instrumentalisation of its identity as an element of soft power would be positive in relations with other countries, whereas having a religious identity and using it as a soft power could have a negative effect on diplomatic relations depending on other countries' perceptions and policies.

In all these propositions, one point is clear from my side: religion serves as a highly salient factor in the transformation of state identity, which works from the domestic political sphere outwards to foreign policy, instrumentalised via a range of transnational tools and apparatuses. Furthermore, the power types of states should be categorised according to the perception of the other countries. All in all, the different situations can be assumed to manifest themselves as an ambivalent structure of religious soft power accompanying an ambiguous state identity.

Notes

1. Öztürk and Gozaydin, 'Turkey's draft constitutional amendments'.
2. Smart, *The World's Religions*.
3. Haghagenghi, *Islam and Politics in Central Asia*, 39.
4. Ben-Porat, *Between State and Synagogue*, 8.
5. Philpott, 'The religious roots of modern international relations', 207–8.
6. Hurd, 'The political authority of secularism in international relations', 237–8.
7. Philpott, 'The challenge of September 11', 69.
8. Berger, 'A bleak outlook is seen for religion', 3.
9. Berger, 'Secularism in retreat', 3.
10. Keddie, 'Secularism & its discontents', 14.
11. Stark, 'Secularization R.I.P.'.
12. Taylor, *A Secular Age*.

13. Modood, 'Moderate secularism, religion as identity and respect for religion'.
14. Mitzen, 'Ontological security in world politics', 344.
15. Lynch, 'Abandoning Iraq', 349.
16. Matsumura, 'The Japanese state identity'.
17. Vössing, 'Transforming public opinion about European integration'; Rumelili and Todd, 'Paradoxes of identity change'; Todd, 'The politics of identity change and conflict'.
18. Dahl, 'The concept of power'.
19. Kreisberg, *Transforming Power*, 41.
20. Morgenthau, *Politics Among Nations*, 5.
21. Arendt, *The Human Condition*, 200.
22. Berenskoetter, 'Thinking about power', 10.
23. Gramsci, *Further Selections from the Prison Notebooks*.
24. Bourdieu, 'Symbolic power', 79.
25. Nye, *Power in the Global Information Age*, 73–4.
26. Nye, *Soft Power*, 2–5.
27. Nye, 'The information revolution and American soft power'.
28. Bates and Huang, 'Sources and limits of Chinese "soft power"'.
29. Lam, 'Japan's quest for "soft power"'.
30. Tsygankov, 'If not by tanks, then by banks?'.
31. Nye, 'Get smart', 160.
32. Lapid and Kratochwil, *The Return of Culture and Identity*.
33. Waltz, *Theory of International Politics*.
34. Wendt, 'Collective identity formation and the international state'.
35. Klotz and Lynch, *Strategies for Research*, 24.
36. Hopf, 'The promise of constructivism', 173.
37. Checkel, 'The constructivist turn in international relations theory', 328.
38. Wendt, *Social Theory of International Politics*, 19.
39. Lim and Putnam, 'Religion, social networks and life satisfaction'.
40. Philpott, 'Explaining the political ambivalence of religion'.
41. Philpott and Keshavarzian, 'State building and religious resources'.
42. Mead, 'God's country?'.
43. Malici, 'Germans as Venutians'.
44. Nye, *Soft Power*, 94.
45. Thomas, *The Global Resurgence of Religion*, 110.
46. Haynes, *Religious Transnational Actors and Soft Power*, 28.
47. Haynes, 'Causes and consequences of transnational religious soft power', 7.

48. Haynes, *Faith-Based Organizations at the United Nations*, 63.
49. Ibid., 403.
50. Öztürk, 'Transformation of the Turkish Diyanet both at home and abroad', 9.
51. Haynes, *Religious Transnational Actors and Soft Power*, 45.
52. Mandaville and Hamid, 'Islam as statecraft'.
53. Koesel, *Religion and Authoritarianism*.
54. Öztürk, 'An alternative reading of religion and authoritarianism'.
55. Sandal, 'Religious actors as epistemic communities'.
56. Sandal, *Religious Leaders and Conflict Transformation*.
57. Fox, 'Paradigm lost'.
58. Cesari and Fox, 'Institutional relations rather than clashes of civilizations'.
59. Yavuz, 'Turkish identity and foreign policy in flux'.
60. Mandaville, *Global Political Islam*.
61. Nasr, *The Shia Revival*, 21.

2

TURKEY IN THE BALKANS: FROM LATE OTTOMAN TO THE 1970S

Throughout my research in the Balkans between mid-2015 and early 2019, the presence of one essential common point could be tallied in the responses of almost all those I interviewed, whether they were socio-political elites or ordinary individuals from the case countries. As they sought to explain Turkey's role in the Balkans, they commenced with the general situation in the late Ottoman period before moving on to the socio-political dynamics of modern-day Turkey. They explained all the historical processes connected to Turkey's domestic political developments, the rationale for its foreign policy and its approach to the Balkans. What is more, they were reading the relations between Turkey and the Balkans in reference to some of Turkey's critical junctures and political leaders. Beyond that, I came to realise that even as the individuals in the field were conversant with Turkey and the Balkans' common religion, history and culture, they mostly gave positive examples from history in their analysis of Turkey's current role in the region. This observation forms the basis of one of the sub-hypotheses of this book: it is hard to understand the political nature of the Balkans without scrutinising developments in Turkey, and vice versa, using a telescopic historical approach.

As a bold example of this observation, I could cite a conversation in which I became involved in one of the coffee shops of Skopje's Old Bazaar in April 2017. Three middle-aged men were talking about recent issues in Turkish politics and their possible effects on North Macedonia–Turkey relations. After a couple of minutes, I went to their table, introduced myself, and asked if I could join their discussion as a researcher. All of them were very talkative and in consequence we had quite a long chat. My first question was about the main reason for their close interest in Turkish politics. Their answer precluded any next questions I might have had in mind and presented the necessity to focus on the history of Turkey in this book.

They underlined that Turkish politics has always been important for them, because it affects their status and living conditions as Muslims in North Macedonia. These people were defining themselves as Turkish Muslim and the grandsons of the Ottomans. One of them summarised their ideas on Turkey and its political dimensions in the following terms:

> Of course, Turkish politics is important for us, because it affects our status and living conditions here as a Turkish Muslims under the pressure of nonbelievers . . . I mean maybe nonbeliever is a tough word . . . Starting from the weak times of the Ottomans we have suffered here a lot. The Ottomans left us here and no one else came for us . . . Okay, it is true that Atatürk has saved the honour of Turks, but it did not have an impact on our situation . . . Maybe Menderes, maybe Özal tried to protect our rights here, but they were very busy with Turkey's politics . . . Now Erdoğan seems to be strong enough to stand behind us, but first of all he needs to be powerful in Turkey . . . Strong leadership in Turkey means a strong Turkey, and only a strong Turkey can protect our values, our culture, our language and our religion here. So that Turkish politics, history, economy and its leadership are important for us . . .

Turkey's strong position with its ramifications for the Balkan region is not unrivalled, but it is also true that it is not exceptional. The current situation, it seems, must be read through the lens of the late Ottoman period under the light of Putnam's approach, namely a two-level game that offers to explain the interactive roles of domestic political actors in international relations.[1] Domestic politics is an important element in any explanation of foreign policy, and efforts to understand this mutual influence are still in progress.[2] In a parallel approach, Turkey is one of those states for which foreign policy preferences are shaped mainly by domestic political developments, as opposed to other factors such as the role of the global economy, the policies of transnational and supra-national organisations, and bilateral relations between states. In the case of Turkey, the main determinants are domestic political debate and significant critical junctures. Any significant change can only stem from domestic politics and then expand into foreign policy. Therefore, transformation in foreign policy needs time, the stable rule of a dominant actor in domestic politics and sustainable public support. In the same vein, any destabilisation of domestic politics would affect the foreign policy area.

On the other hand, Turkey's foreign policy is established in a fixed discourse and the leadership mechanism is important in the transfer of this discourse across generations. Within this discourse is an implicit argument that stronger states, the imperialists, are seeking to destroy Turkey's national unity and independence. The ideational core of the domestic narrative is the need for harmony and homogeneity in order to maintain the territorial integrity of the state.[3] Yet on top of all this, under AKP rule Turkey has been experiencing a new multidimensional change of axis from domestic to foreign policy.[4] Starting from the late Ottoman period, Turkey's foreign policy could be read as an ideological struggle between different major groups that represent different positionality regarding the identity of the state and the role of religion. Indeed, the boundaries between these ideological camps have blurred and they have become intertwined, depriving all of them of theoretical consistency. Yet the current winner in this ideological battle, at least until the beginning of 2021, has been the AKP with its agenda of coercive, ethno-nationalist Sunnification.

The axial dislocation in Turkey's foreign policy is far from being insignificant and merely tactical. Under the AKP's directive, Turkey has been turning away from Europe in particular and the West in general, at both discursive and implementation levels. Retiring from the Western world at the discourse level and the use of foreign policy as an instrument in domestic politics could be seen as a return to a coercive version of a neo-Ottoman mentality, using a top-down approach. The AKP's new understanding of neo-Ottomanism is revisionist in two aspects: reframing Ottoman history by Turkification (ethno-nationalist) and Sunnification (prioritising Sunni Islam), and sorrow for the lost lands that were once under 'Turkish' domination. The AKP's formulation of the new Turkish foreign policy is based on the party elites' repressive tendencies, which include a desire to become the supreme leader of the Muslim world (read Erdoğan). That is, under AKP rule, Turkey's foreign policy started with a pragmatist orientation, and was converted into an ideological one as the major political actor became domestically assertive and reactive. These transformations also necessitate questions that might elaborate the discussion of Turkey's state identity, the position of religion within this identity and the power of the state.

Finally, it would be deficient to read Turkish foreign policy without comparing it with the Ottoman period, since the Republic inherited not only relatively modern institutions from the Ottomans but also the very idea of modernisation itself. Identification of the ruptures and continuities between the two eras can only be illustrative of current discussions on Turkey and its influence on the Balkans.

Late Ottoman Period as the Root of Power Struggles and the Indicator Role of the Balkans

İnalcık, a prominent scholar of Ottoman history, clearly notes the importance of religion and identity for the Ottoman state from its very foundation. According to him, 'the Ottoman state was a small principality on the frontiers of the Islamic world, dedicated to Gaza, the holy war, against infidel Christianity'.[5] The Ottomans started as a vanguard of the other Islamic states and proceeded to become one of the dominant forces of the world. Islam therefore was one of the focal points of the identity, justification and power of the Ottomans. In the era of Süleyman the First (1520–66), Ottoman territories reached far beyond the central Balkans to central Europe and gave the Ottomans the status of a world power. Capturing the Balkan lands was an important juncture in Ottoman enlargement, significantly augmenting its power sources, economy and political influence. Another source of power for the Ottomans was the caliphate, which made the state the representative and prime force of Sunni Islam.[6] However, after the long wars of the seventeenth century, the balance of power turned in favour of Europe and Ottoman hard power declined. The increasing superiority of the Western powers overrode the Ottomans' economic and military capability, rendering the Ottomans dependent on Europe.[7] The continued existence and possible collapse of the Ottomans became a problem for Western politics, and was referred to as the 'Eastern Question'. The political existence of the Ottoman state, under European tutelage and control, officially continued until the beginning of the 1920s.

Even though some argue that the Ottoman state was a Balkan Empire, since its enlargement began in the Balkans and the state incorporated Balkan characteristics in terms of culture and socio-economy,[8] this perspective is deficient. The Ottoman state controlled vast territory including the Caucasus, Western Asia, Eastern Europe and the majority of North Africa. Yet it is also true that the transformation, the modernisation efforts and the inevitable collapse of the state centred on the Balkans. The Serbian independence movement and the independence of Greece – and, chronologically, of Montenegro, Romania, Bulgaria and Albania – were the most visible indicators of the collapse of the Ottomans. The multidimensional transformations started in the Balkans and were always related to the state's identity (religion and ethnic) and power (political, economic and military).

The central administration in Istanbul tried to solve these identity power struggles with a new wave of legal reforms called *Tanzimat* (reorganisation). Among various aims, *Tanzimat* sought to keep the Balkans under firmer control at a critical juncture, but these measures would prove nowhere near enough. The reforms that aimed at a consolidation of the empire failed to stop the tide of nationalism in the non-Muslim Balkan provinces. With a very modern mindset, the *Tanzimat* reforms also aimed at mobilising the population as an efficient force of production, to secure production as a priority.

Indeed, the *Tanzimat* reforms were in part the result of internal power conflicts among different ideological groups. Yet they also resulted from European pressure to protect and privilege the non-Muslim components within the empire. However, by the late 1870s, it became clear that the reforms were not having a significant effect in saving the empire from decline and from the disengagement of the Balkans. For instance, the unification of the Danubian Principalities (Romania), the creation of the Exarchate of the Bulgarian Orthodox church, and the Ottoman–Russian War were the final straws for a failing empire. To make matters worse, Austria and Russia were also trying to influence the non-Muslim components of the Ottoman Empire in the Balkans.[9]

An influential group of intelligentsias, the Young Ottomans, formed in the second half of the nineteenth century, was to play a dominant ideological role in its effort to further reform and sustain the state. The Young Ottomans can also be defined as the first example of a popular Muslim pressure group whose aim was to force the state to take their interests into account.[10] They were also defined as 'pious Muslims and Ottoman patriots, who looked back nostalgically both to a golden era of Islam and the era of the empire's greatness'.[11] Being at the centre stage of major intellectual debates on reforms and relations with the West, the Young Ottomans played a crucial role in putting the first constitution of the Ottoman Empire into practice (1876) and heavily influenced the next generation of intelligentsia with an accumulation of thoughts on modernisation.

Other ideological camps, such as liberals, nationalists and constitutionalists, were suppressed during the reign of Abdulhamid the Second.[12] This can also be interpreted as an identity and power-based struggle through the instrumentalisation of religion in the Ottoman times. The rise of pro-Islamists within the Ottoman state affected the Balkans more than the other regions. One reason for this was that in the 1876 constitution, Islam was identified as the religion of the state – providing justification for the independence movement of Greek Christians in Crete in the following year. Western states started to exert more pressure on the Ottoman regime, with the purpose of protecting the rights of non-Muslims in the Balkans. Even though in 1908 the Ottoman administration restored the 1876 constitution, which had been suspended with the outbreak of the Turko-Russian war in 1877, and wanted to establish a multi-ethnic state with religious equality, the disintegration of the Balkans could not be prevented. Most of the Balkan peoples in North Macedonia, Albania, Greece and Bulgaria had either already become independent or were on their way there.

The period of Abdulhamid the Second saw the formation of opposition groups, which organised in military academies, schools of medicine, schools of administration and law schools. The core of this opposition movement was called Ittihad-I Osmani Cemiyeti (Ottoman Unity Society) and had as its aim to reinstate the constitution and the parliament. Yet they could not compete with the Sultan's intelligence agency and were either arrested or escaped, mostly to Paris. Members of the group in exile formed a committee called İttihat ve Terakki Cemiyeti (Committee of Union and Progress, CUP). The CUP organisation became active in many parts of the empire, some of which had already gained independence. The Balkan version of the CUP endorsed an activist wing, which formed the Ottoman Revolutionary Party. CUP organisations in Bulgaria participated in the opposition movements.[13] Yet even though the CUP and the Young Turks grew rapidly and resulted in the 1908 revolution that opened the second constitutional era of Ottoman history, this was not enough to reunite the Balkans under the Ottoman flag. Turkish nationalism, as the very basis of the CUP, created enmity towards non-Muslims. In North Macedonia, for example, local guerrillas started to organise, and Albanians staged a rebellion against Istanbul. These were radical changes in the balance of power in the Balkans.

At the end of the first decade of the twentieth century, Serbians and Bulgarians established a coalition against the Ottomans. Even though the Young Turks became the major ruling power in Istanbul at the beginning of the 1910s, they could not manage to keep the Balkans under control. At the end of 1911, Greece and Montenegro joined the coalition of Serbia–Bulgaria, with the encouragement of Russia. This was the unofficial flashpoint for the First Balkan War of 1912–13. Serbia and Greece came out of the war as the main victors, both acquiring huge new territories. Bulgaria had won much less; therefore, it declared war on its former Ottoman allies. This became the official cause for the Second Balkan War. The central administration of the empire came out as the biggest loser of these wars and in the follow-up the region fell into disarray in many ways. Moreover, after these two wars, Balkan nationalism grew and the power vacuum in the region caused the total fall of the Ottoman Empire.[14] The ethno-religious conflicts and expansionist desires of the great powers sparked the fire of the First World War in 1914, and this brought the empire to the brink of total destruction.

The official identity of the CUP was formulated during the early years of the Young Turks. It would be the ideational foundation of Republican Turkey, since the founding father of modern Turkey and the following two presidents were former CUP members. The leading cadre of the CUP also represented one of the ideological blocs of contemporary Turkey, with their nationalist and secularist (*laikci*) ideas. Therefore, they tried to shake off the influence of religion in the judicial and educational systems and this further undermined the position of the *ulema*.[15] A significant portion of Westernisation, including the provision of civic rights, was the legacy of the CUP, incarnated in the founding father of modern Turkey, Mustafa Kemal Atatürk.[16]

Formative Years of the Republic (1920s–1946): Identity Construction and the Importance of the Balkans

The Bulgarian Muslim community, officially called the Muslim Denomination, is administered by the Supreme Muslim Council, which consists of thirty members. At the core of the Supreme Muslim Council, the Office of the Grand Mufti has held executive power for more than a hundred years. Currently, the office represents almost all of the 1.5 million Muslims in Bulgaria on national and international platforms and delivers religious services to this community, getting its financial support from Turkey's Diyanet. This renders the office mutually important for Bulgaria and Turkey. In 2017, the staff of the Grand Mufti's Office recommended that I talk with Dr Ismail Cambazov, who had written a book of two volumes on the history of Bulgarian Muslims. He would present the historical point of view regarding the perspectives of Bulgarian Muslims on Turkey. After multiple failed attempts, the interview was finally conducted on 8 April 2016. His descriptions of Turkey's foundation were interesting and very controversial:

> Atatürk founded a nonbeliever Turkey, of course Turks were Muslims who devoted themselves to the values of Islam, but the state had a nonbeliever character. And what did that state do for the Muslim brothers in Bulgaria? Nothing. While we were suffering here, Turkey was busy creating new relations with the Western world. Thank God, the situation has gradually faded away and currently Turkey has a Muslim leader, Erdoğan.

The approach taken by Cambazov was quite similar to the ideas presented by the three coffee drinkers at the *Baklavacı Teyze* in North Macedonia's capital city Skopje, alongside many other Muslim citizens of not only Bulgaria, but also other Balkan countries. That is, consciously or not, these individuals claimed that there had been a religion-oriented identity change from Turkey's foundation era to the present day. They also claimed that this transformation had influenced Turkey's position in the Balkans, and its influence on the Muslims of the Balkans.

The irreversible decline of the Ottomans and the occupation of Anatolia by the victors following the First World War paved the way for a national independence movement to regain the territories that were designated by the Misak-ı Milli (National Pact) in the congresses of Erzurum and Sivas in 1919. Following the War of Independence, the Republic was proclaimed as an independent state in 1923. Even though Western and Eastern Thrace had been discussed by the Ankara government many times, the founding fathers decided not to go beyond the borders of Edirne, because of the decreased capacity of the army. Thessaloniki, the birthplace of Mustafa Kemal, remained outside Turkey's border. That is to say, from the beginning of the 1920s the Balkans had become a matter of foreign policy subject to reciprocity in the articles of the Lausanne Treaty. The population exchange that was to follow further alienated the region from Turkey.[17] Under the agreement with Greece, between 1923 and 1927 around four hundred thousand Greek Muslims were accepted into Turkey and an Orthodox Christian population of around nine hundred thousand, including the Turkish-speaking Christians, was sent to Greece.[18] Furthermore, religion- and ethnicity-based questions such as the Alevi and Kurdish issues also started to take shape during the early Republican period.

The socio-political state of mind of the young Republic became Kemalism, and the objective of early Kemalist ideology was the establishment of a powerful state structure within the territories of the country. Kemalism categorically rejected ethnic forms of nationalism but defined all subjects and different demographic components of the Republic as Turks. This meant that being a Turk was more than an ethnic identity, but not totally political or voluntary in terms of nationhood. Those who migrated to Turkey from former Ottoman territories were accepted as Turks. The people from the Balkans were also in this category.

The Kemalist transformation under the guidance of the founding and ruling Republican People's Party (Cumhuriyet Halk Partisi, CHP) had three core normative sources: Westernisation of the state and society as an aim, and establishment and protection of Kemalist nationalism and *laiklik* as duties. The historical background of these aims and duties would indicate that the early Republican elite can be categorised as the winners of the Ottomans' ideological power struggles. This winning elite set out to construct its ideal state and society accordingly. The Kemalist regime tried to ensure the new identity via legal enforcement and institutions, which in practice functioned as guardianship mechanisms.

Turkey's *laiklik* journey has a multidimensional character, which at first glance looks like an ideological construction. Although Turkey has been constitutionally defined as a *laik* country since 1937, actual practice is not that simple. The institutionalised mechanisms for controlling religion make this situation even more complex. Although the Diyanet's assigned duty is religious, its structural and legal mechanisms are *laik*, and it has an exceedingly political position. At the state level, the heritage of the Ottoman period is strongly relevant to this complicated issue. From the imperial period to the current context, the state has always controlled and managed religions. During the Ottoman period, the Caliph/Sultans had an absolute authority to appoint and dismiss the heads of religious affairs: Shaykh al-Islams (*Şeyhülislam*). Moreover, Shaykh al-Islams ran religious affairs on behalf of the Sultan. This meant that the state controlled, managed and regulated religion with the purpose of protecting the state, in a coercive way. Thus, the founding cadres of the Republic had complicated relations with religion. On the one hand, they recognised the necessity of religion for the consolidation of society. On the other hand, they were sceptical about the influence and power of religion and religious figures in Turkish society.[19] They aimed to neutralise the regulatory and mobilising capacities of religion. Furthermore, they wanted to use it as a social and political regulator on behalf of the state and the ruling elite. Thus, *laiklik* was the concept preferred by Turkey's Republican elite in all affairs of the state.

The Turkish understanding of *laiklik* meant that the state should not be totally disconnected from religious issues but should avoid religious regulation and management in any affairs of the state. Therefore, religious bodies should obey the general arrangements of the legal system, even while the state retained infused elements of Islam in its mentality, as a historical construction. The sensitivities of Sunni Islam implicitly determined the state habitus. In this way, the Republican elites did not entirely relinquish the hegemonic power of religion despite the country's *laik* constitutionality. In spite of fundamental changes in the Republic's claims as a new order, neither state structure nor its mentality was radically different from the Ottoman state habitus. Starting from the Byzantine era to the Ottomans and thence to the Republican era, religion was always put under the state umbrella, which is to say it was state controlled in implicit and explicit ways. The Diyanet is a clear manifestation of these continuous habitus, and with its multidimensional functions and capacity it has been increasing its sphere of influence since its inception. As a guardianship mechanism, the Diyanet was used not only as a tool to support new the *laik* administrative structure, but also effectively to regulate Turkish society by protecting it from 'undesirable' faith-based ideas.

In the early Republican period, the authorities tried to gather together all Sunni-Islamic activities under a single roof in an effort to control Sunni Islam, which constituted the 'official Islam' of the Turkish republic. By delimiting the boundaries of what was acceptable in the framework of official Islam, the Turkish state burnt bridges with a host of religious actors, who in time developed into 'unofficial Islam'. Endorsement of an official Islam is an existential part of Turkish *laiklik*. In 1925, dervish lodges were closed, the tombs of the Ottoman sultans and saints were abolished, and their ceremonies were prohibited, on pain of criminalisation. In 1932, the Diyanet (read government/state) mandated the call to prayers (*ezan*) to be performed in Turkish. Furthermore, a *tefsir* or a Turkish translation of the Qur'an was published by the Diyanet in 1938. Apart from the official face of Islam or the formal *laiklik* implementations, the Kemalist regime defined the former mobilisations of Islam in derogatory terms and regarded them as the unwanted reality of the Ottoman past, in the age of science and reason.

As for Kemalist nationalism, the new regime established institutions to reconstruct the language and history in line with the mentality of the new elite. The Turkish History Society in 1931 and the Turkish Language Society a year later would serve precisely this aim of reconstructing the language and history[20] as guardianship mechanisms. Thus, the transformation of the state structure from a traditional, semi-civic, semi-theocratic empire into a new nation-state, that is to say the modernisation of the state, was based on three main pillars: *laiklik*, Turkish nationalism and Westernisation. The acceptable citizen of the Turkish republic was *laik*, but culturally a Sunni Muslim who willingly defined herself/himself as a Turk. Until the death of Atatürk in 1938, Kemalism thus formed the core of Turkey's socio-political system. Yet it is hard to claim that this new Kemalist ideology was based on a broad consensus of people's preferences. Rather, it was a top-down process implemented by a bureaucratic and relatively repressive political elite whose ideology was grounded in official *laiklik*, nationalism and statism. One might therefore define the founding mentality of Turkey as nationalist coercive *laiklik* within the frame of Westernisation.

The construction of the new state identity also provided a new arena within which to reformulate the foreign policy behaviours for the new state. Since Westernisation was one of the main pillars of the state, the new foreign policy prioritised peaceful relations with the Western countries with whom the Ottoman Empire had fought over the centuries. The West was the very epitome of absolute development and power, yet the Kemalist elite had some reservations because of the recent traumatic past. The Sevres Treaty of 1920 created concern about and suspicion of the West. Furthermore, Turkey was a medium-sized power with limited power resources during the early Republican period[21] and the regime's main aim was to consolidate a *laik* and Westernised nation state within its own borders first. In this regard, neither democracy nor liberal values were a priority in the early Republican period.

In the early Republican period, Turkey became a member of some newly established intergovernmental organisations including the League of Nations. This highlights three different points. First of all, it signalled a certain 'balance'[22] in policy for a country with medium-power characteristics, indicating that Turkey was aware of the limits of its power and preferred not to take an adventurist position. Second, Turkey was beginning to become integrated into the international system and establish economic relations with the other members of this club. Third, a priority for the Kemalist regime was to establish peaceful relationships with neighbouring countries, particularly with Greece. After the Greco-Turkish War in 1930, Turkey and Greece agreed to normalise their relations. This normalisation process affected Turkey's Balkan policy in a positive way.

The Balkans was important for the Kemalist regime since it was a former territory and there were still strong historical, religious and cultural ties. The Balkans also had personal significance for the founding elite of Turkey. Along with Atatürk's own Thessaloniki roots, out of fourteen people in key leadership positions in 1938, only three came from mainland Anatolia. The other eleven came from the Balkans, the Aegean region and southern Europe. Six out of fourteen came from areas that had been lost in the Balkan Wars. This trend was to continue: from the mid-1930s on, fully half of the members of the government were born in the Balkans.[23] Nonetheless, the homeland of Turkey's founding fathers did not enjoy a peaceful and stable environment, even in the first and second quarters of the twentieth century. In the 1930s, the Balkan economies were thrown back on their local resources, partly by the rising fascism in Italy and a number of small-scale conflicts among the Balkan countries.[24]

The Balkan countries and Turkey shared some common problems, such as the fascist movements in continental Europe. The countries of the Balkans thus tried in various ways to establish friendship agreements both with each other and with Turkey. The first such attempt was the First Balkan Conference held in 1930 with the attendance of Albania, Bulgaria, Romania, Turkey, Greece and Yugoslavia. The Second Balkan Conference was held in Istanbul in 1931 and was followed by two more conferences in 1933 and 1934. At the end of all these conferences and as a response to the growing Italian expansionist ambitions in the Aegean Sea and the Balkans, the Balkan countries and Turkey agreed upon the Balkan Pact in 1934 with the signatures of Romania, Yugoslavia, Greece and Turkey.[25] Bulgaria and Albania stayed out of the Pact because of their strong ties with Italy. The Balkan Pact essentially aimed to protect the territories of the signatory states against the expansionist policies of Italy. Furthermore, each of the signatory states gained particular benefits from the Pact. Turkey prioritised its border security against a possible coalition between Greece–Bulgaria and Italy.[26]

Turkey tried to maintain a neutral position in the Second World War. Its policy-makers were aware that Turkey was tired country after the War of Independence and needed a recovery period. Any kind of adventure could prove too costly for the future of the country, engendering the possibility of a total collapse. However, Turkey as a middle-power country occupied an exceptional geopolitical position during the Second World War, making it very difficult for it to remain uninvolved. It managed by instrumentalising some of the contradictions between the antagonists. While it made it through the war without participating in any armed conflict, however, both the war and its aftermath were to change Turkey's domestic and foreign policy mentalities, as will be explored in the next section of this chapter.

In sum, the early Republican period can be defined in the light of identity, religion and power sources. The period was one of the holding points in the history of modern Turkey in regard to identity struggles. On the strength of their advantage in having 'saved the country', the leading cadres defined the new state identity as a combination of coercive nationalist *laiklik* and Westernism. This identity formulation was not the *terminus ad quem*, rather it was the pivot for the next moves in the power struggles among different camps, because the Kemalist ideology and identity could not successfully eliminate the conservative identity proposals. Most of the conservatives, Kurds and other ethno-religious camps found ways to be active in politics and society after the single-party period.

In another perspective, however, in terms of state–religion and religion–society relations the early Republican period could be defined as a period of dichotomies. On the one hand, the Turkish republic's founding fathers preferred to manage religion within the political mindset they had inherited from the Ottoman and even Byzantine periods. On the other hand, the early Republic's top-down reforms and coercive *laiklik* implementations could not eliminate all non-recognised Islamic bodies. It is true that most of the non-recognised Sunni-Islamic structures were offered the opportunity to exist by keeping a low (not to say invisible) profile, and they did so. But they did not melt away. Immediately following the single-party period they started to exert influence in both society and politics.

Period of Fluctuations (1946–80): The Rise of Unofficial Islam and Mediocre Relations with the Balkans

The Second World War affected the young Republic profoundly in terms of economic and social conditions, eventually resulting in the foundation of the Democrat Party (Demokrat Parti, DP). The DP was the first 'real' opposition party, unlike the previous political parties, which were founded by Mustafa Kemal mainly to promote the multi-party system but were forced to shut down when opposition power camps started to organise under their umbrella.[27] No genuine opposition had been tolerated. In order to understand the foundation and subsequent electoral victory of the DP, it is necessary to take a brief look at the socio-economic and political conditions under CHP rule between 1945 and 1950. This was the beginning of the post-Second World War period and

Turkey had not yet managed to repair the economic damages it had suffered. During the war, people on fixed incomes became poorer while those engaged in trade and industry grew richer. Under these circumstances the Turkish economy was characterised by black-market dealings in essential items, shortages and rising prices.[28] The CHP government levied a heavy capital tax (*Varlik Vergisi*) that aimed at placing the burden on profiteers, intermediaries and businessmen who had benefited most from the war economy.[29]

In 1945, the CHP government proposed a land reform law to gain the favour of landlords, triggering a major divide in the party. While İnönü supported the reform, some prominent members of the party such as Adnan Menderes (who himself was a landlord) and Refik Koraltan took a stand against the distribution of land to the peasants. Instrumentalising this issue, on 7 June 1945 Adnan Menderes and three other members of the parliament, Fuad Köprülü, Celal Bayar and Refik Koraltan, submitted a proposal for changes in the CHP's domestic by-laws and requesting a free and transparent party body and election structure. In January 1946, these opposition figures established the DP with the permission of İnönü.

The DP quickly gained popularity and easily established party branches in almost every city in Turkey. Even though the 1946 general elections were held in a rather unorthodox way, that is to say by open ballot and secret tally, the DP managed to gain sixty-one seats. In 1950, it won the elections by criticising the practices of the Kemalist regime. The victory of the DP was the very beginning of centre-right political parties, including the AKP in the 2000s. It was also a reaction to the Kemalist regime's hegemonic identity construction project and a popular expression of desire to be vocal and organised against the CHP's top-down statism, coercive nationalist understanding of *laiklik* and economic failures. After the elections, the DP controlled the parliament and Celal Bayar, a founding figure of the DP, assumed the office of the presidency.

This new situation gave the DP the power to regulate political and social systems more quickly and influentially. However, the guardianship mechanisms of the Republic, that is to say the state apparatuses, reacted. This was the first tension between elected officials and the mighty bureaucracy of Turkey. In spite of appearances, however, it is almost impossible to claim that the DP was totally against the Kemalist policies. The general argument and complaint of the DP directly concerned the bureaucratic guardianship mechanism and its intervening nature. According to the leading cadre of the DP, the interventionist bureaucracy was the main obstacle standing between Turkey and a modern democracy. It is also not possible to lump the ten years of DP power together in the same basket, since it stood on many different grounds in political terms. Most DP political implementations were designed to please its conservative and Islamist electoral base. The DP's prime minister Menderes and the other leading figures of the party were aware that repressive implementations of *laiklik* were not welcomed by a broad mass of Turkish people, even though they had not evidenced any direct reactions to the CHP.

The DP period is important to an understanding of the relations and meeting points of official and unofficial Islam in Turkey. Official and unofficial Islam were defined by the official endorsements of the Republic and the Diyanet was positioned as the only representative of official Islam. Yet the coercive implementation of *laiklik* facilitated the formation of unofficial Islamic movements. The DP period was the time when these movements started to become visible. The unofficial Islamic paradigms did not necessarily create an anti-Republican political attitude. On the contrary, they supported the Republic as a nation state but the Kemalist proposition of national identity and politics was not acceptable to them. During the DP period, some of the unofficial religious groups explicitly supported the DP and started to take positions in a relevant bureaucratic institution, the Diyanet.

The first example of unofficial Islam was the Nurcu community, whose paradigm was developed by (Bediüzzaman) Said Nursi (1876–1960) on the basis of traditional Sunni Islam and openness to modern science. Even though Nursi did not engage directly in politics, by the 1950s he announced that it was incumbent upon his followers to support the DP.[30] Another movement that came into being around the same time was the Süleymancılar, referring to its eponymous founder the Nakşibendi Sheikh Süleyman Hilmi Tunahan (1888–1959).[31] Religious groups found an opportunity to enter the Diyanet and meet with official Islam during the DP period. As such, this was a sort of 'cocoon period' for such groups to grow both socially and politically. Speaking of the position of Süleymancıs and Nurcus in the institution, former Diyanet president Mehmet Görmez declared:

During the early Republican period we did not have enough educated individuals with the ability to serve in our organisation. At the beginning of the
1950s persons who ran this big institution realised that some of the imams
who were educated in some of the medreses and religious groups such as
Nurcu and Süleymancı could help us. But the real engagement with these
communities occurred between 1965 and 1980.[32]

Indeed, this sort of political, social and bureaucratic relationship based on
mutual interests between the DP and these religious communities stood in
opposition to the Kemalist *laik* identity. Therefore the military, as a leading
guardianship mechanism, and the Kemalist components of society started to
be discomforted by the radical changes brought about by the DP. To them,
the DP had simply interrupted the identity project of the Republic. Apart
from the socio-political transformations in Turkey under DP rule, there was
significant economic development. The boost for this development was foreign aid under the conditions of the Cold War. The Western Bloc supported
Turkey after the Second World War. Even though most of the supportive
agreements with the West and the USA were signed during the CHP period,
the DP was positioned to reap the main benefits. The most visible effect of
this aid was seen in the agricultural sector. Yet after 1957, even though the
economic conditions were better than during the war years, the DP governments were unable to control rising prices and the rate of inflation.

With both its positive and negative aspects, the DP decade was the first
real experience of democratic practice in Turkey. The guardianship mechanism, however, did not allow the situation to continue. Economic turbulence
and ensuing repression by the DP soon paved the way for the Turkish military
to intervene. On the morning of 27 May 1960, the Turkish Armed Forces
declared that they had taken over the rule of the country. The parliament was
closed for the first time in the history of Turkey. The constitution was also
suspended. The declaration of justification issued by the army underlined its
protection of the Kemalist revolution, the democratic system and the people
of Turkey. This intervention had symbolic and concrete significance in terms
of different identity proposals and power struggles. First of all, it positioned
the Turkish military as the foremost institution of Kemalist guardianship and
paved the way for future intervention in civilian politics. Second, it was the
first indication of what the different identity camps could do to take the

reins of power into their own hands. The successful coup conducted by the *laik* Kemalist camp via deployment of the military was just the beginning of the long-lasting tensions between different identity groups – tensions that continue today.

Turkey's 1961 Constitution introduced freedom of association and speech as well as autonomy in universities and public broadcasting. However, it was a 'programmatic' constitution, re-institutionalising the state structure via new guardianship mechanisms such as the National Security Council, the Constitutional Court and the Council of State, with additional powers.[33] All of these institutional changes strengthened the Kemalist identity of the state, but at the same time empowered anti-Kemalist mobilisation in society and politics. The new constitution augmented the ideological diversity of the country, rendering the era between 1960 and 1980 a vibrant yet conflictual period in recent Turkish history, rife with instability and socio-political struggle.

The military junta envisaged political rule with dominant and sustainable CHP governments, consolidating the *laik,* nationalist and Kemalist society. Global dynamics, under the effects of the Cold War, brought an open era in Turkey's domestic politics. This new era has special relevance to an understanding of both the general role of religion in Turkey and the discussions that followed in the early 2000s. After a five-year transition period, Turkey's people gave a chance to a new political actor, Süleyman Demirel, and his Justice Party (Adalet Partisi, AP), which was the ideological follow-up to the former DP, and was shut down by the junta in the 1960 intervention. In the 1960s, two more political movements were formed: the Workers' Party of Turkey (Türkiye İşçi Partisi, TİP) and the Republican Villagers Nation Party (Cumhuriyetçi Köylü Millet Partisi, CKPM). Even though the 1960s witnessed Islamic movements and their political effects, it would be fair to say that this decade was dominated by the AP and its conservative, populist, Islamist and Western capitalist mentality, and transformations of identity in line with these.

In the AP era of the 1960s there were significant changes in the realm of Islam and politics. First of all, whereas there had been only twenty-six İmam Hatip Schools from the late 1940s to 1965, the AP opened forty-six new such schools between 1965 and 1970.[34] In 1965, the size of the Diyanet and the scope of its activities significantly expanded. These new regulations reflecting the policy preferences of the AP were not against the understanding of Turkish *laiklik*, which was defined as the management of religion, but were directly about the forceful control of the state over religion. By enlarging the areas of influence of religion both in state and society they caused other issues, including the germination of religious communities within the political system.

Another critical intervention by the military came on 12 March 1971, resulting in the resignation of the government albeit without abolition of the parliament. The main reason for this intervention was the violent conflicts between left- and right-wing political movements. The 1971 military intervention was not of an isolated nature: there were similar interventions in 1973 and in 1997. These interventions aimed at 'regulating' society according to the military's Kemalist identity proposals and taking the state back under their control.

The relatively liberal constitution of 1961 and the conservative AP's close relations with the religious communities facilitated socio-political processes that may be regarded as preliminaries to the formation of the AKP in the early 2000s. In this regard, Necmettin Erbakan entered Turkish political life with the Islamist National Order Party (Milli Nizam Partisi, MNP) in 1970 and, after its closure by the constitutional court on grounds of anti-*laik* behaviour, Erbakan moved on to the National Salvation Party (Milli Selamet Partisi, MSP). All the parties that were formed by Erbakan and shut down by high courts in Turkey formed the tradition of political Islam, which was dubbed the National Outlook Tradition (Milli Görüş Geleneği).[35] Between 1970 and 1980 the MSP was successful in participating in the National Front (Milliyetçi Cephe, MC) governments, holding a key position.

MC governments were established twice by the right-wing, conservative and nationalist political parties, the AP, National Action Party (Milliyetçi Hareket Partisi, MHP) and MSP. Their popular support and followers in the state bureaucracy were not strong enough to change the state identity. However, the relations of these governments and the MSP with religious communities did pave the way for an identity change in Turkey. The majority of the supporter base of the MSP came from Muslim Sufi *tarikats* and Islamic movements. Among them, a powerful element was the Nakşibendi groups. This was the first time in Turkey's political history that a religious group played a determinant and crucial role through its backing of an Islamist political party. It was perceived as a fundamental challenge by the Kemalist elite and was positioned against the *laiklik* project of the Republic. The rise of Islamic and nationalist tendencies in politics had a significant social base stemming from socio-economic and political problems. Indeed, the subsequent rise of the AKP would tell a similar story.

The 1970s also witnessed the changing role of official Islam and the structure of the Diyanet. The changes can be divided into two interlinked categories. At the national level, the organisational structure and capacity of the institution were enlarged under the National Front governments. It was domestically utilised to overcome the violent conflicts and polarisation that characterised the decade, becoming a national unity tool. At the international level, the Diyanet became a transnational state apparatus in the 1970s. In 1975, the Türkiye Diyanet Vakfı (Turkish Diyanet Foundation, TDV) was founded by top-ranking Diyanet officials and received tax-exempt status three years later by ministerial decree. The foundation has come to play a very important role in financially supporting the activities of the Diyanet, at home as well as abroad.[36]

After the Second World War, a significant number of Turkish citizens migrated to continental European countries as guest workers. Turkey constructed a new policy to protect, support and bring them together under the same identity and started providing religious services for Turkish Muslims, as well as Muslims from other countries. This newly acquired duty gave the Diyanet a further boost: in 1978, Religious Services Consultancies (Din Hizmetleri Müşavirliği) were established within eighteen Turkish consulates in Germany, and twenty-one Attachés for Religious Services (Din Hizmetleri Ataşeliği) were appointed by the Diyanet at Turkish embassies and consulates in Europe, the Unites States and Australia.[37]

The multi-layered social, political and economic chaos of the 1970s ended with the military coup of 12 September 1980: an extremely important development for religion, identity and power relations in Turkey. The main argument put forward by the military was that they were the best and only true guardianship mechanism against chaos, and would therefore lead the country to a better future. In the coup declaration, the military put it clearly:

The aims of this operation are to safeguard the integrity of the country, sustain national unity and fraternity, prevent the existence and the possibility of civil war and internecine struggle, re-establish the existence and the authority of the state, and to eliminate the factors that hinder the smooth working of the democratic order'.[38]

Yet the 12 September coup did not establish a peaceful and democratic regime. It did, however, transform the state identity, the social structure and the role of Islam in socio-political life, as will be addressed in Chapter 3.

In this period, Turkey's foreign policy affected the gloomy atmosphere of the Cold War. At the very beginning of the Cold War period, official recognition came with the Truman Doctrine in 1947, membership of the OECD and the Council of Europe in 1948 and 1949 respectively, and admission to NATO in 1952. Turkey applied to become a member of the European Economic Community (EEC) in July 1959, following the application by Greece.[39] Turkey could not, however, establish normative Western political values in the fullest sense of concepts such as democracy and separation of religion and state. Yet it was a significantly important country that was geographically very close to the Soviet Union and was accepted as a coalition partner of the West as a buffer zone against the Soviet frontiers. Even though there was a pragmatic policy based on the instrumentalisation of alliances during the DP period, after 1960 policies started to change.

In line with this identity-based domestic conflict, two turning points were important in the 1960s and 1970s in terms of Turkish foreign policy: the Cuban missile crisis and the Cyprus issue. During these crises, Turkish society and the decision-making elite started to question the rationality of membership in the 'Western club'. However, Turkey's desire to gain acceptance as a European state has remained intact as an important objective of Turkish foreign policy. Even though Turkey's journey of application did not go very well during the 1960s and 1970s, this did not change its position. Erbakan's stance against the EU constitutes the only exception to this orientation. According to the Islamist policies of Erbakan, the EU was a Christian club and therefore something to be avoided at all costs. This anti-Western and anti-European orientation was a central and foundational factor in the identity and policies of the Islamist parties in Turkey.

The Balkans, meanwhile, had been heavily affected by both Second World War and post-war conditions, and the region witnessed a huge diversity of notions and moments, descending from hope to chaos and ambiguity in the middle of the twentieth century. Turkey did not have the luxury to remain apart from of all these problems, because of its historical and geographical ties with the region. One issue in particular is very important, not to say determinant, in regard to the Balkan people's perspectives on Turkey: that of immigration from the Balkan countries to Turkey after the Second World War. Although it was not the first migration wave from the Balkans to Turkey, it was the most significant one in terms of Turkish–Balkan relations.

The establishment of a communist regime in Bulgaria in 1944 created a new situation for Turks and other Muslims in the country. The new regime began to implement new policies to transform the Bulgarian multi-ethnic, multilingual and multi-religious structure.[40] This new policy affected Turks and Muslims negatively. Even though Ankara governments declared their concern in diplomatic ways, the Bulgarian government did nothing to improve the rights and living conditions of Turks and Muslims. These minority groups started to establish mass protests against the Bulgarian government. The Bulgarian government could not control the street protests and demanded the Turkish government accept a total number of 250,000 ethnic Turks. Because of its economic and structural problems Turkey welcomed only around 150,000 Bulgarian Turks who were forced to migrate.[41]

After Bulgaria, the greatest waves of migration to Turkey came from Yugoslavia, mostly from today's North Macedonia, where all Muslim people were classified as Turks by the Yugoslavian authorities, even though the majority of that population were Bosnian and Albanian Muslims, groups that did not feel secure under the communist regime. Therefore, largely forced migrations were initiated by the central government of Yugoslavia during the early 1950s and continued in the 1960s and 1970s. In the period between 1946 and 1970, a total of 182,505 people moved to Turkey and were placed in Kırklareli, Tekirdağ, İstanbul-Üsküdar, Ankara and İzmir.[42]

In terms of domestic politics, power struggles and identity tensions were the most significant features of the period between 1946 and 1980. Socio-political polarisation and the use of force by the guardianship mechanisms of the state shaped this era. Furthermore, the rise of political Islam, the resurrection of the Islamic movements and the transnationalisation of the Diyanet are important in terms of their effect on the country's future and its relations with the Balkans. In these decades, Turkey did not deviate from its historical priorities: security and Westernisation. It set out to animate its historical and cultural ties with Muslim and Turkish individuals and groups in the Balkans.

Notes

1. Putnam, 'Diplomacy and domestic politics'.
2. Milner, *Interests, Institutions, and Information*; Hudson, 'Foreign policy analysis'.
3. Mansour, *Statecraft in the Middle East*.
4. Although it is hard to find precisely this claim, there are various studies that discuss foreign policy changes in Turkey and the role of leadership within such changes. See for instance Görener and Ucal, 'The personality and leadership style of Recep Tayyip Erdoğan'; Özpek and Demirağ, 'The Davutoğlu effect in Turkish foreign policy'.
5. İnalcık, *The Ottoman Empire: 1300–1600*, 3.
6. Quataert, *The Ottoman Empire, 1700–1922*, 83–4.
7. Lewis, 'Some reflections on the decline of the Ottoman Empire'.
8. İlber, *İmparatorluğun en uzun yüzyılı*.
9. Mazower, *The Balkans*, 102–3.
10. Ahmad, *The Making of Modern Turkey*, 28.
11. Zürcher, *Modern Turkey*, 59.
12. Bozdaglioglu, *Turkish Foreign Policy and Turkish Identity*, 41.
13. Hanioğlu, *The Young Turks in Opposition*, 109.
14. Todorova, 'The Balkans: From discovery to invention', 455.
15. The word *ulema*, which is widely used in the Islamic world, is used to refer to community-based scholars. Ottoman *ulema* was a basic element of the state and society, presenting progressive visions particularly during their formative and developing phases and despite all their deficiencies, creating dynamism in society.
16. Göçek, *The Transformation of Turkey*, 70–8.
17. Hirschon, *Crossing the Aegean*.
18. Zürcher, *Modern Turkey*, 163–5.
19. Öztürk, 'Turkey's Diyanet under AKP rule'.
20. Kadioğlu, 'The paradox of Turkish nationalism', 186–8.
21. Oran, *Türk Dış Politikası*, 29–31.
22. Güçlü, 'Turkey's entrance into the League of Nations', 199.
23. Zürcher, 'The Balkan wars and the refugee leadership', 665–78.

24. Mazower, *The Balkans*, 128–9.
25. Oran, *Türk Dış Politikası*, 350–3.
26. Türkeş, 'The Balkan pact and its immediate implications', 140–1.
27. Hale, 'The Turkish Republic and its army', 191–201.
28. Türkeş, 'The Democratic Party, 1946–1960', 120.
29. Aktar, *Varlık vergisi ve „Türkleştirme" politikaları*.
30. Mardin, *Religion and Social Change in Modern Turkey*, 98.
31. Yavuz, *Islamic Political Identity in Turkey*, 144–9.
32. The interview was conducted by the author at the Diyanet headquarters on 14 January 2016.
33. Heper and Keyman, 'Double-faced state', 264.
34. Sakallioğlu, 'Parameters and strategies of Islam–state interaction', 239.
35. Yıldız, 'Politico-religious discourse of political Islam in Turkey'.
36. Bruce, *Governing Islam Abroad*, 103–4.
37. Çıtak, 'Between "Turkish Islam" and "French Islam"'.
38. Cited in Tachau and Metin, 'The state, politics, and the military in Turkey', 27.
39. Müftüler-Bac, *Turkey's Relations with a Changing Europe*, 53.
40. Kirişçi, 'Post Second World War immigration', 65.
41. Kostanick, 'Turkish resettlement of refugees from Bulgaria'.
42. Kirişçi, 'Post Second World War immigration', 71–2.

3

TURKEY AS A NASCENT POWER IN THE BALKANS: FROM THE ÖZAL YEARS TO THE AKP

Between 2015 and 2018, almost all the political elites in Bulgaria, North Macedonia and Albania answered my questions about the AKP's regional policies by comparing them to Turkey's policies in the 1980s and 1990s. The AKP was largely juxtaposed with the Motherland Party (Anavatan Partisi, ANAP) of the 1980s. Likewise, these respondents also mentioned both the similarities and the differences between Erdoğan and Turgut Özal. Among those referring to similarities, the words of Ferdinand Xhaferraj[1] in a May 2017 interview are striking:

> Turkey's influence, Diyanet, religion, neo-Ottomanism, soft-power, Gülen Movement and so on and so forth – they did not start with the AKP. Özal was the founder of all and everything. Of course, the world, the Balkans and Turkey had very different conditions, but it is so clear that Özal was the first political actor who understood the role of Turkey in the Balkans truly. Therefore, only a comparative approach with Özal and Erdoğan can be rational to understand the policy differences of Turkey in the Balkans. Özal's Turkey was more kind, diplomatic and had a global perspective; Erdoğan's Turkey is oppressive, and in their relations they do not know any better.

The socio-political instability and violent conflicts of the 1970s paved the way for a military that then defined itself as the main guardian of the Republican values, that is to say a variation of Kemalism, in the 1980s. Yet

73

the 12 September 1980 military coup did not protect the *laik*, Kemalist and middle-power identity of Turkey. Instead, it acted as a trigger for the identity transformation that is still going on under AKP rule. The new regime created a new ideological combination that is called Turkish (nationalism)-Islamic (religion) Synthesis. The new regime also expanded the Diyanet's authority and assigned it the duty of carrying out its mission within the framework of the principles of the Turkish understanding of *laiklik*, with the purpose of achieving and maintaining national solidarity and integrity. Within this new duty, the understanding of *laiklik* has gained a wider function that can be defined as instrumentalisation for the socio-political aims of the power-elite. Thus, the Diyanet was transformed into a multifunctional and transnational state apparatus with the duty of management and instrumentalisation of religion. Furthermore, it was also assigned with a new function: supporting and promoting the new type of nationalism using the tenets of Islam.

The 1982 military constitution made significant changes in Turkey's identity by re-regulating the role of religion in and for the state and society, but the real change came with the 1983 electoral victory of the ANAP, a political party established as the socio-political merger of all the different colours of Turkey's right-wing political tradition: conservatives, nationalists and Islamists. The influential leadership of Özal was an important factor in the electoral success of the ANAP. Özal had recognised the social transformation that Turkey was going through in the 1970s and identified the key issues to which the current political actors were failing to give proper responses. In founding the ANAP he became the focus for appeals on such issues. The ANAP, with its 'catch-all' party structure, consummated the identity transformation of the country. The changing conditions of the Cold War and global neo-liberalisation further affected both the success of the ANAP and Turkey's identity change.

The Özal period can be situated within three major concepts: economic neo-liberalisation, the establishment of patrimonialism and nascent Sunnification of the state identity. It was economic neo-liberalisation that brought about patronage and patrimonialism and sowed the seeds for Sunnification, albeit indirectly. Rodrik prefers to conceptualise these achievements as premature liberalisation and incomplete stabilisation. According to him, the Özal governments implemented mixed economic policies: liberalisation with politics of patronage.[2] Özal's leadership had a decisive impact on the neo-liberal transformation of the Turkish economy but the transformation was based on populism and top-down regulation by the government. That is, Özal's economic policies were populist, top-down and autocratic. This autocratic style of policy implementation tended to undermine representative institutions and paved the way for personalised politics.[3] Moreover, during the ANAP period, the close relations between political power holders and some of the supporting groups gave them opportunities to form and grow middle-size businesses. Called the Anatolian Tigers (Anadolu Kaplanları), these businesses played an important role in the successful integration of the Turkish economy into global markets, due to their vibrant and competitive nature. Most of these supporting groups came into being via political support and had conservative, Islamist links with the Özal governments.[4] They also acted as the locomotive of Sunnification.[5]

The Özal period could also be defined as a period of improvement for the Islamic communities or 'unofficial' Islamic structures such as the Gülen Movement and Nakşibendies. There were two major factors behind this boost. First, even though the military junta insisted that *laiklik* was still one of the main identity sources for Turkey, a Turkish-Islamic synthesis was becoming an almost acceptable ideological norm for those Islamic communities that were not defined by fundamentalist Islamic ideas. Second, there was a symbiotic relationship between Özal's ANAP and these communities. While Islamic communities were supplying electoral support and human resources for the ANAP governments, Özal's ANAP was helping them to access higher levels both in the state bureaucracy and in financial circles. The characteristics of unofficial Islam started to change during the Özal period. Under the shadow of the Kemalist guardianship mechanisms, Islamic communities tried to stand up against the *laik* identity of state power. Adding to these multidimensional relations with unofficial Islam during the ANAP period, the increasing number of mosques, Islamic publications and Islamic content in textbooks and in the media were other indicators of the public visibility of Sunni Islam in Özal's Turkey. A further sign of nascent Sunnification was the establishment of private financial institutions such as the Al-Baraka Türk Private Finance Institution and the Faisal Finance Institution, which were oriented towards Saudi Arabia.

Eventually Özal's position started to erode due to economic problems, exacerbated by the return of old political actors such as Süleyman Demirel, Bülent Ecevit, Alparslan Türkeş and Necmettin Erbakan, who had been banned by the 1980 military coup. The Özal era ended with his sudden death in 1993. However, Özal's ANAP had opened a new phase in the transformation of Turkey's socio-political identity, affecting in particular one key issue: *laiklik*. For instance, during Özal's funeral ceremony, a huge mass of people gathered together and shouted slogans such as 'Müslüman Türkiye Laik Olamaz' ('Muslim Turkey cannot be *laik*'), 'Müslüman Halka Müslüman Lider' ('A Muslim leader for the Muslim people') and 'Ya Allah Bismillah ('In the name of God, God is the greatest').[6] These slogans represent significant identity transformations in the Özal era. From a different perspective, they could be seen as a result of the 1980 coup, which aimed to establish national unity through a combination of Sunni communities (unofficial Islam), the Diyanet (official Islam) and nationalist principles.

The post-Özal years were ones of chaos and instability. Between 1991 and 2002 Turkey experienced eight different coalition governments and two single-party governments, each lasting five months. The main aim of the 1980s coup leaders was to narrow the bases of political participation, enforce the functions of the guardianship mechanisms and weaken the core of parliamentary democracy.[7] They aimed to establish a society that was at the same time modestly Sunni, nationalist and *laik*. They succeeded in establishing something different: a synthesis of Islam, conservatism, patrimonialism and a patronage-based neo-liberal economic structure, in a less-than-harmonious society that meanwhile was dealing with problems ranging from the Kurdish issue to state violence.

In the 1990s a milestone in Turkish political history occurred: the local victory of the Welfare Party (Refah Partisi, RP). The RP was the last political party to be directly founded by the first Islamic political actor of Turkey, Necmettin Erbakan. This local election victory of the RP opened up spaces of opportunity for some relatively new political actors, for instance Erdoğan became the RP's municipal mayor of Istanbul in 1994. Defining the RP is important to an understanding of the AKP's leading cadres. While it was on the one hand a moderate Islamic political movement, on the other hand the RP had certain authoritarian leanings, such as strong and undisputable party discipline and leadership.[8]

The rise of political Islam against Kemalism can of course be linked to globalisation and post-modernisation. The RP spoke the language of socio-economic justice and equality in poor urban neighbourhoods and its voice resonated. It brought together peripheral segments of the business class with people from the working class and attempted to unite them around a common Islamic identity.[9] Repressive leanings, conflict with the Kemalist *laik* identity, struggles with the hegemonic Kemalist bureaucracy and representation of the poor urban masses were the founding elements of the Islamic movements. These elements also explain how Islamist politics gained a foothold on the political stage in Turkey. Yet being the executive branch of the Turkish state during the 1990s, under the guardianship mechanisms of the Republic, was not an easy task for the RP and its leader Erbakan.

In the second half of the 1990s, the centre-right True Path Party (Doğru Yol Partisi, DYP) and the RP established a coalition, making Erbakan the prime minister. Also, in the second half of that decade, legitimising its power through the relevant constitutional article designed to protect the country against separatism (*bölücülük*) and religious fundamentalism (*irtica*), the Turkish Armed Forces started to be more assertive in daily politics. While the separatism in question concerned the Kurdistan Workers' Party (Partiya Karkerên Kurdistanê, PKK) and the Kurdish issue, religious fundamentalism was stretched to include most Islamic communities, given their rising visibility in the public field. The pressure exerted by the Turkish military and the Kemalist *laik* establishment on Erbakan's coalition government intensified in February 1997, culminating in an ultimatum issued by the military during the National Security Council meeting on the last day of that month. After three months of resistance and attempted negotiation, Erbakan finally dissolved the coalition government in June and resigned as prime minister. In January 1998, the constitutional court shut down the RP on the grounds that the party was running anti-*laik* activities, and banned its leading members from active politics. The military intervention of 28 February 1997 put its stamp on history as a post-modern coup that justified itself as protecting the *laik* identity of Turkey.[10] Even though the supporters of the 28 February process claimed that the effects of this correction would endure for more than a century, it actually ended up creating another Islamist political movement, the AKP, itself a hegemonic power of considerable proportions. In a general frame, it might be argued that the 1980 coup, the transformations during the Özal period, the traumatic socio-political atmosphere in the 1990s and the 28 February military intervention reveal the fragility of Turkey's *laik* identity, proving its incompatibility with the nature of the general society and the state structure.

During my fieldwork in the case countries, political elites and local experts preferred to divide the foreign policy approach of neo-Ottomanism into two different categories: Özal's neo-Ottomanism and that of Davutoğlu. Even though Davutoğlu rejected the concept of neo-Ottomanism as defining his foreign policy approach, his policies were described in this way by both academics and politicians, albeit with slight differences from those of Özal. For instance, in 2017 Ivo Hristov, a member of the Bulgarian parliament from the Socialist Party and a lecturer in political science and international relations, underlined that while it is impossible to say whether Özal's or Davutoğlu's neo-Ottomanism was better for the Balkans, one point is obvious concerning the Özal period: economic interactions took priority over cultural and religious activities. By contrast, during the AKP period religious and cultural policies have been more visible. Indeed, Hristov's claim has merit. First of all, Özal's foreign policy was much more active than that of previous periods, and with the end of the Cold War Turkey improved its relations with the Balkans. Second, Turkey began to emphasise its affinities with the Islamic world. Finally, Özal tried to establish stronger relations with Western powers, notably by applying to the EU for full membership in 1987, because he was well aware that without Western support it would prove difficult to maintain the democratic regime in face of the guardianship mechanisms in Turkey.

The fusion of official and unofficial Islam, the rise of political Islam on a global scale, and the Turkish-Islamic synthesis of the 1980 coup were the main catalysts of this transformation, as the Islamic values of the Turkish context managed to reproduce themselves in relation to the ongoing social, economic and political transformations.[11] Özal's neo-Ottomanism was a combination of different factors: culture, the economy, Islam, nationalism and global changes. Thus, although not directly Islamist, it had ethno-religious components that allowed it to be read as an early version of neo-Ottomanism, later to be intensified in the AKP's version. Indeed, it was a new attempt to reconstruct Turkey's state identity. During the Özal period, furthermore, Turkey not only entered agreements with different countries via official diplomatic channels, but also started to use its transnational organisations, such as the Gülen Movement and its education centres. In this regard, Özal's new foreign policy approach and instrumentalisation of transnational organisations created the basis of Turkish soft power resources, and this would be even more pronounced during the AKP period after 2010.

Yet Özal's proactive foreign policy almost disappeared with his death. Economic crises, armed conflict with the PKK, the post-modern coup and the unstable and short-term coalition governments between 1993 and 2002 all obstructed or reversed most of the changes that he brought to Turkish foreign policy. The Özal period posed a significant challenge to Turkey's established state identity and this shift was reflected in foreign policy. But the impetus was not of sufficient duration to change Turkey's state identity and policies in any permanent way. Turkey's Balkan policies are a testament to this.

At the very end of the Özal period three Balkan countries, Bulgaria, North Macedonia and Albania, opened their doors to Turkey, and the Diyanet was the first Turkish institution to enter these countries other than the official diplomatic presence. In the 1980s, there had been early steps establishing the grounds for these invitations. and Özal holds a special place for most of the Muslim elites in these three countries. For instance, in Bulgaria, Cambazov and the Grand Mufti underlined the importance of Özal, who during the late 1980s and early 1990s both directly and indirectly supported them against the Bulgarian regime. Even though some of the legal regulations had taken religious and national identities under protection during the communist period (1946–90), Bulgarian Muslims suffered due to the prohibition of mother-tongue education, Turkish names and Islamic practices. The harsh policies of the Bulgarian communist regime punished Turkish and Pomak Muslims of Bulgaria. who then started small-scale rebellions against the government. In late 1989 Thodor Zhivkov, the president of Bulgaria, called on the Turkish government to open its doors for Bulgarian Muslims to migrate to Turkey. Turkey initially complied with this request and committed to taking 250,000 Bulgarian Turks from Edirne and Kıklareli, but this mass migration was stopped by Özal. As Ivanov argues, Özal's aim was to accept the Bulgarian Turks into

Turkey as promised, but Zhivkov's officials substituted thousands of gypsies in the migrant groups. When Özal saw this intention he closed the doors, since some of the individuals from these gypsy groups were known to be criminals. But Özal's plan did not end there. He encouraged the Gülenists to change the situation.

Even though it seems that the Gülen Movement has always aimed to enter the Balkans, Özal's encouragement accelerated the process. Almost all the representatives of the Gülen Movement in the Balkans noted that even though they came to the Balkans under the inspiration of Fethullah Gülen, Özal's normative, political and bureaucratic support was imperative.[12] For instance, the Bulgarian representative of the Gülen Movement boldly underlined Özal's support for the Movement in Bulgaria. With this support, the Gülen Movement's Bulgarian association signed an official sponsorship agreement with the Grand Mufti's Office and provided that institution with money and human resources. They also undertook to supply teachers for Momchilgrad, Shumen and Ruse İmam Hatip high schools. Lastly, they established the Bulgar–Turk Demokrasi Vakfı (Bulgarian–Turkish Democracy Foundation), but the Gülen Movement lost its impact during the 28 February process, since Turkey put pressure on the Bulgarian state and the Diyanet entered the stage as a new actor. The Diyanet and the TDV thus signed the first financial support agreement with the Bulgarian Grand Mufti to eliminate the role of the Gülen Movement, but according to the Grand Mufti Mustafa Hadzihi, until the AKP period Turkey was unable to pay for all the items in the agreement.

In the light of this evolution, one may claim that Turkey had a mixed identity in the eyes of the Bulgarian political cadres in the 1990s. The Bulgarian policy-makers sought to establish relations with Turkey and utilise its religious state apparatus, the Diyanet, because they wanted to entrust the control of their Muslim components to a *laik*, moderate and Western country. The makers of foreign policy did not see Turkey as a threat. Yet at the same time Turkey's decision-makers had supported one transnational Islamic movement, the Gülenists, for almost a decade. Following the changes in domestic politics, Turkey wanted to replace the Gülenists with its legal religious body, the Diyanet.

Even though Turkish–Albanian relations had always been reasonably good, the fall of the communist regime took these relations to a whole new level of economic and military cooperation. Alongside economic, military and diplomatic relations, Turkey and Albania started to establish different sorts of relations via both the Diyanet and the Gülen Movement at the very beginning of the 1990s. The Gülen Movement had entered the country with a positive reference from Özal. Likewise, as the Gülenist spokesperson in Albania, the representative of the Gülen Movement in Bulgaria noted the importance for Albania of Turkish understanding of Islam and the Gülen Movement in the 1990s, against the Salafist groups and Wahhabism. According to his accounts, members of the Gülen Movement very quickly established the first school complex, with the support of both Turkey and Albania, and it was opened by Özal in 1992. As an example of warm intentions, Fethullah Gülen advised that Özal's name be given to this school. Currently, Kolegji Turgut Özal is the oldest Gülenist school in Albania with campuses in two different cities, Tirana and Durrës. They then opened a madrasa in Elbesan. Currently, the Gülenists run a chain of non-religious schools, from nursery to university level, which are operated by the non-religious foundation. The madrasas are run by the Movement's religious foundation in Albania. Yet the Gülen Movement is not alone in the field of Turkish-origin Muslim activity in Albania.

Albanian Muslims used to be represented by the Albanian Muslim Community, a traditional institution founded in 1923 and operational until 1967. The Community then resumed operations in 1990. On paper, it is a legal institution and a non-political community, independent from the Albanian state. It serves as the governing and representative establishment for all Muslim institutions including madrasas, mosques and religious universities. The personal story of its current chairman, the leader of the Albanian Muslim Community, Skënder Bruçaj, is a telling exemplar by which to understand the complicated positions of Turkey, the Diyanet and the Gülen Movement in 1990s Albania, and their interpenetrating structures. According to him, conducting religious obligations was a repressed need for Albanian Muslims during the communist period. With the commencement of democracy, their institution needed new, educated religious personnel, and with the help of the Albanian state Albanian Muslims established contact with the Turkish Diyanet, because Turkish Islam was safely distant from the support of radicalism. In 1992, the Albanian Muslim Community sent approximately one hundred students to a religious education centre run by the Diyanet in the

Turkish city of Bursa. Skënder Bruçaj was one of them. Sometime later, the Diyanet was unable to provide their basic needs. Yet there was an official agreement in place and the Diyanet started to plan the opening of its office in Tirana in reciprocity. Still, the students found themselves in an abandoned position and a couple of months later, the Diyanet transferred them to a dormitory in Istanbul, Çamlıca, which they learned was opened with the legal permission of the Turkish state and run by the Gülen Movement. This relocation took place under the guidance and permission of the Diyanet.

The last country in the Balkans to extend an invitation to Turkey was North Macedonia. North Macedonia was the only country that had reached its independence without internal conflict after the Yugoslavia period. Starting from the first visit by Özal, Turkey was invited to the country for religious assistance. As in the Bulgarian case, the official invitation of the Diyanet to North Macedonia took place after the 28 February process. However, as in the other case countries, one Turkish initiative was already at work in North Macedonia: the Gülen Movement. Indeed, the story of the Movement's involvement is very similar in all of the cases.

Although in some ways resembling the case countries in this study, no other Balkan country officially invited Turkey and utilised its state apparatuses; neither did they diplomatically refuse Turkey's request to establish offices of its transnational state apparatuses. For instance, Turkish diplomatic representatives in Belgrade, Serbia, explained that the Serbian state did not permit an official Diyanet consultancy in any region of the country. However, the Diyanet had been organising some activities of religious assistance with local actors, particularly in the region of Sandžak, where the majority of the population is Sunni Muslim. The main reason for Serbia's reluctance is based on its concerns about national sovereignty and its relatively greater power compared to other Balkan countries. Similarly, Bulgaria did not allow TİKA offices to be opened in the country. Süleyman Gökçe, former ambassador to Turkey, claimed on 7 April 2017 in Sofia that 'the refusal of Bulgarians to open a TİKA office was a missed opportunity for them [Bulgarians]'. On 10 April 2017, Bulgarian deputy minister of foreign affairs Todor Stoyanov expressed his discontent: 'Enough is enough! Turkey has Diyanet, embassy, consulates and many agreements with us and local municipalities. No other state has that many arms in Bulgaria.'

Throughout the 1990s, even though Turkey was unable to open offices in the Balkans, it started to establish collaborations in various Balkan countries via TİKA, the Diyanet and municipalities. Due to political and economic instability in Turkey, none of these collaborations was able to reach a consolidated level. However, Turkey continued to play important roles under the umbrella concept of security. For instance, Turkey recognised Bosnia and Herzegovina as an independent state on 6 February 1992 and established diplomatic relations on 29 August of that year. In the Bosnian War, President Süleyman Demirel mediated between Bosnia and Croatia when both countries signed the Split Agreement on a joint defence of Bosnia against the Serbian forces. Furthermore, Turkey played a balancing role in the international arena concerning Serbian aggression against former Yugoslavian countries. In Kosovo's name crisis *vis-à-vis* Greece, Turkey has always supported the former.

To return from the details of the Özal era to the overview, in the period between 1980 and 1999 Turkey's foreign policy was shaped by its internal issues and identity conflicts. This period is important for an understanding of the AKP's foreign policy on the Balkans, because it represented the initial workings of the neo-Ottomanism taking shape under the influence of the Turkish-Islamic synthesis of the 1980 military coup. This new approach included more elements of culture, history, language, kinship and religion and the Balkans was very ripe for this policy. However, it would be fair to say that this neo-Ottomanism was only a preliminary phase, since Turkey had relatively limited state capacity during this period.

To conclude, one might argue that states construct their identities before they form their political systems, and these identities inform both citizens and the state elite as to the identity of friends and enemies, as well as what the nation's targets should be and how these might be reached. Further, states form their policy preferences based on their corporate identities and start interactions with other states in accordance with these identities. Thus, identities shape the regional, national and international missions and impacts of states. State identities may be based on such factors as values, cultural codes, race and religion, all having historical coexistence. Religion is an integral part of the state as well as of society, and influences both domestic and foreign policy. As noted in the theoretical chapter, states construct their identities at the intersection of the domestic and the international, in a competitive process between different groups with different identity conceptions and interests. The winning groups gain the representative position and set out to define the *normal* but it is not easy to change state identity quickly and permanently. During the formation and re-formation of state identity, socio-political crises are likely to occur. In this regard, complicated relations between states and religions influence both domestic and foreign policy, through interests and institutional aims.

The establishment of Republican Turkey was based on a Turkish under-standing of secularism, termed *laik. Laiklik,* in the Turkish experience, concerns both state and society and implies that religion has to be managed by the state and regulated in line with the positivist ideas of the founding fathers. Furthermore, the state is the ultimate determiner of the 'good', the 'proper' and the 'acceptable', and thus Turkey is the controller of religion via its state apparatus, the Diyanet. Turkey is therefore a country that defines the 'true religion' and employs it as one of the resources of its power. Turkey was established as a Muslim majority yet *laik* country with middle-sized power and capacity. This unique identity provided it with significant influence in particular areas where Muslim populations could be an issue: areas such as the Balkans.

Republican Turkey has been pulled in different directions by different socio-political actors and state apparatuses. While the political majority has always been formed by the centre-right parties, high-level state bureaucracy has mostly sided with secular politics, acting as guardians of the Republic. While the guardianship mechanisms have tried to consolidate Turkey in a coercive *laik,* nationalist and Western-oriented position, the majority of the population has supported the right-wing political actors who voiced the religious sensitivities of the masses that were ignored and suppressed by the *laik* elite. Even so, the right-wing parties did not have an agenda to change the *laik* identity of the country and Turkey constructed its relations with the Balkans in this context. Turkey's Muslim majority, yet *laik* and Western-oriented identity formation, gave it power to influence the countries in the Balkans until the beginning of the new millennium.

Notes

1. Xhaferraj is an Albanian politician from the Democratic Party who served as a Member of Parliament between 1992 and 2011 and as Minister of Tourism, Cultural Affairs, Youth and Sports between 2009 and 2011.
2. Rodrik, 'Premature liberalization, incomplete stabilization', 25.
3. Öniş, 'Turgut Özal and his economic legacy', 126.
4. Tugal, *Passive Revolution*, 132.
5. The term 'nascent Sunnification' emerged in a comparison between the Özal and Erdoğan periods. The differentiation between nascent and coercive Sunnification derived from the two leaders' characters as well as their relations with the Kemalist foundation and *laiklik*.
6. Çemrek, *Özal's Politics with Special Reference to Religion*, 91.
7. Cizre-Sakallioglu and Yeldan, 'Politics, society and financial liberalization', 496.
8. Önis, 'The political economy of Islam and democracy', 123.
9. Gülalp, 'Globalization and political Islam'.
10. Ozel, 'Turkey at the polls', 82.
11. Yavuz, 'Turkish identity and foreign policy in flux', 22–3.
12. Öztürk, 'Delectation or hegemony'.

Part II

TURKEY'S INTENSE TRANSFORMATION UNDER AKP RULE

Introduction

On 13 February 2018, I was taken on a trip from Stockholm to Strasbourg to present a paper at a workshop entitled 'La Turquie "moderne": Concepts et controverses dans l'Histoire contemporaine de la Turquie' ('Modern Turkey: Concepts and Controversies in the Contemporary History of Turkey'). While I was awaiting the train at Mulhouse station around 22:30, a man in his late twenties asked me for a cigarette. He had a very familiar accent and therefore I asked him, 'Are you from Turkey?'. He responded immediately with the same question: 'No I am from Kosovo, are you from Turkey?'. Suddenly his tone changed, he made a victory sign and he spoke quickly using words that included *inşallah*, *maşhallah*, Islam, Erdoğan and Afrin.[1] It was very difficult to understand him, so he reverted to English and said: 'İnşallah Erdoğan will be very successful in Afrin and show the power of Muslims to everyone.' I was eager to find out more, but there was no time for it. The questions I was keen to discuss are of considerable relevance to this book: What is the relation between Erdoğan's (actually Turkey's) Afrin operation and the power of Muslims? Why is Erdoğan viewed as a Muslim leader and/or Turkey as a Muslim country? And, is this kind of perspective common among the Muslims of the Balkans?

Of course, the words of one Kosovan cannot be taken to represent the views of all people from the Balkans regarding both Turkey and Erdoğan. Yet after more than two years' participant observation in the Balkans, I can attest to the fact that the ideas expressed by the young man are not unique, particularly among lower-middle-class Muslim individuals and groups in the Balkans. Furthermore, some political elites and leading Muslim figures share the same perspective. Thus, the main questions should be: How has a country that is constitutionally *laik* come to be perceived as a religious state – and what are the main determinants of how this process came about?

Many of the critical junctures and determinants of Turkish history are directly and/or indirectly related to notions of state identity, power sources and religion. Yet among various critical junctures, the AKP period is arguably one of the most important for both Turkey and the Balkans.[2] Indeed, this period encompasses a significant number of internal and external turning points, each of which could be seen as a critical juncture in its own right. As such, Turkey's time under the AKP deserves special attention in order to understand Turkey's position in the Balkans of the new millennium. Even though every such juncture has its own unique characteristics and multifaceted effects on Turkey's internal and external politics, they all share four common features. First of all, it is not important whether the critical junctures occurred within the foreign policy arena or in the domestic political environment: all of them had the capacity to affect Turkey's general political state of mind. In this regard, their aftershocks and reflections on other areas have the capacity to constitute new situations in the overall politics of Turkey.

Second, all the critical junctures have influenced Turkey's identity; and indeed, the establishment of the country's founding identity was itself one of the biggest determining moments of the country's history. From the 1920s until comparatively recently, the norms around which the Turkish state is institutionalised have comprised various instantiations of the six principles of Kemalism: republicanism (*cumhuriyetçilik*), populism (*halkçılık*), nationalism (*milliyetçilik*), secularism (*laiklik*), etatism (*devletçilik*) and reformism (*devrimcilik*). These principles diverge significantly from – and indeed broadly stand in opposition to – the prevailing ideology of the late Ottoman period as well as contemporary Turkey, particularly Islamism and political Islam. Identity and power struggles thus lie at the core of both the historical critical junctures and emerging developments. To be more precise, even though Turkey's political history appears to be an example of 'failed democratisation', it has been shaped by political elites whose particular idea of state identity can be summarised in one sentence: Turkey has to be a modest power (middle-power), Western-oriented (in terms of foreign policy), nationalist (Turkish) and coercive *laik* (management of religion via state apparatus) in character.

The third common feature, which relates directly to the second one, concerns religion. One of the fears of Turkey's Republican founding fathers was the dominance of uncontrolled, unofficial Islam within the country's corridors of socio-political power. Therefore, Islam and *laiklik* are important focal points of all these critical junctures and their multifaceted outcomes. In this regard, one could argue that each subsequent juncture has resulted in the weakening of Turkish *laiklik*, including the enforcement of the guardianship mechanisms to protect it against unofficial Islamic groups and their supporters.

The last common feature stands at the crossroads of Turkey's domestic and foreign policy arenas and constitutes one of the key arguments of this book. It suggests that the critical junctures of Turkey's internal and external political journey have directly and indirectly affected the country's policies and perspectives concerning the Balkans. The relationship between Turkey and the Balkans is based on cultural, political, religious and linguistic ties, as well as their kin-based history. Furthermore, their geographical proximity and the Balkans' position as metaphorical bridge between the political systems of the East and the West have given rise to opportunities as well as obstacles for both Turkey and the Balkan countries.

It is worth reiterating here the importance of the first years of the new millennium as one of the most important stages in Turkey's political history. This period saw the initiation of Turkey's transformation in terms of identity and power resources. The beginning of the 2000s was marked both by the major economic crisis of 2001 and by the rising power of the former Islamic cadres of the National Outlook Movement who organised under the flag of the AKP. In its initial years, the AKP was a phenomenon that required considerable effort to understand, even for scholars familiar with Turkey. Despite its roots in political Islam, the party's leadership claimed that it had changed, and began playing to the centre-right of the political spectrum. Defining themselves as conservative democrats, the party's ruling elite started making policies that compromised with the *laik* system, embraced a West-leaning, neo-liberal agenda and created significant momentum for EU membership. These measures enabled the party to construct itself as a reformist actor. Yet this discourse was not to last, and the AKP has subsequently started to be a phenomenon again, though in a very different way.

The Story of the AKP: An Explanation of the Party's Rapid Transformation

In recent years, numerous international indices have tracked a rapid deterioration in fundamental democratic freedoms in Turkey. For example, the World Justice Project's 2017–18 Rule of Law Index ranked Turkey at 101 out of 113 countries, indicating the absence of effective judicial checks on government and significant governmental interference in judicial processes. Additionally, Freedom House's 2018 report places Turkey in the 'not free' category for the first time in the country's history, noting that 'after initially passing some liberalising reforms, the government has shown growing contempt for political rights and civil liberties in recent years, perpetrating serious abuses in areas including minority rights, free expression, associational rights, corruption, and the rule of law'.[3]

Over the years, Turkey has gradually moved to a contemporary one-man rule. While the AKP retains an autonomous party structure on paper, it would be fair to say that Erdoğan and the party have become almost synonymous. In a sense, Erdoğan's political and social charisma transcend his official position as the president of Turkey. It is no surprise that most of his supporters refer to him as *reis* (chief/boss) or *halkın adamı* (man of the people). His speeches have excessive influence not only on politics but also on the judiciary and every function of the bureaucracy. After the failed coup d'état on 15 July 2016, Erdoğan has intensified his position within the context of the state of emergency, using his popularity and influence on his supporters as well as on the party and the bureaucracy.[4]

This significant drift since the beginning the new millennium has posed a challenge to scholars attempting to define the AKP's domestic and foreign policy preferences. In this regard, while some studies viewed the AKP's 2002 victory as an opportunity for the country's liberalisation,[5] a decade later new studies noted concerns regarding the ideological background of the party's leading figures, their radical statements in the past and their potential conflicts with Turkey's establishment. Additionally, a number of studies detail Turkey's 'Islamisation' or Sunnification under AKP rule, directly referencing concepts of state identity and *laiklik*.[6] Furthermore, the positive atmosphere present before 2010 has gradually dissipated and a new subject has become popular: Turkey's coercive transformation under AKP rule. The AKP's repressive policies are blamed for the fall of the Turkish model and the collapse of Islamic liberalism.[7] Furthermore, the prolongation of the state of emergency instituted after the 15 July 2016 attempted coup has made the country's situation much more complicated. In this regard, the change in scholarly approaches is only a reflection of the changing reality of the situation. The transformation of the AKP also means the transformation of Turkey, because of the party's dominant and hegemonic structure.

Turkey's drift under the state of emergency and hegemonic leadership can be explained by way of reference to the ideas of Carl Schmitt and Giorgio Agamben. In his *Political Theology*, Schmitt establishes an essential proximity between the state of emergency and political sovereignty. To Schmitt, the state of emergency is a legal concept based on the political sovereign's ability to transcend the rule of law in the name of the public good.[8] Departing from Schmitt's perspective, Agamben employs a similar concept: the state of exception. A state of exception imbues one person or government with a power and authority that extend far beyond the boundaries of law. In the state of exception, logic and praxis become blurred, enabling the disappearance of the boundary or mutual dependence between politics and law and the transfer of unprecedented power to political leaders. Under this condition, legal regulations cease to constitute a sufficient check on political processes. In such a system, democracy is reduced to elections that are questionable in terms of freedom and fairness, and basic rights are entrusted to the will and capacity of the leader. This is often referred to as *raison d'état*, which has a direct relation to state identity and power.[9]

Throughout the AKP years each critical juncture has been instrumentalised. Thus, Erdoğan has managed to use some of the exceptional conditions to provide political gain, to consolidate his supporters and to functionally instrumentalise the transnational state apparatuses of Turkey.[10] Indeed, Turkey's transformation directly affects its identity and foreign policy behaviour, and Turkish foreign policy under AKP rule has become more 'individual-centric' than 'government-centric'. Furthermore, Turkish foreign policy has also undergone significant changes, turning to ambiguous/uncertain power by using ethno-religious discourses and policy implementation methodologies.

President Erdoğan has also used Islamic rhetoric in his post-2010 foreign policy agenda, and the ideational father behind the AKP's foreign policy, Davutoğlu, has argued that Turkey could become a global power in the post-Cold War context if it follows an expansionist foreign policy based on 'Islamist ideology'. Thus, after 2010, under the influence of Davutoğlu, the party's foreign policy agenda started to offer an alternative state identity that is decidedly more ethno-religious in orientation. Even though Erdoğan elbowed Davutoğlu out of the prime ministership in 2016 in response to domestic political struggles, Davutoğlu's foreign policy agenda is still very much alive; indeed, one can argue that coercive Sunni Islam with an ethno-nationalist discourse is a key identity component of contemporary Turkish foreign policy, in stark contrast to the classical *laiklik* state of mind of the Republic of Turkey.

Given the ties introduced in the early chapters of this book, what happens in Turkey can easily impact the Balkans in one way or another. Turkey's critical junctures are thus also important for the Balkans, particularly where it has official transnational state apparatus offices beyond embassies, as in Bulgaria, North Macedonia and Albania. Most of the political actors in these three Balkan countries have underlined the importance of Turkey and Turkish politics for the countries themselves. For instance, in an April 2017 interview conducted with a political figure in Albania, who also served as a former foreign ministry in the first decade of the new millennium, the respondent stated that:

> Erdoğan and his friends with their pro-EU, liberal and democratic perspectives were very much welcomed by us and they were very active in a positive way . . . Their political strategy, which was compatible with Islam and democracy, was also a kind of an antidote to some of the fundamentalist movements in the region. But, especially after 2010, with the aggressive tone towards the EU, and increasingly repressive policies, Turkey has started to lose both influence and prestige in the region.

Even though these sentences appear aptly to describe the general frame of the AKP's journey and the perceptions of local actors in the Balkans, they fail to detail some of the more complex factors at play. Arguably, the AKP's journey is better explained by examining the interlinkages between structures of domestic and foreign policy. Under such a frame, the overall political processes and the critical junctures of the AKP since 2002 can be divided into four sequential periods, each forming the basis for the next, as follows:

1. 2002–8, the period of survival in the context of the classical guardianship mechanisms;
2. 2008–13, the period of takeover via popular support and the marriage of interests with an unconventional and interest-based coalition partner (the Gülen Movement);
3. 2013–16/17, the period of unexpected change and fatal war with the Gülen Movement; and
4. 2016 and the following years, the period of hegemony and challenge through polarisation and policies of coercive, ethno-nationalist Sunnification in the post-coup attempt era, after July 2016.

Phases of the AKP's journey

Period	Critical junctions	Party's attitude
2002–8, survival	E-memorandum Republican meetings	Defensive
2008–13, takeover	Ergenekon and Sledgehammer (*Balyoz*) trials Closure of AKP trial KCK operations	Active
2013–16/17, challenge	Gezi Park protests 17–25 December corruption investigations	Reactive
After 2016/17, hegemonic	15 July failed coup attempt and state of emergency	Aggressive

Notes

1. Afrin Operation or Operation Olive Branch is the name given to the military operation of the Turkish Army and pro-Turkish forces, such as the Free Syrian Army, in the northern Syrian Kurdish-majority Afrin Canton. It was started in January 2018 under various international discussions.
2. Öztürk and Akgonul, 'Turkey: forced marriage or marriage of convenience with the Western Balkans?'.
3. For the full report, please see https://freedomhouse.org/report/freedom-world/2018/democracy-crisis (accessed 5 June 2020).
4. Christofis *et al.*, 'The view from next door'.
5. Yavuz, 'The AKP and normalizing democracy in Turkey'.
6. Yesilada and Rubin, *Islamization of Turkey under the AKP Rule*.
7. Tugal, *The Fall of the Turkish Model*.
8. Schmitt, *Political Theology*.
9. Agamben, *State of Exception*.
10. Baser and Öztürk, 'In lieu of an introduction', 9–10.

4

DEFENSIVE AND ACTIVE YEARS
OF THE AKP

Compared to other political structures that have been examined in research on Turkish political history, the AKP deserves a special definition under the discussions of its party structure. In arriving at such a definition, the relevant question should be: How can we define a party that has retained power in all elections since its establishment, but is also weakening the general norms of contemporary democracy via the personalisation of executive power (centred on Erdoğan), the imposition of ever stricter constraints on freedom of expression and civil liberties, and the growing use of the state's coercive capacity to suppress dissent? The electoral success of the AKP is another aspect that requires specific attention in a country like Turkey, which was governed by fifteen different coalitions between 1947 and 2002, each coalition governing for an average of only sixteen months. In this context, defining the AKP is important for understanding its hegemony and longevity.

To understand the AKP's party structure and its relationship with contemporary liberal democracy, it is useful to define what democracy means. As democracy is a concept with many interpretations, such a definition is not straightforward. To start with, however, democracy requires not only free, fair and competitive elections, but also the freedoms of organisation and expression that make such elections truly meaningful, as well as alternative sources of information and institutions to ensure that government policies reflect the votes and preferences of citizens.[1] During the early 1990s the dominant concepts within democratisation studies were Huntington's theory of the 'third wave'[2] of democratisation and Fukuyama's 'end of history',[3] both of which predicted democratic transitions and the globalisation of liberal democracies. Yet these theories did not prove to be hardwearing in the new millennium and they have yielded to democratic grey zones and hybrid regimes. Therefore, new definitions have been developed by scholars who have sought to interpret the concept of democracy within authoritarian contexts.

The broad-based expansion of electoral authoritarianism in the developing world has fascinated scholars since the start of the twenty-first century. The challenge of defining these complex regimes has led scholars of comparative politics to apply a range of concepts, including semi-democracy[4] and illiberal democracy.[5] While emphasising different regime elements, all nonetheless point to the decay of democracy in one way or another. Despite holding elections regularly, such regimes neglect the basic tenets that have come to be associated with contemporary liberal democracy. Elections even become instruments to legitimise increasing authoritarianism. Similarly, Levitsky and Way define regimes that combine democratic institutions (including elections) with authoritarian behaviour as competitive authoritarianism. According to their conceptualisation, democratic institutions exist in form but not in substance because electoral, legislative, judicial, media and other institutions favour those in power.[6]

Accordingly, in these situations of 'problematic' and 'limping' democracy, it has been argued that hegemonic parties emerge by ensuring success at the ballot box over consecutive elections in multi-party settings, establishing an authoritarian atmosphere within one of these 'destitute democracies'. Within this definition, five criteria have been outlined for classifying a party as hegemonic, and these are relevant to the case of the AKP. A hegemonic party: (1) has the largest seat-share in parliament; (2) maintains a hegemonic bargaining position within the party system; (3) retains its governing position over multiple elections; (4) cultivates overarching support from society for its general political agenda; and (5) exhibits clear authoritarian tendencies to retain its position.[7] It is hard to stray from these criteria when considering Turkey's main democratic indicators and political issues under AKP rule. A comparison between the AKP's vote percentages and levels of democracy clearly highlights that the AKP's increasing vote percentage is accompanied by decreasing levels of democracy.

AKP votes and the levels of Turkish democracy

Year of election	Vote share (percentage)	Freedom House rating	V-Dem index
2002	34.4	4.5	0.49
2004	41.7	3.5	0.5
2007	46.6	3	0.47
2009	38.8	3	0.42
2010	57.8	3	0.43
2011	49.9	3	0.41
2014	44.1	3.5	0.3
2015-1	40.8	3.5	0.28
2015-2	49.5	3.5	0.28
2017	51.4	3.2	0.12
2018	52.5	3.2	0.12

The AKP is now a hegemonic party within the state, even though the story did not start like this. It is also difficult to define the 2020 AKP regime in Turkey as a competitive authoritarianism or illiberal democracy because it is almost impossible to compete with the ruling structure. Even though in the local elections in 2019, Erdoğan and his party lost the main metropolises including Istanbul, it is still very difficult to defeat the Erdoğan regime within the state structure because of its hegemonic cadres in the main institutions. Particularly since the official declaration of the state of emergency and after the constitutional referendum of 16 April 2017, all the bureaucratic, judicatory and executive structures have been controlled by one system: the party and its leadership. Peaking after the constitutional referendum, and right after the 2018 snap election, the persona of Erdoğan himself has become more key than the party structure.

Erdoğan's visible political career started at the local level in Istanbul. Running for mayor in 1989, he presented a relatively moderate figure in the political tradition of Islamism. However, following his election as mayor of the city in 1994, Erdoğan gradually lost his mid-field attitude and reverted to a confrontational Islamist discourse. He stated publicly that he was in favour of imposing *sharia* law and prohibited the serving of alcohol in all municipally run facilities.[8] Under the 28 February process atmosphere, Erdoğan was punished by the guardianship mechanisms. He was convicted and spent four months in prison, an episode that served to spur his struggle with the classical guardianship mechanisms. Upon his release, Erdoğan claimed a new political orientation as a conservative democrat and established a new political movement with the reformist camp of his former comrades. He publicly stated: 'I took off the shirt of National Outlook', asserting his transformation and a total departure from Islamism. This short sentence and the metaphor that it contains speak volumes about his pragmatism, in that he regards ideologies as garments to be put off and put back on again depending on their utility.[9]

The political methodology and the results of the conflict between Erdoğan's AKP and Turkey's classical guardianship mechanisms find an explanation in political theory. Recall Schmitt's and Agamben's explanations of law-politics and the concept of sovereignty as having a direct relation with state identity and power; Agamben is critical of the way that Schmitt presents the state of exception as a dictatorship, since this, in Agamben's eyes, inevitably leads to a distinction between the exception and the rule. In pointing to the connection between totalitarianism/authoritarianism and democracy as well as between exception and rule, he claims that while the authority has the ability to regulate normal political and social conditions through established law, it is also bound by the law. Exceptions and anomalies that can be neither predicted nor circumscribed effectively will arise, and when they do, extraordinary measures that are not regulated by law are required. When the exceptions appear as a danger to the very existence of the state, a state of exception and measures taken in this context become the only way to survive.[10] In light of this argument, between 2002 and 2008, the AKP and Erdoğan were unable to retain total authority and, in place of this, the guardianship mechanisms tried to exclude the AKP and its leading actors from the political arena in different ways.

The AKP's 2002 victory owes a great deal to the emergence of a new middle class comprised of conservative small business owners in Anatolia. Market-friendly liberals also celebrated the party's victory over the ultra-secularist Kemalist bureaucracy.[11] There was, in short, something in the party's programme for all reform-minded actors, and the party came into office amidst an atmosphere of optimism and hope for positive change. The Kemalist *laik* elite and the guardianship mechanisms, however, have always been sceptical of Erdoğan's real intentions, and created a rather disorganised opposition consisting of the Turkish armed forces, the high judiciary and the CHP. This ideological camp is most accurately described as a coalition that aimed to establish various obstacles. The CHP arm of the informal coalition worked on the parliament. The high judiciary represented a sword of Damocles that had the power to close down the party. The army represented another such sword, that had the capacity to (attempt to) dominate the democratic political arena. One might claim that the primary aim of the coalition members was to preserve their privileged position within the political system, by coercive means.

This loose coalition acted in tandem during the presidential elections of 2007, a time when the Turkish political arena was shaken by a new kind of military intervention: the e-memorandum (*e-muhtıra*). The Turkish Armed Forces officially 'warned' the AKP government via its website. Considering the recent history of the country, such warnings are taken extremely seriously, both by political figures and by the general public. The CHP, then the only opposition party in the parliament, opposed the nomination of Abdullah Gül, a close comrade of Erdoğan. It was also a war of symbols in that Gül's wife wore the headscarf, which was considered a threat by the *laik* coalition. Opposition groups organised large demonstrations known as Republican Meetings (Cumhuriyet Mitingleri), where they expressed hard-line secularist sentiments entwined with ultranationalist and anti-Western messages.[12] The issue evolved into a political crisis. The head of the Turkish Court of Appeals (Yargıtay), Sabih Kanadoğlu, claimed that the election of the president could not have happened without a two-thirds majority of the parliament in the Turkish Grand National Assembly (Türkiye Büyük Millet Meclisi, TBMM). The armed forces' 'e-memorandum' was issued in a context of political polarisation and must be evaluated accordingly. The chief of general staff, Yaşar Büyükanıt, later backed down, saying that he had penned the memorandum himself and it was only a press statement. However, this retraction did not ease the tension, and the memorandum was still considered by the public and the international community as constituting a threat by the armed forces to the AKP. Erdoğan and his party were again targeted by the guardianship mechanisms, only to come out stronger. In a counter-declaration, the government stated that the general staff is accountable to the government and reminded the army of its position under the constitution. The disorganised *laik* coalition had failed; Gül was eventually elected president and the AKP increased its votes by 10 per cent in the 2007 general elections.

These domestic political developments affected the position of Turkey's foreign policy under the AKP. Domestic political struggles were one of the opportunity points for the AKP in its foreign policy between 2002 and 2008. It was on the one hand more active than in previous years, but on the other hand unable to establish its unique stamp on Turkish foreign policy. Even so, this period saw a number of critical junctures that enabled the AKP to build a relatively positive foreign policy record.

The 2003 US invasion of Iraq was the first and one of the most significant critical junctures for the AKP. The incidental rejection of military operations on Turkish soil was a turning point: the AKP realised the importance of foreign policy decisions in mobilising popular support for their rule. In 2003, it was widely assumed that Turkey would join the US-led 'coalition of the willing', even though public opinion was overwhelmingly against the war. The AKP was at the forefront of parliament's rejection of Turkey's involvement in an American war in Iraq. This constituted a turning point for the AKP to gain leverage over the Kemalist military and state elite who were allusively and silently in favour of joining the US-led coalition.[13] By highlighting the need for Turkey to consider different policy options in relation to its Middle Eastern neighbours, Erdoğan began to present a new identity for Turkey,[14] best described as 'populist and proactive, but ambiguous'.

The AKP government's active but relatively low-profile approach to foreign policy was appreciated by the EU and other Western powers. Hence, Europeanisation and harmonisation with EU norms allowed the AKP ruling elite to downplay civil–military relations in favour of civilians in politics.[15] Even though the AKP could not manage to reduce the influence of the guardianship mechanisms in domestic politics, it was able to instrumentalise foreign policy successes and popular support. The party implemented a mutual instrumentalisation policy concerning both domestic and foreign issues. While it drove forward in its domestic difficulties in the EU process, the AKP also relied on its EU relations to protect itself from the *laik* guardianship mechanisms.

The EU reform process has been the main facilitating factor used by the AKP to weaken the institutions designed to protect Kemalist interests. In contrast to the expectations of EU officials and *laik* sections of the Turkish society, the AKP accelerated the reform process mandated by the EU. This was an astute move in terms of gaining the consent of the EU and the *laik* public, both of which were otherwise very suspicious of the new ruling elite. Moreover, via this policy the AKP gained the increasing support of liberal intellectuals who had the ability to promote its policies both at home and abroad. This also means that the EU membership process helped the AKP ruling cadre to capture power in its struggle with the coercive *laik* elite, who had up until this point occupied a privileged position within the administrative and economic structures of the state. The EU process provided an excuse for the AKP to make the Kemalist bloc's institutions more transparent and more accountable. In a way, these reforms helped the AKP to remove the classical guardianship mechanisms over politics. This relatively more transparent aura became the conduit for the AKP to consolidate its power.

Experiencing domestic political struggles and conscious of its lack of experience in foreign policy, the AKP was reluctant to articulate its policy preferences openly. As such, it is not possible to state that the AKP brought about a total or even a particularly remarkable identity transformation. Even though it can be argued that for the first time in Turkey's history the Islamic political actors aimed for Turkey to become a member of the EU, one cannot read too much into this since no particular change occurred in either the AKP or Turkey's political identity. Yet the proactive foreign policy opened some doors, which could be considered a power transformation. For instance, according to data from 2007, EU member states imported more than 40 per cent of Turkish exports and provided more than 57 per cent of the country's total imports. Turkish exports to the EU market totalled around 45 billion euros in late 2007. Furthermore, in the same year, Turkey received more than 12 billion euros in capital inflow from Europe.[16] Despite these positive developments in Turkey's relations with the West, it is hard to discern any visible change in its policies towards the Balkans during this period.

Between 2002 and 2007 TİKA primarily, and later the Diyanet and other transnational state apparatuses, became more active in Central Asia than in the Balkans. A remarkable discourse change occurred during the AKP's first term based on its ideology, but that was all. In spite of this, during Gül's term at the foreign ministry in 2003 he signed an official document/letter that instructed Turkey's missions abroad not to hinder the activities of the

Gülen Movement or those of other religious communities. Furthermore, the official document advised that Turkey's foreign ministry missions should help primarily the Gülen Movement. Although it articulating positions contrary to the ideological and identity codes of *laik* and Turkey's Western-oriented foreign policy, Erdoğan also supported this official document. At roughly the same time, the national security courses that portrayed the Gülen Movement as a threat to the state were abolished and all circulars and orders against religious communities that were issued during the coup of 28 February were cancelled. However, newspapers reported that in a National Security Council meeting held in August 2004, Turkey's armed forces revealed that the Gülen Movement had acquired significant capabilities.

The year 2004 marked the start of the unconventional interest-based coalition between the Gülen Movement and the AKP. Even though the Gülen Movement and the AKP emerged from different traditions in Turkish political Islam and possessed different worldviews and organisational and political styles, as well as completely different historical roots and traditions (not to mention socialisation practices), their agendas coalesced around common interests, particularly in relation to foreign policy. The Balkans represents an important area given its intersection of interest in the AKP and the Gülen Movement, and what is more it affords a crystal-clear view to explore the limits of these interest-based relations. For instance, during interviews conducted in May 2016 as part of the fieldwork process for this book, a high-ranking Turkish diplomat in the Balkans underlined that:

> . . . we are commissioned officers of Turkey and we must obey orders. After Mr Gül's official document we started to be in contact with the members of the movement in our duty countries. But I have to say that most of us including me did not volunteer to do this. They started to knock on our doors about every single issue and made many requests for help. To help them was not our primary duty. I believe in a *laik* Turkey and we the official missions are the real representatives of Turkey that should not be in touch with them. Ultimately, after the 17–25 December process we [were through with] relations with this sneaky organisation.

Expressing a contrary opinion, a representative of the Gülen Movement in North Macedonia, in April 2016, claimed that the close relations between

Turkish diplomats and members of the Movement were against the civil structure of the community and now the Movement is suffering the consequences of this overly close relationship. However, the Albanian representative of the Gülen Movement did not share the same point of view. According to him, after the 'dark' times of the 28 February process, it was very nice to gain acceptance from the Turkish state, but this did not make a great difference to their situation in Albania. On the very same issue, the current Grand Mufti of Bulgaria, Mustafa Hadzihi, stated on 9 April 2017:

> With the 28 February process the members of the Gülen Movement started to be more invisible, but with the beginning of the AKP period they became more and more active. It was so important that the official government of Turkey put them under their protection. After this process, they started to take office inside the Grand Mufti Office until the 17–25 process. Now everybody knows who they are.

Considering these different ideas about the relationship between the Gülen Movement and the AKP, one point is particularly important. Under the AKP, Turkey, with the Gülen Movement and other transnational state apparatuses, became more visible in foreign counties and particularly in the Balkans. This visibility was interpreted as the result of Turkey's newly emerging soft power. Furthermore, the positive diplomatic and commercial relationships developed with various parts of the world promoted a more positive image of Turkey. Thus, the AKP was pursuing soft power approaches through the adoption of a multilateral, cooperative, win–win foreign policy. The AKP believed that Turkey, as the successor to the Ottoman state, should play a responsible and proactive role in the maintenance of regional peace and stability in the Balkans and the Middle East.[17] Yet at this point, it would be well to remember Haynes's arguments regarding the difficulties some countries experience in seeking to establish and control, especially religious soft power, and these should be borne in mind when evaluating such claims. While the AKP had ambitious intentions, in reality the emerging soft power was fragile, and this would make it an ambiguous power resource. Thus, between 2002 and 2007 Turkish foreign policy tested its potential to establish real transformation for the future. However, the AKP's policy-makers were very much aware that real transformation could only be brought about through a complete change in the country's power and identity.

Takeover Period (2008–13): Popular Support and a Marriage of Convenience with Unconventional Coalition Partners

By 2008 Erdoğan and the AKP realised that although they were the ruling party in an elected government, they did not have the ability to manage the bureaucracy, judiciary and military due to existing checks and balances in Turkey's democratic system.[18] The only way for them to maintain power was through popular support, since the guardianship mechanisms were opposed to the establishment and the party's leading figures. Therefore, between 2008 and 2013, the AKP worked to establish a new political discourse and policies to take control of critical state apparatuses and consolidate their power by instrumentalising popular support and exploiting the opportunities afforded by certain critical junctures.[19] During this period, the AKP instrumentalised exceptional situations, taking advantage of them for its own benefit. Throughout, the party leadership referred to election results to justify their actions, citing their legitimacy as a function of the 'national will' (*milli irade*), and endeavoured to become a real sovereign. As Schmitt outlines, the sovereign must decide both that a situation is exceptional and what to do about the exception in order to be able to create or recover a judicial order when the existing one is threatened by chaos. Agamben identifies two main schools of thought on the legality of the state of exception. The first views it as an integral part of positive law because the necessity that grounds it is an autonomous source of law.[20] He codifies this thought within international law, however, whereas the AKP instrumentalised the internal law to establish an exceptional situation to discourage the old guardianship mechanisms. In this regard, this period was the first indication of the blurring of the boundary between law and politics.

During the struggle against the guardianship mechanisms, Erdoğan and the AKP were not alone. The Gülen Movement was one of the biggest and most well-known supporters of the governing structure. These two different structures had not cooperated very closely in domestic politics, with the exception of a five-year period during the AKP's first term. Even though there was a low-level partnership during the first years of the AKP, the visibility and impact of this informal coalition reached a peak only during the AKP's second term. This kind of coalition was well suited to the nature and characteristics of the AKP and the Gülen Movement. On the one hand, even though the AKP had its roots in the National Outlook Movement as well as one full term of experience in governing, it did not have a sufficient number of cadres eligible to serve in the state bureaucracy and some of the key organs such as higher judicial bodies. On the other hand, even though the Gülen Movement had been trying to occupy some of the critical positions in the state structure, former governments and the guardianship mechanisms did not give them right of free entrance due to their religious and non-transparent structure. Turkey's guardianship mechanisms and *laik* components consistently viewed the Gülen Movement as anti-*laik* and harmful to the established codes of the Republic of Turkey.

From this unconventional informal coalition, it is possible to assert three main arguments:

1. One of the main aims of the Gülen Movement–AKP collation was to occupy the sovereign position and reshape state identity according to their common worldviews.

2. If we are talking about the mutual paving of the way for the power struggle in the areas of media, civil society and the judiciary, it appears that the discourse between the AKP and the Gülen Movement on democratisation and fighting against the guardianship mechanisms remained at a discursive level. That is, the power struggle between these two informal coalition partners and the classical guardianship mechanisms were not about the liberation of the state, but rather a battle to control and re-regulate the state's identity.

3. Echoing its alliance in domestic politics, the coalition gave a good account of itself in the foreign policy arena. The transnational branches of the Gülen Movement carried out lobbying activities in favour of the success of the AKP governments, and the AKP governments tendered some opportunities and assistance for the Gülen Movement activities abroad. For instance, while the Gülenist Journalist and Writers Foundation (Gazeteciler ve Yazarlar Vakfı) established a number of organisations that were indirectly for the benefit of the AKP government, some of the

transnational state apparatuses, such as the Diyanet and TİKA, supported the activities of the Gülen Movement abroad. Among these transnational state apparatuses, even Turkish Airlines helped the Gülen Movement.

In 2016, one of the senior figures of the Gülen Movement in the Balkans corrected these claims concerning the benefits of the informal coalition:

> During the 'peace times' with the AKP, we had a respectable position in the offices of Turkish Airlines, for instance when we needed something for our offices here from Turkey they did not take a delivery charge from us, and we could easily upgrade our tickets or buy promotional tickets, but now they started to change their ways when they saw us in the street.

The coalition's opening clash with the old guardianship mechanisms dates back to 2007 but the first real blow was struck at the beginning of 2008 with the Ergenekon and Sledgehammer (*Balyoz*) allegations that flag officers were plotting to overthrow the AKP. The cases were handled in a questionable manner from the beginning and reflected the AKP's interest in ending Turkish military influence in politics. For example, the government chose particular prosecutors who had mostly organic relations with the Gülen Movement and the court, on terms that were sympathetic to the AKP. Even though the judicial process has to be independent from politics, in reality the cases were highly political and based on the outcome of the power struggle in the AKP–Gülen coalition. Pro-government media members and pro-Gülen news organisations aggravated the situation by supporting the trials publicly. Further, party spokespeople defended the trials by claiming that they were part of a war between those with a pro-coup mindset and the AKP. Concurrently, the AKP and the Gülen Movement incorporated their supporters into the military in place of Kemalist and pro-*laik* army officers.[21] The AKP government established prosecutors endowed with special authority, and Erdoğan publicly declared himself to be 'the prosecutor of these cases', thereby blurring the line between the executive and judiciary as per Agamben's claim.

Consistent support by Gülen-affiliated news organisations reinforced a perception among the public of an alliance between the Gülen Movement and the AKP government. Erdoğan and the Movement had managed to touch the untouchables. This power struggle diminished the prestige of the army in the eyes of the people. The Turkish Army was one of the most powerful defenders and representatives of the *laik* Turkey and one of the determinants of 'real' sovereignty. As such, according to Turkey's *laik* citizens the unconventional coalition had targeted the Achilles' heel of *laik* Turkey, enabling them to establish themselves as a dominant force.

On another front, the cooperation between the AKP and the Gülen Movement regarding the Kurdish issue reached a peak in this period. Even while employing the rhetoric of establishing a peace process,[22] they aimed to discredit Kurdish civil actors. The underlying motive was their desire to be the dominant voice in the region of Turkish Kurdistan, where the majority of the population is Kurdish. Furthermore, the Gülen–AKP coalition was underpinned by a Turkish nationalist ideology. Trials against the Kurdistan Communities Union (Koma Civakên Kurdistan, KCK) were particularly emblematic. The KCK is a Kurdish political organisation committed to implementing Kurdish leader Abdullah Öcalan's political views of democratic confederalism. It operates as a branch of the Kurdish movement in urban areas. The KCK was investigated for its political activities by the AKP government, and 562 arrests were carried out between 2009 and mid-2013. Erdoğan and pro-Gülenist media outlets were openly cited as being supportive of the process.

But here the narrative runs ahead of itself – let us return to the evolving events of 2008. As part of the guardianship mechanisms' counter-attack, the Attorney General of the Supreme Court of Appeals initiated a closure case against the AKP, on the grounds that the party had violated the basic principles of *laiklik*. Eventually, the court found the party guilty of becoming a centre for anti-*laik* activities but ruled against forcing it to disband.[23] There was also a 50 per cent reduction in state funding for party activities, but this did not constitute an existential threat to the AKP. Erdoğan and his party had just passed another vital test, posed this time by the judicial bureaucracy, another indicator that the old guardianship mechanisms had started to lose power.

After the closure case, Erdoğan and the AKP started to vocalise the old slogan: 'we are the government, but we do not have the authority'. There was an unspoken understanding in the party elite about the need to take over the bureaucracy and major state apparatuses. Past victimisation by guardianship mechanisms was utilised to this end: whoever victimised them had also victimised the people's will, since the AKP was fighting for the people against the tutelary system. Learning by hard experience, Erdoğan had come to recognise the lack of accountability within the high bureaucracy in the Turkish state structure. In the minds of the Gülen Movement and Erdoğan's AKP, bureaucratic tutelage and the guardianship mechanisms were evil only when someone else controlled them. Identifying an opportunity, they again appealed for popular support.

The 2010 referendum on constitutional change and the general election in 2011, which the AKP won by 58 per cent and 49.5 per cent respectively, evidenced that Erdoğan had garnered sufficient popularity to confront the classical guardianship mechanisms successfully. The 2010 referendum amendments consisted of an incoherent mixture; while some of the amendments promoted universally accepted norms of liberal democracy, others were controversial and prompted heated public debate. The amendment that favoured women, children and disabled people through affirmative action was largely applauded, but radical changes to the Constitutional Court and Supreme Board of Prosecutors and Judges (Hakimler ve Savcılar Yüksek Kurulu, HSYK), such as restructuring their size, election and assignment processes, were disputed. The referendum was the most significant intervention of the AKP and the Gülen Movement against the guardianship mechanisms up to that point, and it constituted a victory in the ongoing power struggle.

During the takeover period, the AKP pitted itself against the guardianship mechanisms in an effort to 'advance democracy', but also displayed increasingly repressive tendencies by discrediting and delegitimising political and civil society actors it did not agree with, in large part aided by the Gülen Movement. On one hand, they tried to justify their struggle against the guardianship mechanisms under the general umbrella of liberalisation and civilian governance. On the other hand, they started to establish a new guardianship mechanism and small executive groups that lacked transparency. Thus, the discourse of democratisation was used strategically to eliminate the old mechanisms. However, in reality, this coalition transformed Turkey by shifting power from the coercive nationalist *laik*–conservative Kemalist elite to coercive ethno-nationalist Sunni AKP–Gülen coalition cadres. This period also showcased some of the strategies that Erdoğan would later employ as leader. For instance, during this period Erdoğan openly expressed his desire to convert Turkey's governance structures to an executive presidential system and repeated his commitment to a new 'religious generation'.[24] The period thus provided clear and early indicators of the AKP's shift from a dominant to an increasingly authoritarian and hegemonic party. It also demonstrated the party's attempts to influence the judiciary and civil society.

During this takeover period punctuated by conflict with guardianship mechanisms and bolstered by informal partnership with the Gülen Movement, the AKP was starting to develop the capacity of the transnational state apparatuses and to establish new structures. Here, three institutions deserve special attention: the Diyanet, the Yunus Emre Foundation and the YTB, this last operating primarily outside Turkey. Furthermore, TİKA's activities increased during this process, through the coordination of the Diyanet, the Yunus Emre Foundation, the foreign ministry and some of the major AKP municipalities.

Under the 2010–17 presidency of Professor Mehmet Görmez, the Diyanet gained support both at home and abroad with the political, bureaucratic and economic backing of the AKP. The AKP as a pro-Islamic single-party government used the official religious apparatus to implement its socio-political aims. In this way, the Diyanet's growth did not save it from becoming one of the most politicised and disputed transnational state apparatuses in Turkey under AKP rule. Beyond that, its structure, budget, administrative capacity and activities entered a process of gradual expansion, and its policies became synchronised with the policies of the governing AKP. Indeed, the Diyanet began to issue *fetvas* and press statements that reflected the AKP's political discourse. Thus, the Diyanet was strategically employed in the domestic context to legitimise the AKP's policies via religious approval mechanisms, suppressing opposition movements and actors. These changes should be read not only as characteristic of the takeover period per se, but also as early notifications of Turkey's identity change under the AKP, paralleling the establishment of a more Sunni Islamist and nationalist-oriented project.

The increasing activities of the Diyanet were not limited to domestic politics, but played out in the foreign policy arena as well. Methodically enacting the new Turkish foreign policy and religious identity, the Diyanet eventually established sixty-one branches in thirty-six countries. It has now published and distributed Qurans and other religious books in twenty-eight languages and provided financial support to official Muslim institutions in the Balkans, Continental Europe and Africa via the Turkish Diyanet Foundation, and has supplied educational and material support for foreign countries' imams. Finally, the Diyanet has undertaken the organisation of official meetings such as the Balkan Countries' Islam Council, and Latin American Countries' Muslim Summit.

The second major institution established within the AKP's identity-shift project was the Yunus Emre Foundation. Its primary aims are to promote Turkish language, history, culture and art on the world stage, to provide education in these subjects and to improve relations between Turkey and other countries through cultural exchange. However, the foundation and its cultural centres also have an important role in Turkish foreign policy. As Ahmet Davutoğlu notes:

> Foreign policy is not carried out solely with diplomacy but also through cultural, economic and trade networks ... The mission of the Yunus Emre Foundation is related to Turkish foreign policy's strategic dimension and the popularisation of Turkish language, the protection of Turkish cultural heritage, and the dissemination of Turkish culture to the outside world. This will enable us to place our historical and cultural richness in our current strategy.[25]

An argument may therefore be made that the presence of the Yunus Emre Foundation and its activities seems to be strengthening Turkey's soft power. Turkey has started to promote its cultural identity as a foreign policy tool. Despite its Muslim majority, the *laik* and Western-oriented Turkey of earlier decades already had a positive soft power impact. The country's drift towards a less *laik* and less Western identity can be perceived as an initiative towards the establishment of hegemony in certain areas – such as the Balkans.

The third of these transnational institutions, the YTB, became active in 2011. Its main aim is to create strong relations with the Turkish diaspora[26] and kinship groups in the fields of socio-economic affairs and culture.[27] Beyond this primary purpose, even though the YTB has no official representation in the Balkans, it is among the active Turkish-origin transnational state apparatuses. Leveraging its ever growing financial capacity, it has been organising Balkan Youth Forums (Balkan Gençlik Forumları) and providing support to students at various levels through Turkey Scholarships (Türkiye Bursları);

Albanian, Bosnian, Bulgarian and North Macedonian students together form one of the biggest groups taking up such scholarships.[28]

With these and certain other active transnational state apparatuses, the AKP's Turkey has been endeavouring to construct Turkish state impact, influence and most probably a normative hegemony by employing its religious, cultural and historical background. Yet in order to achieve this goal such apparatuses require ideological support. This has come from the top positions of the AKP government and specific changes in the country's foreign policy during the takeover period. Indeed, this transformation was directly related to the power resources and identity structure of Turkey.

Alongside the domestic political changes and their reflection on external issues, the dominant determinant of the changing foreign policy was staging of new actors. Witness here Ahmet Davutoğlu and his theory of *Stratejik Derinlik* (Strategic Depth), as an example of the importance of policy-makers themselves, as manifested in foreign policy. In the context of the Balkans, Davutoğlu's ideas are crucial to understanding the underlying logic of Turkish foreign policy change. The central claim of Davutoğlu's thesis is that Turkey, as a result of its Ottoman past and its shared cultural identity and religion with both old Ottoman territories and the Islamic world, could utilise its geostrategic location to enhance its standing in the world. In this way, Turkey has the potential to be a pivotal state in global affairs. This represents a rebuke of two of the main characteristics of classical Turkish foreign policy. First, Turkey preferred to define itself as a *laik* and Western country, whereas Davutoğlu argued that the core of Turkey's character stems from its Ottoman background and religion. This was a groundbreaking identity shift for Turkey.

Second, Turkey traditionally played a middle-power role, which offered a number of advantages including being a negotiator and a centre of attraction for numerous other countries. Pivotal-state status however holds greater prestige than middle-power status and offers a new definition of power for Turkey at the global level. Davutoğlu also offers an alternative worldview by instrumentalising religion. He focuses on the ontological difference between Islam and all other civilisations, particularly that of the West, and asserts that the differences between Western and Muslim paradigms create an obstacle for the study of contemporary Islam as a subject of the social sciences, especially of international politics.[29]

Davutoğlu's problem with the Western modernist paradigm lies in its distancing of revelation as a primary knowledge source,[30] and thus he characterises the emergence of the Islamic state as a response to the imposition of Western nation-states on the world. He posits that the core issue for Islamic polity is to reinterpret its political tradition and theory as an alternative world system rather than merely as a programme for the Islamisation of nation-states. Davutoğlu believes that governments in the Islamic world cannot derive their legitimacy from the same sources as Western states (such as elections and representative institutions), but instead must have a religious basis. In this reading, the Ottoman Empire collapsed due to its separation from the Muslim-majority Middle East, not its separation from the Balkans.[31] Davutoğlu considers that nationalism will eventually come to an end in the region and that Turkey can – indeed, should – lead this pan-Islamic political project. However, this vision applies not to all Islamic or Muslim-majority states, but specifically to the Middle East, the birthplace of Islam.[32] Davutoğlu also notes that Turkey is a key part of Islamic civilisation and can take its rightful place on the world stage again only if it embraces leadership of the Islamic world, as it did when the caliphate was based in Istanbul. This is indeed a major thematic, as Davutoğlu repeatedly drives forward a Turkish nationalist ideal supported by glorification of the Ottoman era.

According to Davutoğlu, the new Turkish foreign policy has five pillars that also comprise the country's policies regarding the Western Balkans. First, Turkey should establish a balance between security and democracy. Second, it has to eliminate problems with immediate neighbours and the wider region. Third, it should work at developing economic and political relations with surrounding regions and beyond. Fourth, it must implement a multidimensional foreign policy within a synchronisation mentality. Lastly, Turkey should utilise 'rhythmic diplomacy' in its bilateral and multilateral relations. The Balkans appears to be a suitable context in which to implement these foreign policy aims, since it is located within Turkey's geographical, cultural and economic realm of influence. Furthermore, Davutoğlu suggests that the Balkans is in a new era comprising restoration, cooperation and construction: restoration in the sense of restoring shared cultural, economic and political ties; cooperation in the sense of developing a new spirit of joint action; and construction in the sense of a way both to overcome the legacy of past decades and to respond to the challenges of the new decades to come.[33] This claim is a fit for Turkey's new foreign policy mentality, which is proactive in character and based on fundamental principles including zero-problems with neighbours and win–win policies.

However, it is difficult to know whether Davutoğlu's pronouncements have been received positively in the Balkan countries. Here, two examples are relevant. First, in his speech at the opening ceremony of a conference on the Ottoman Legacy and Balkan Muslim Communities Today, held in Sarajevo in October 2009, Davutoğlu set out his view that under the Ottoman state, the Balkan region became the centre of world politics in the sixteenth century. This was the Golden Age of the Balkans. He went on to propose that the Balkan countries could escape the destiny of being on the periphery or a victim of geostrategic competition between great powers by re-establishing the successes of the Ottoman period. In this sense, the empire is presented as a positive example and as the model for the solution to ethnic and religious conflicts.[34] Contrary to Davutoğlu's panegyric declarations regarding the Ottoman past of the Balkans, however, most of the Balkan countries celebrate the date of their defecting from the Ottoman Empire as a national holiday.

A second example comes from my fieldwork in Bulgaria in 2017. Even though most of the local experts and elites criticised the ideas of Davutoğlu and his ethno-religious desires for the Balkans, Turkish officials did not enter into such discussion. Then, in my second meeting with Turkey's ambassador to Sofia, we spent considerable time on Davutoğlu's ideas. The ambassador vehemently rejected the claims of axial dislocation under the AKP governments and claimed that this was the continuation of classical Turkish foreign policy. He asserted that Davutoğlu's ideas had been accepted by most 'logical' Bulgarian political elites. After voicing these views, he gave me a Bulgarian translation of Davutoğlu's book, *Strategic Depth*. He informed me that 'this was translated by Bulgarian scholars with our help and they did a book launch in the Faculty of Political Science at the University of Sofia during the term of prime minister Ahmet Davutoğlu in 2015'. After hearing so many pejorative statements in the Balkans about Davutoğlu's strategies it was interesting to see that this translation was in the possession of, and being used by, the biggest state university in Bulgaria. The plot thickened when the following day, during an interview with one of the Bulgarian members of parliament, I learned that right after the book launch the academic and administrative staff responsible

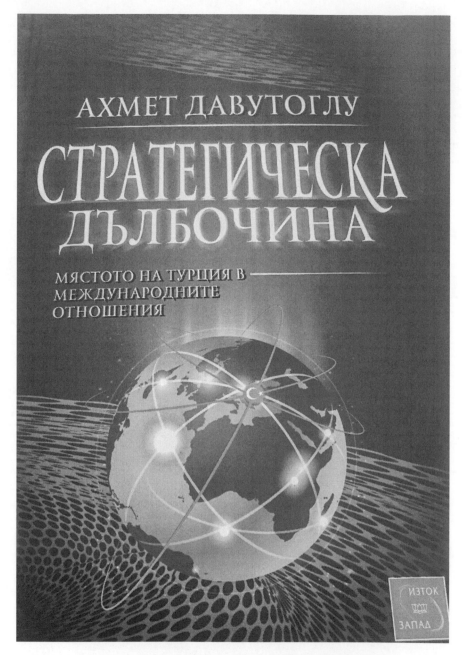

Figure 4.1 The Bulgarian translation of Davutoğlu's book. Photo by the author.

were retired from their offices by the Bulgarian state. Furthermore, it is almost impossible to find the book in any Bulgarian bookshop, since Bulgarians find Davutoğlu's ideas hegemonic, Islamist and colonialist against Bulgaria.

Aside from the Balkan policies, during the takeover period Turkey implemented a number of foreign policy initiatives that brought to the fore questions about the country's identity and power in a regional and global context. For instance, diplomatic tensions with Israel, the establishment of a new partnership with Kurdish leader Mesoud Barzani and the opening of the Turkish Consulate in Erbil ran counter to the classical mindset of Turkish foreign policy. Indeed, on the one hand, these were also important messages to the equilibrants of domestic politics, such as the Kurdish vote. On the other hand, Iraqi Kurdistan does not have a pejorative connotation in the eyes of the Turkish state since its people and regional government are mostly critical of the PKK. These positive attempts through the Kurdistan Regional Government in Iraq, however, were not destined to be permanent, and disappeared under the pressure of coercive ethno-nationalist Sunnification in Turkey.

Turning now to the claim that during the takeover period Turkey involved itself in a range of political issues globally as part of its proactive foreign policy agenda, it is obvious that this effort was beyond the government's capacity and consequently it started to make mistakes. Two events can certainly be considered here under the rubric of critical junctures for the AKP: the Arab uprisings and the Syrian civil war. Political crises in the Arab world and in Syria provided an opportunity for the AKP, and particularly for Erdoğan as its leader, to promote Turkey as the protector of Sunni Muslims in the region, but this was a direct indicator of an identity change in Turkey. That is to say, even though Turkey traditionally assumed a mediator role fitted to its *laik* identity, it had now become a Sunni Muslim actor. Although this policy pleased Turkish conservatives and religious sections of society, it changed the perception of Turkey regionally and globally. For instance, the AKP's leading cadre openly supported Egypt's Morsi and invited the United Nations Security Council to take a visible responsibility. Furthermore, the AKP's leading cadre, but primarily Erdoğan and Davutoğlu, believed that Syria's Assad would soon be ousted from power as a result of his mistreatment of his people. Yet at the same time, Turkey began to promote and support pro-Sunni groups against the Assad regime, and this is also a reversal of its classical approach.[35]

Summarising the workings of this chapter, three main assertions can be made concerning the domestic and foreign policy of the takeover period. First, it was a time of rapid transformation. On the one hand, the struggle against the classical guardianships was almost finished, but on the other hand the early stages of authoritarianism were starting to emerge. These processes saw the transfer of power from the classical Kemalist guardianship mechanisms to the unconventional, unofficial AKP–Gülen coalition. Second, to justify increasing authoritarianism, both Erdoğan and other leading AKP figures started to instrumentalise Sunni Islam, a development linked to the change in Turkey's *laik* identity. Despite appearances, there was not much change in regard to the methodology of the management of religion, but at the discursive level the use and foregrounding of religion were highly salient. Lastly, perhaps the most significant change concerned foreign policy. It can be claimed that the main shifts in Turkish foreign policy have been from a *laik* structure to Sunni Islam initialisation, from a realist orientation to an ideological one, and from a controlling and modest nature to a proactive one. Therefore, it is possible to define the AKP's new Turkey between 2008 and 2013 as a country of newly emerging coercive, ethno-nationalist Sunnification.

Notes

1. Diamond and Morlino, *Assessing the Quality of Democracy*.
2. Huntington, *The Third Wave*.
3. Fukuyama, 'The end of history?'.
4. Case, 'Semi-democracy in Malaysia'.
5. Case, 'The rise of illiberal democracy'.
6. Levitsky and Way, *Competitive Authoritarianism*.
7. Cinar, 'Local determinants of an emerging electoral hegemony'.
8. Heper and Toktaş, 'Islam, modernity, and democracy in contemporary Turkey'.
9. Carroll, 'Turkey's Justice and Development Party', 6.
10. Agamben, *State of Exception*,19.
11. Çarkoglu, 'Turkey's November 2002 elections'.
12. Çınar, 'The electoral success of the AKP'.
13. Coskun *et al.*, 'Foreign policy as a legitimation strategy', 88–9.
14. Aras and Gorener, 'National role conceptions and foreign policy orientation'.
15. Akça and Balta Paker, 'Beyond military tutelage'.
16. Kösebalaban, *Turkish Foreign Policy*, 156.

17. Oğuzlu, 'Soft power in Turkish foreign policy'.

18. Özbudun, 'AKP at the crossroads'.

19. Irak and Öztürk, 'Redefinition of state apparatuses'.

20. Agamben, *State of Exception*, 22–6.

21. Rodrik, 'Ergenekon and Sledgehammer'.

22. Somer and Liaras, 'Turkey's new Kurdish opening'.

23. Keyman, "Modernization, globalization and democratization in Turkey', 315.

24. Keyman, 'Creating a pious generation'.

25. Kaya and Tecmen, 'The role of common cultural heritage', 11.

26. Öztürk and Taş, 'The repertoire of extraterritorial represion'.

27. Ünver, 'Changing diaspora politics of Turkey', 186.

28. Ekşi, *Kamu Diplomasisi ve AK Parti Dönemi Türk Dış Politikası*, 355.

29. Ozkan, 'Turkey, Davutoğlu and the idea of pan-Islamism'.

30. Cornell, 'What drives Turkish foreign policy?'.

31. Davutoğlu, *Stratejik derinlik*, 193–202.

32. Ozkan, 'Turkey, Davutoğlu and the idea of pan-Islamism'.

33. Davutoğlu, 'Turkey's foreign policy vision'.

34. Türbedar, 'Turkey's new activism in the Western Balkans', 140.

35. Coşkun *et al.*, 'Foreign policy as a legitimation strategy'.

5

REACTIVE AND AGGRESSIVE YEARS OF THE AKP

The period 2013 to 2016 saw a move from a *de facto* state of exception to the legalisation of a state of emergency under repressive, Islamist, one-man rule. The state of exception relies on a systemic disbelief in the potency and problem-solving capacity of legislation; it therefore implies weak faith in the will of the people. Proponents of the concept argue that in such extreme situations there must be a powerful decision-maker who performs on behalf of the people; however, an ultimate lack of accountability negates the sovereign's claim to represent the collective will. Under the conditions that necessitate the state of emergency, the sovereign empowers himself to rule by exception, and creates the necessary conditions to prevent a return to juridical order. The duration of the state of emergency is also decided by the sovereign. Therefore, the sovereign, who decides on the state of emergency in terms of scope, penetration and duration, transcends checks and balances and is thus able to attain sufficient power to navigate existential threats successfully. Over time, the authority of the sovereign becomes absolute and needs no further justification.[1] Between 2013 and 2016, Erdoğan and the AKP instrumentalised the exceptional situations to establish exceptional leadership mechanisms, not only in relation to the old guardianship mechanisms, but also concerning their former allies.

From the mid-2013 onwards, the AKP faced new and different power struggles and conflicts despite its dominance in Turkish political life.

Consolidating his power within the AKP, Erdoğan attained the status of indisputable leader. He created a personality cult around himself and, along with the AKP membership, attributed all political challenges to both domestic and foreign actors attempting to attack Turkish society. Five episodes help to elucidate this:

1. The Gezi Park protests;
2. The 17–25 December corruption investigations;
3. The conflict between the AKP and the Gülen Movement;
4. The 15 July 2016 coup attempt;
5. The 16 April 2017 constitutional referendum.

These turning points are important for two main reasons. First, all the processes served as catalysts for the changes in Turkey's identity and power resources. Second, they also constituted the main determinants of Turkey's relations with the Balkans and the changing perception of the Balkans towards Turkey. Reflecting into the Balkans via the transnational state apparatuses, these events served to determine socio-political outcomes of all sorts in regard to Turkey.

One of the most important episodes in the AKP's authoritarian turn was the Gezi Park protest, which has been comprehensively instrumentalised by the party elites. The protests began on 27 May 2013 when excavators attempted to demolish the Taksim Gezi Park, a rare urban green space in Istanbul city centre, in order to develop the site for commercial use.[2] This project was in line with the AKP's neo-liberal urban policies.[3] However, citizens from the pro-EU and pro-*laik* middle class came together with pro-Kurdish groups to save the park and protest against Erdoğan's increasingly repressive tendencies. For many, the demonstrations were not only about the park, but rather about saving democracy, freedom of opinion and diversity in Turkey. The protests turned into a nationwide uprising with an estimated three million participants, spreading to seventy-nine cities across Turkey. The AKP responded with police brutality directed at the demonstrators, demonising them with the slur *birkaç çapulcu* (bunch of hooligans). Erdoğan threatened opposition groups by calling his own supporters to the streets to counter the protests. In total, eleven people were reported killed and some eight thousand injured (many severely) across thirteen cities.[4] The result of the Gezi

Park protests was a hardening of Erdoğan's position *vis-à-vis* the opposition. Gezi had turned into a political crisis and Erdoğan would not hesitate to utilise it to build his absolute rule within the AKP, thereby paving the way for exceptional leadership.

Erdoğan's harsh reaction could be interpreted as stemming from a fear of losing power, in view of recent experiences in the Arab world. In other words, his actions were based on a fear that the uprising could potentiate a total power reversal in Turkey. Yet these very actions were also used by Erdoğan to consolidate his power. Agamben discusses the concept of necessity as the foundation of the exception. He points out that the theory of the state of exception can be wholly reduced to the theory of the *status necessitatis*. Necessity fulfils the main function of freeing the state of exception from the burden of legitimacy. Agamben also points out an extreme aporia in that necessity implies 'an objective situation', a 'pure facticity' that carries no trace of the previous normative – and thus subjective – judgement.[5] The idea of necessity as an objective situation turns it into a legitimating force. From this point of view, Erdoğan's reaction to the protests serves as a prime example of subjective judgement.

The second episode was the 17–25 December corruption investigations. Despite facing allegations of corruption, Erdoğan strengthened his personality cult following the 17–25 December corruption investigation process in late 2013. This episode represents the first highly visible power and interest-based conflict between the Gülen Movement and the AKP. Prior to this, other issues had arisen, such as the Mavi Marmara Flotilla,[6] the Hakan Fidan issue[7] and the private education system change,[8] but the corruption case was of much greater significance and the ripples of the interest-based conflict spread to the Balkans and beyond.

The corruption case, which was directly related to Erdoğan, four ministers of his cabinet and their relatives, was the main turning point for the conflict between the AKP and the Gülen Movement. Erdoğan presented this issue as a coup attempt against Turkish democracy and his administration. Thus, to protect itself the AKP developed a traitor narrative against all those who questioned the party or Erdoğan, not only nationally but also on an international scale. In particular, this narrative targeted the AKP's former coalition partner, the Gülen Movement. AKP loyalists, aided by media outlets, stated that police officers loyal to the Gülen Movement had initiated the corruption investigation. Erdoğan also directly blamed the Movement itself, asserting that there was no basis for the accusations against him. Within days, police officers leading multiple investigations were replaced by new prosecutors.[9] Further, Erdoğan started to wage a war against his old ally, and individuals who were members of the old guardianship mechanism were replaced. A government decree quickly followed, which removed hundreds of detectives and police officers, including the chiefs of the units dealing with corruption and organised crime. The original prosecutors who led the investigations were eventually reassigned, demoted and finally dismissed. According to Agamben, necessity transforms the subjective judgement of the political authority into the objective requirements of the situation.[10] Indeed, in the case of the Gülen Movement and the AKP there is another dimension, which can be named as domestication and step-by-step extermination of the Gülen Movement under the AKP's new Turkey.

Indeed, it is possible to pick up the reflection of this conflict in locations around the world, particularly where both the AKP and the Gülen Movement are active. Yet the directions of force are quite different according to countries and regions. Thus, while in the Turkic Central Asian countries the fate of the AKP is significant because of Turkey's good relations with these states, in some African countries, such as South Africa, the Gülen Movement has been able to hold sway as a result of long-standing and strong ties to influential political actors and local elites. The Balkans is one of the most complicated contexts in which to examine the impacts of conflict, since the AKP is a very strong and influential actor with its transnational state apparatuses, and the Gülen Movement is well established within civil society institutions, schools and media institutions.

Erdoğan and the AKP emerged stronger from the Gezi Park protest and the corruption investigations, aided by less-than-democratic but popularly successful management. The AKP went on to further its political success by winning the 2014 local elections. Erdoğan took more than 52 per cent of the vote and became the twelfth president of Turkey, assuming the role for a five-year period from 2014 onwards. Since the president has to be non-partisan under the Turkish constitution, Erdoğan was obliged to leave the chair of the AKP. With the new presidency, Davutoğlu took the position of prime minister, providing the green light for enactment of his foreign policy approach by Turkey under AKP rule. However, Davutoğlu lost his parliamentary majority in the June 2015 elections for the first time in the AKP's political journey. Erdoğan managed the situation skilfully, assuming three different roles simultaneously: head of the party, prime minister and president.

Despite the fact that the results of the June 2015 election necessitated a coalition government, it was not established. The AKP government initiated a series of military operations against the PKK in Kurdish-dominated south-eastern cities and declared a regional state of emergency, upon Erdoğan's orders. Following several fatal explosions in Istanbul and Ankara, Erdoğan declared a war against terrorism in this same period, as Bush did before the Iraq War. The government started military operations against the PKK in a number of eastern cities and declared a regional/local state of emergency. Erdoğan continued to lobby for a stronger presidential system, promising it would reduce violence and increase stability. With the fight against terrorism Erdoğan became bolder, more nationalistic and less accountable. His firm stance paid off and once again the AKP won a majority in the October 2015 elections. Interestingly, neither the violence nor the military operations stopped, and the societal desire for a strong leader remained. Terror and general instability, as exceptional situations, had brought him closer to exceptional leadership. In this regard, he has started to use his exceptional leadership and different types of persecutions against every single group that managed to stand up to his decisions. For instance, the scholars who signed a petition in favour of pursuing a more peaceful agenda with the Kurds in south-eastern Turkey[11] suffered under the Erdoğan regime.

2016 and Afterwards: Establishing Coercive Ethno-nationalist Sunnification

The hegemonic period was triggered by a failed coup attempt in July 2016 that Erdoğan himself referred to as 'a gift from God' – or in other words a permanent state of emergency, legitimising the exceptional situation. Since the beginning of the coup attempt, both the AKP government and the other political groups have been emphasising that the coup leaders were directly linked to the Gülen Movement. Five days after the coup attempt, the AKP government declared a state of emergency that remained in place for two years, until Erdoğan was re-elected president in 2018.[12] As noted previously, the logic behind the sovereign's decision on the exception appears simple: once the sovereign decides that an emergency situation exists, all subsequent steps are considered dictates of the 'conditions of urgent necessity'. A situation emerges and becomes a threat to order, the emergency and urgency of the situation require the sovereign to decide and act immediately, and thus the law turns into an obstacle that prevents the sovereign's capacity to act immediately and take the necessary measures. Hence, the sovereign suspends the law for the sake of the juridical order itself. However, defining a situation, an event or an act as an exception is very much linked to the sovereign's perception of order, security and threat. In this case, the coup attempt was the main legitimacy point and opportunity for Erdoğan to establish his platform of exception.

The night of 15 July 2016 represents one of the most important moments in contemporary Turkish political history. A group of Turkish Army flag officers attempted to mount a coup against Erdoğan and the AKP government. While there have been different types of military intervention in Turkey since 1960, this was a terrifying attempt for a country that had suffered from military tutelage periods, but it was repelled with the support of opposition parties and devoted civilians. During the coup attempt 265 people died and 2,797 were wounded. Shortly afterwards, Erdoğan, backed by other politicians and media outlets, accused the Gülen Movement of being behind the move.

One of the quickest and strongest responses to the coup attempt came from the Balkan countries. While the EU and the USA refrained from immediate response, preferring not to react directly to the coup attempt, the Balkan countries – particularly Bulgaria, Albania and North Macedonia – came out in support of Erdoğan and declared they would fight the Gülen Movement in their countries. For instance, the Bulgarian government condemned the coup attempt on the morning of 16 July. Likewise, the Albanian president Bujar Nishani reiterated his 'full support for the constitutional order in Turkey', and underlined how Albanians and the people of Turkey are close friends and that in this spirit of friendship the Albanian state hoped for peace and legitimacy for Turkey. Indeed, he also focused on the importance of Turkey's political stability for Albania and the rest of the Balkans.

Edi Rama ✓
@ediramaal

Takıp et

I lumtur per popullin vella te Turqise dhe mikun e çmuar Presidentin Erdogan per daljen me sukses te plote nga nje nate tejet e veshtire!

00:35 - 16 Tem 2016

90 Retweet **310** Beğeni

💬 26   🔁 90   ♡ 310

Figure 5.1   Albanian prime minister Edi Rama's tweet

Additionally, the Albanian prime minister Edi Rama tweeted that he was 'happy for the brotherly people of Turkey and precious friend president Erdoğan for emerging from a very difficult night with full success'.

Under the conditions of the state of emergency, the government then started ruling the country via statutory decrees, in which the parliament had no say and government had no judicial accountability. Democracy was practically suspended. The justification for the state of emergency was that the conditions were serious, and the government needed to take swift and effective measures. The lingering shock and trauma of the incident meant that the government faced little opposition during the first few weeks of the state of emergency. Erdoğan stated repeatedly that the people and the state of Turkey were facing an existential threat and the measures being taken by his government were essential to their survival. Therefore, the extraordinary and extra-legal measures need to be evaluated in this context. Law was not enough to remove the threat, and Erdoğan alone – as sovereign of the country – held the power to decide what the exception was.

However, the measures he implemented far exceeded what was justifiable in the context. Many were actually unrelated to the coup attempt. Within the first three months of the state of emergency, thirty-five medical establishments, 934 private teaching institutions, 109 private student dormitories, 104 foundations, 1,125 associations, fifteen private universities, nineteen unions, forty-five newspapers, fifteen journals, eighteen TV stations and twenty-nine publishing houses, most of which were run by the Gülen Movement, were closed down. More than 111,000 civil servants were fired from public institutions; seven thousand of them were employed in the judiciary, while 10,000 were army officials and another fifty thousand were employed by the education ministry. Two thousand, five hundred journalists lost their jobs. More than thirty-six thousand people were arrested. The buildings that were confiscated from Gülen-affiliated institutions had an estimated worth of around 5 billion US dollars. Thousands of small and middle-sized private businesses were shut down by the AKP government on the accusation that they had provided financial support to the Movement.[13]

Since under this onslaught the Gülen Movement no longer represented a strong threat, Erdoğan turned his attention to the Kurds,[14] and almost all pro-Kurdish print and visual media organs were shut down in the post-coup process. The autonomy of the judiciary was lost altogether, and prosecutors acted as persecutors of the opposition. The co-chairs and some of the municipal governors of the pro-Kurdish People's Democratic Party were arrested. That is, Erdoğan set about seizing by force the areas that the AKP had lost in the elections. Another crackdown in the post-coup process targeted the country's *laik* and Kemalist daily paper, the *Cumhuriyet*. A group of *Cumhuriyet* columnists and editors were arrested on accusation of aiding the PKK and the Gülen Movement. The accusations were less than convincing because it is very difficult to juxtapose the PKK and the Gülen Movement. It is implausible to associate the *Cumhuriyet* with either of these groups, and yet more so to conceive the three of them acting in concert.

At this point, it is worth noting that neither the issues concerning the Kurds nor the problems of the Kemalist groups in Turkey are of much interest to either ordinary individuals or elites in the Balkans. In the Balkans, socio-political elites interact with three subject areas: Erdoğan, the Gülen Movement and Turkish-origin transnational state apparatuses. During interviews conducted in 2017, the former Albanian foreign minister and the board chairman of the Albanian Institute for International Studies think tank, Besnik Mustafaj, shared his thoughts:

> We, as the Albanians and as part of the Balkans, of course are interested in Erdoğan, Gülen and other visible issues in Turkey and here. The rest – leftists, liberals and Kemalists – are not visible actors for us. Our people do not know

anything about them, but issues and actors concerning religion, finance and politics are important for us because they determine some of the equilibriums in Albania and other countries. So, ask me about Erdoğan, Gülen and their fight in Albania, but do not ask anything about the CHP or others since they are not relevant topics for us.

Thus the power transitions, identity transformation and role of religion are of considerable importance to the Balkans when discussing issues related to Turkey. Increasing authoritarianism would be a central concern. The gradual process of authoritarianism matured after the abortive coup, which posed as great an opportunity as it did a crisis. The process involved constant violations of law in the run-up to the coup attempt. However, as the official state of emergency was declared after the coup attempt, extra-legal practices were not only legalised but also expanded and accelerated. In time, the coup attempt has turned into a pretext to silence the opposition using crackdowns against political actors as well as civil society and media enterprises. Yet the real power and identity change happened on 16 April 2017 with the constitutional referendum that led to the transformation of Turkey's system to a presidential one.

The most obvious instrumentalisation of the failed coup attempt was ordered by Erdoğan. This was the drafting of the new constitution, which enshrined the change from a parliamentary to a presidential regime. It was swiftly approved in the parliament with the support of the nationalist MHP. The new constitution was drafted under the blanket of a state of emergency that went far beyond measures against military and bureaucratic tutelage, without the consent of the other parties in parliament. Opponents of the amendment, including the CHP and the HDP (Halkların Demokratik Partisi – People's Democratic Party), argued that transferring the executive authority of the parliament to the president and affording him immunity in relation to judicial accountability would effectively turn Turkey into a dictatorship. By allowing the president to maintain party affiliation, they asserted, single-party rule would result in the destruction of minority parties and the weakening of vital checks and balances. In the context of the deep polarisation that Turkey had been struggling with, this new divide over regime change would further deepen the cracks in the fabric of society. Upon completion of the referendum campaign period, Turkish citizens went to the polls, delivering a result that ranks as one of the most marginal in Turkish election history. A total of 24.3 million voters (51.2 per cent) cast their ballot for 'Yes' against 23.1 million (48.8 per cent) for 'No'.[15] Yet it is fair to say that no one was happy with the result, since it indicated a high level of polarisation among the general public. Although Erdoğan's supporters view the results of the referendum as the official start of a 'new Turkey' era, power struggles between various groups continue.

I spent the period immediately prior to the referendum in Skopje and later cast my own vote at the Turkish embassy in Sofia. I also joined a street demonstration in Skopje on the night of the referendum in order to observe participants. Immediately after the referendum, I was in Albania and it was obvious that Albanian elites were apprehensive about the increasing authoritarianism and religiosity in Turkey and their possible impact on their region. These issues will be explored in greater detail in the next chapter; however it is worth recalling here a quote from the Bulgarian Mihail Ivanov: 'We – not only the Bulgarians, but also the people of the Balkans – know that religious fundamentalism and unchecked power are harmful for society and as far as I can see, Erdoğan has been facilitating both in Turkey.' Indeed, the election results indicate that the AKP has been able to consolidate its power through increasing authoritarianism and the polarisation of society. What, then, is the role of religion in this context?

In mid-2017, Bose claimed that the 'Turkish secular state is dead'. Emphasising the AKP's hegemonic Sunni-majoritarian policies, he noted that the 'secular state is literally no more than a memory'.[16] There are some obvious indications that *laiklik* in Turkey might be in danger. For example, the Diyanet's budget has quadrupled under Erdoğan's rule and Turkey's national school curriculum has been rewritten, omitting evolution and adding the concept of *jihad*. The number of students enrolled at religious schools, officially known as İmam Hatip, has risen from sixty thousand to more than 1.2 million since 2002.[17] The biggest mosque in modern Turkey is currently being built on Çamlıca hill overlooking Istanbul. It will be visible from everywhere in Istanbul, Erdoğan declares. It is one of hundreds of mosques that have been built across the country in recent years. Indeed, it has been reported that the number of mosques has reached more than ninety thousand under AKP rule. Today, Turkey has twice as many mosques as the Islamic Republic of Iran, despite the two countries having roughly the same population. On the one hand these are worrying signs and ought to be taken seriously, on the other hand they are indicators of how the AKP regime has enlarged its capacity for influence in Turkey.

Another point requires closer examination when considering the power conflicts, identity changes and establishment of the AKP's hegemony: the organisational structure and organisational power of the AKP. The AKP's organisational structure has played a significant role in its rise to hegemony within Turkey, and interestingly also in Turkey's activities in the Balkans. While municipalities within Turkey and the role of the AKP's organisational structure will be addressed in the next part of this study, it is worth mentioning here the words of current political actors in North Macedonia regarding the AKP's activities in their country via municipalities. These actors have persevered in repeating that Erdoğan's interest in the Balkans and particularly in North Macedonia started with his major term in 1993–4 and remained at the level of municipalities and local branches of his party. He first visited Harabebaba Tekkesi in Tefora in 1994 and promised a contract to help, but he did not do anything since the region was full of non-Sunni Muslims. According to them, Erdoğan instead provided financial support to Sunni North Macedonians using resources from the municipalities of Istanbul and Bayrampaşa. They also noted that during Erdoğan's period as prime minister, he started to attend to the region through not only big institutions but also municipalities and local branches of the party via bilateral agreements between Muslim municipalities in North Macedonia and Turkish municipalities of the AKP. Furthermore, the AKP's big organisational structures such as the AKP's Istanbul Provincial Directorate, as well as certain universities and companies such as Istanbul Sebattin Zaim University and Metro Tourism, which have very close relations with the AKP, have provided support to projects in North Macedonia.

Here, let us further examine the AKP's institutional structure, municipal power and network relations between formal and informal Turkish institutions, since the role of the dominant party structure is directly related to its impact on the Balkans. Since the establishment of the AKP, Erdoğan and the party leadership have exerted considerable effort to increase the AKP's membership and its visibility in local communities. This is mainly due to his experiences of *realpolitik*, along with those of other members of the leading cadres. According to Court of Cassation figures from 2018, the AKP has more than 11 million members, corresponding to around 20 per cent of the electorate. The number of members is around nine times higher than the next strongest party, the CHP. Turkey's other party, the HDP, has only 37,511 registered members. Accordingly, the AKP's numerical superiority provides an indicator of its hegemonic position and influence at both the national and transnational levels. Furthermore, the AKP is the only political structure that has formal representative bodies in all major cities, districts and within particular neighbourhoods across the country. As such, they have ensured their availability to citizens.

Moreover, the AKP has many permanent (or, during election periods, temporary) representative offices in other countries where the influence of the party is significant. My observations from Skopje during the presidential referendum process are relevant here. At that time, a visitor to the Muslim-majority part of Skopje might easily have guessed that the city was a strong backer of the AKP. Streets, mosques and most of the shops were bedecked with AKP flags and posters of Erdoğan.

Since its early years, the AKP has relied on three segments of Turkish society for support: women, youth, and small and rural communities. The AKP successfully encouraged women who had not previously been politically active to become involved in the party's women's branches and take part in political events. They were able to reach out to housewives across the country who could become voters and active participants within the party. In a similar vein, the youth branch has become one of the most active branches of the party, focusing on voter engagement among young people. There are youth branches organised from within party headquarters in each local district, which is particularly effective considering that the average age of voters in Turkey is 29.6 years. Finally, the AKP has opened branches for voters from small and rural communities in larger cities across Turkey, to account for internal migration patterns[18] that have been prevalent since the early Republican period.[19]

Figure 5.2   Skopje before the 2017 Turkish constitutional referendum. Photos by the author.

Yet this engagement process is by no means democratic. There is no transparency in who is chosen to head internal branches, which the party leadership explains as a measure to ensure unity in the party. Further, party representatives serve mainly to propagate Erdoğan's ideas in parliament, across the bureaucracy, in municipalities and throughout the society more generally. Despite the fact that many party members experience 'political alienation' by identifying themselves with Erdoğan, they remain absolutely committed to both him and the party.[20] The AKP's electoral success is not limited to general elections; it also performs very well in local elections. For instance, in the 2014 local elections, the party controlled almost 60 per cent of all municipalities as well as eighteen out of twenty-seven metropolitan areas. This is significant in that the party is able to assign particular functions to its supporters in these municipalities. Thus, the AKP has been in charge of designating local and countrywide bureaucratic positions across Turkey since 2007 as patronage and patrimonial relations remain significant. The party's electoral success is limited only in cities in the south-east of Turkey where Kurds are the dominant demographic, and cities in the west where secular and Kemalist voter support is strong.

Under these circumstances, the period of AKP rule between 2013 and 2018 was characterised by three main features. The first is the AKP's propensity to initiate brief but intense periods of infighting with mostly Western countries and local actors in order to consolidate power in the domestic arena. Second, there is de-Europeanisation and de-Westernisation in foreign policy discourse and implementation. Third, there is a turn towards an ethno-religious discourse. Even though these policy changes started with Davutoğlu's period in the foreign ministry and picked up speed under his prime ministership, they have not changed with his resignation. Indeed, one may claim that, contrary to the post-Davutoğlu motto of normalisation of foreign policy, the axial dislocation has become more visible since 2015.

Since the beginning of the Gezi Park protest, Erdoğan and the AKP's leading cadre have been trying to consolidate their support by initiating crises rather than reacting. Furthermore, they have been presenting these crises as both a target and a movement against the national unity and development of Turkey. This argument can be substantiated through recourse to many examples. For instance, immediately prior to the constitutional amendment referendum, European countries voiced their apprehension about the erosion of democratic principles in Turkey. Moreover, as noted previously, they also criticised Turkey's record in relation to human rights and freedom of speech, particularly in light of the measures taken by the Turkish state to crush dissent in the aftermath of the attempted coup.

To conclude, one might argue that from 2013 onwards, Erdoğan even began to believe that there was a Western conspiracy to topple him, to which he responded with a furiously anti-Western agenda. Islam – or more precisely, a kind of Islamic nationalism – began to play a greater role in this latter-day AKP ideology. The West is depicted as not just the enemy of Muslims but their very antithesis. Muslims are moral, honest, decent people, whereas the West is corrupt, degenerate and hypocritical. Indeed, all of these processes affect the relations with the Balkan states, which stand between the EU and Turkey. In short, the case can easily be made that Turkish foreign policy has acquired a new, anti-Western orientation. At the same time, an emerging ethno-religious discourse is effectively bringing about a coercive ethno-nationalist Sunnification process in Turkish foreign policy. The effect of this new position on the Balkans has been specified as one of the priorities of the EU agenda for the foreseeable future.

A number of assertions can thus be made about Turkey's recent identity shifts and their enactment at home and abroad. It is crystal clear that Turkey has experienced increasing authoritarianism under the hegemonic party structure of the AKP and the exceptional leadership of Erdoğan since 2011. One of the effects of this rising authoritarianism is the increasing fragility of Turkish *laiklik* both at home and abroad. This authoritarian and less *laik* Turkey has become more aggressive, adventurist and anti-European. Finally, Turkey's new state identity (ethno-nationalist Sunni) has made it as an ambiguous power in the international arena, particularly in the Balkans. These claims are addressed in detail in the third and final part of this book.

Notes

1. Humphreys, 'Legalizing lawlessness'.
2. Öztürk, 'The presidential election in Turkey'.
3. Elicin, 'Neoliberal transformation of the Turkish city'.
4. Arat, 'Violence, resistance, and Gezi park'.

5. Agamben, *State of Exception*, 66–9.
6. The Erdoğan–Gülen rift began with the *Mavi Marmara* incident in 2010, when Turkish charity İHH organised an international flotilla to deliver aid to the blockaded Palestinians of Gaza. Following the failed attempt to break the Israeli blockade, which resulted in the killing of nine Turkish activists when Israeli commandos raided the *Mavi Marmara* in international waters, Gülen expressed his disapproval of the mission.
7. Hakan Fidan is the head of the Turkish National Intelligence Agency (Milli İstihbarat Teşkilatı, MİT). The Gülenists led an ultimately unsuccessful smear campaign against Hakan Fidan and tried to prosecute him. But Erdoğan did not allow this move by the Gülen Movement.
8. In the autumn of 2013, Erdoğan ordered the closure of preparatory schools around the country – a significant source of income for the Gülenists, who operated about a quarter of these schools.
9. Saatçioğlu, 'De-Europeanisation in Turkey', 138.
10. Agamben, *State of Exception*, 71.
11. Baser, Akgönül and Öztürk, '"Academics for Peace" in Turkey'.
12. Öztürk, 'Lack of self-confidence of the authoritarian regimes'.
13. Öztürk and Gözaydın, 'Turkey's constitutional amendments', 216.
14. Gurses, *Anatomy of a Civil War.*
15. Esen and Gümüşçü, 'A small yes for presidentialism'.
16. For the full version of the article please see www.openthemagazine.com/article/essay/the-death-of-secularism, accessed 3 June 2020.
17. To view the numbers please see www.turkeyanalyst.org/publications/turkey-analyst-articles/item/437-the-islamization-of-turkey-erdoğan's-education-reforms.html, accessed 3 June 2020.
18. Baser and Öztürk, 'Turkey's diaspora governance policies'.
19. Doğan, *Mahalledeki AKP.*
20. Ibid., 73–5.

Part III

THE AKP'S NEW TURKEY AND ITS REFLECTION IN THE BALKANS

Introduction

The previous pages can be encapsulated in four claims that are directly and indirectly related to Turkey's policy preferences on the Balkan Peninsula. By focusing on these claims, this last part of the book sets out to explain the complicated relationship among state identities, power and religion, and their impact on foreign policy in the case of Turkey under AKP rule.

First, religion can manifest itself in domestic politics and international relations either as an instrument or a purpose, or as a combination of the two. Thus, it may be used as a socio-political tool for justification and mobilisation purposes. It may also be used to establish and reshape various socio-political structures within societies. More frequently, it is used as a combination of instrument and purpose, which can be summarised as the instrumentalisation of religion to establish a socio-political environment designated by mostly, but not always, religious political actors. Even in secular/*laik* systems, governments instrumentalise and regulate religion for the purposes of management and mobilisation of society, and regulate the relations between state and religion, and between society and religion, in non-secular ways. In a similar fashion, the instrumentalisation of religion could be used to convert societies and states into a more religiously defined orientation. In all these possibilities, religion acts as a great influencer that may be utilised to transform policy preferences, identities, power norms and relations between states at the international level.

Second, transformations in domestic politics have an immense ability to reshape the identity, preferences, interests and power structures/resources of states – and these are the main determinants of foreign policy. Domestic political transformations and struggles might affect the corporate identity of states as well as their behaviours, leading them to re-organise their foreign policies. This claim falls in line with the constructivist approach and provides a significant explanatory power for the case of Turkey. Thus, the axial dislocations that Turkey has been going through reflect the power conflicts in the domestic socio-political arena since the late Ottoman period. Two points are crucial in the recent history of Turkey: the role and/or the position of religion, and the hegemonic, coercive effect of leadership.[1] Certainly, both the role of religion and the impact of leadership on the transformation of state identity are issues that have been scrutinised in the scholarly literature, but the Turkish case gives us the combined effect of the two. A key determinant for Turkey's domestic politics is the form of the relationship between religion and state, with the regulating role of political leaders. Erdoğan's leadership, the AKP's hegemonic position and the power of religion have consolidated to dislodge the *laik* structure of the state and of foreign policy preferences. Turkish state identity has been re-oriented on the basis of normative national Sunni-Islamic values and priorities. This process is described as Sunnification in this study. Since ethno-nationalist policies and religion have much in common in their conception of purity, boundaries and order, in the case of Turkey they have come together at the state level, in a coercive way, under the rule of a hegemonic authoritarian regime. Thus the identity change experienced by Turkey is defined as a process of coercive ethno-nationalist Sunnification.

Third, state identity is strongly relevant to state power and its resources. Being a democratic country that values and protects human rights and promotes religious freedom accords a certain influence on the state. States interact with each other and affect the international community, through their identities alongside their negotiation powers. Every state has a certain capacity of hard power according to its sanction capabilities in mainly military and economic terms. Soft power, however, is based mostly on identities, lifestyles, belief systems and any other normative capacity to exercise influence on others. The functions of soft power tools can be utilised for different policy preferences, depending on the policy choices of the ruling elite.

Fourth, the religion-oriented, identity-based power transformations of states might not be exportable to every foreign country since the host country might have different identity preferences. A common historical experience and similarities in issues like religion, ethnicity, language and culture constitute major determinants. For these determinants to be influential, the countries must be willing to interact with each other, and offer and accept relevant services. The nature of the relations between some Balkan countries and Turkey affords an interesting example of such interaction. Furthermore, because of Turkey's established foreign policy approach, which prioritises security, the country has always tried to play a part in Balkan politics. Any instability in the Balkans would affect Turkey's domestic politics in one way or another. In the same vein, some Balkan countries have had similar approaches to Turkey because of their significant Muslim populations, but mostly as a 'belonging' category. Thus Turkey's ongoing religion-based transformations in domestic politics and power relations reflect on its Balkan policies fairly directly.

The AKP's long-lasting hegemonic power in domestic politics under Erdoğan's assertive leadership, which involves the instrumentalisation of religion, has accumulated enough capacity to convert the identity of the state. Even though in its initial stages Erdoğan's Turkey was defined as a weak democracy with competitive authoritarianism, it has rapidly become authoritarian via its use of states of exception. The process of coercive ethno-nationalist Sunnification of the state has also been intensified with this authoritarian turn. The potent role of Islam within the state structure is termed 'hegemonic Islam' by Cesari. In her hegemonic Islam, religion is not only absorbed within the state structure, but also enacts the national identity.[2] At first appearance, Cesari's definition of hegemonic Islam seems to be very much applicable to the situation of Turkey, particularly in the second decade of the 2000s. However, Turkey has another defining characteristic that differentiates it: hegemonic authoritarianism and influential ethno-nationalist tendencies. That is, Sunni Islam has reached a hegemonic position within the state institutions and has been transforming the state and the national identity under an authoritarian regime. Authoritarianism, therefore, is one of the driving engines of the coercive ethno-nationalist Sunnification in state and society in the hands of authoritarian pro-Islamist leading cadres. The reflection of this transformation on state identity, power and foreign policy preferences carries the elements from the two processes that together create the AKP's new Turkey.

All of these transformations have different effects on different Balkan countries due to their different characteristics. For instance, while the Bulgarian Muslim population is around 557,139, which roughly constitutes 7.5 per cent of the overall population, and a significant number of Bulgarian Muslims are Sunni, according to the 2002 census for North Macedonia,[3] a multireligious (mainly Orthodox Christian and Muslim) and multi-ethnic (mainly North Macedonian and Albanian) country, there are more than 650,000 Muslims, who constitute 35 per cent of the overall population. Albania is the only Muslim-majority country among the three, with its more than 1.5 million Muslim citizens (including Sunnis, Bektashis and others), almost 60 per cent of the overall population. These three countries have been hosting transnational state and semi-state apparatuses of Turkish origin: foundations and groups that are active in socio-political life. Moreover, there are also pro-Turkish and pro-Muslim political parties and pressure groups that are influential in these countries. Bulgaria, North Macedonia and Albania are inside Turkey's sphere of influence via not only the Diyanet, but also many other organisations which mostly became active during the AKP period. Therefore, Turkey's recent coercive ethno-nationalist Sunnification reflects on these countries as the domestic issues are exported through transnational apparatuses. Thus, after more than two years of fieldwork and observations, I argue that it is possible to define in four different categories Turkey's changing face as reflected in these three Balkan counties. These categories are: (1) increasing investment as a service to the Ummah, (2) the export of domestic conflicts via formal and informal transnational apparatuses, (3) involving 'others' in the political arena for the purpose of enlarging the sphere of influence and (4) destabilising the secular environments of host countries.

Notes

1. Büyük and Özturk, 'The role of leadership networks'.
2. Cesari, *The Awakening of Muslim Democracy*, xiv.
3. This was the last census that was open to the public. Due to the demographic conflicts, the Macedonian state prefers not to announce new population statistics.

6

SERVICE TO THE GLOBAL UMMAH

Almost all the political elites, public figures and ordinary people I talked to in the streets of North Macedonia's Skopje and Tetovë mentioned the significant support provided by Erdoğan's administration during the flood disaster in 2016. They underlined what a difficult time this was for the North Macedonian people because the infrastructure of North Macedonia was poor, and the state's own resources were insufficient to deal with a disaster of this magnitude. Yet thanks to Turkey's prompt and long-term support, they managed to cope with the effects of the flood. Particularly in Skopje's Old Bazaar, where the majority of the population is Sunni Muslim, it was possible to see aid bags bearing the label of Turkey or Turkish Presidency some two years after the flood. Due to this and similar support provided by the administration, most of the people in the Old Bazaar spoke very highly of Erdoğan.

Indeed, this is not the only example provided by locals in the Balkans regarding Turkey's comprehensive aid activities, investment and economic power. Turkey's involvement is not limited to hard times in the Balkans. In 2017, Bulgaria's Chief Mufti Mustafa Hadji underlined that the material and non-material support provided by Turkey had been gradually increasing since 2006–7. Even though it is not enough, Turkey has been sending around two million Bulgarian levs each year, in accordance with the official agreement with the Grand Mufti's Office in Sofia. According to Hadji, they can also ask for material support from the Diyanet and the Turkish Diyanet

Foundation. For example, during the Eid periods, Turkey sends sacrificial lambs to Bulgarian Muslims.

Despite the abundance of affirmative and grateful opinions expressed by Sunni Muslim groups in the Balkans regarding the aid and investment offered by Turkey the world leader of the Bektashi Order, Grandfather Hajji Baba Mondi (Haxhi Baba Edmond Brahimaj) maintained a critical distance. On 25 April 2017, he was asked about the financial support of the Turkish state to Bektashis in both Albania and the rest of the region. His answer was remarkable:

> We do not want to ask anything from the Turkish government because we believe that politics and religion have to be separate like his holiness Husseyin suggested. But sometimes, we might find ourselves in a position to ask very small things from our friends. Indeed, Turkey is among these friends . . . I told Davutoğlu, 'you constructed many mosques, but did not do anything for our lodges'. Then he promised to help us, but we never ever got any financial support. In 2011, Turkey promised to renovate Harabati Baba Tekkesi (*Арабати Баба Теќе*) in [North] Macedonia. This did not happen and TİKA with the Diyanet tried to build a mosque just next to our lodge.

Figure 6.1   Grandfather Hajji Baba Mondi and Ahmet Davutoğlu, 2016. Photo by the author.

These different viewpoints coming from different groups invoke the possibility of sectarian discrimination in Turkey's aid and investment. When the AKP's Balkan policy is considered through the lens of imposing an ethno-religious discourse on the region along with coercive Sunnification, this possibility becomes more substantial. Yet according to Turkey's official records, its investment and aid are not limited to Sunni groups or Muslims and issues related to them. For instance, in 2015, upon the request of the Macedonian National Conservative Centre, TİKA provided aid for Saint George Church near Kumanovo, in Varna. TİKA also helped in some of the minor construction and renovation projects of the Macedonian Orthodox Church Dominion of the Most Holy Virgin Mary, which is an important house of worship for the Orthodox population of North Macedonia. These examples suggest that under the soft power policy approach of the AKP governments, Turkey has been trying to show its presence among different groups in the Balkans. Yet as noted earlier, states need to have a certain level of economic well-being to exercise soft power.

Turkey is a country where economic crises are fundamental determinants of the political situation. The 2001 economic crisis indicated the correlation between the economy and political success, as it immediately preceded the AKP's accession to power in 2002. After a decade of economic failure and coalition governments, the AKP was perceived as a new hope offering promise of change.[1] To start, the party based its economic policies on the plan set in place by the previous government and the IMF, which had two main aims: increasing GDP and establishing a monetary policy with a target of price stability.[2] The AKP governments, particularly between 2002 and 2008, tried to solve some chronic problems plaguing the Turkish economy and created new and alternative sources for the treasury. Under a strict regime, the Turkish economy made some headway against its entrenched difficulties, but the global economic turbulence of 2008 affected the Turkish economy negatively. Negative impacts also ensued from the string of consecutive and significant political disturbances: the Gezi protests, the 17–25 December corruption investigation, the struggle between the Gülen Movement and the AKP, the failed coup attempt and the enduring state of emergency. As it has been noted in table 3, the Turkish economy has not really improved since 2009, when the GDP per capita reached around $10,500. Even though, according to 2017 economic indicators, Turkey's GDP has grown more than 5 per cent, the Turkish lira has been plunging without restraint since 2018.[3] The exchange rate has depreciated steadily since mid-2017. Intensified market pressures in August 2018 led to a further depreciation of around 30 per cent, followed by a partial recovery. Under conditions of backsliding democracy and political tension, the economy has remained an issue of major debate in Turkish politics in both 2019 and 2020.

Changes in GDP per capita in Turkey, 1998–2016 (source: Turkish Statistical Institute)

	Mid-year population	Value	Change	Value	Change
	(000)	(TL)	(%)	($)	(%)
1998	62,464	1,151	–	4,442	–
1999	63,364	1,691	46.9	4,003	–9.9
2000	64,269	2,656	57.0	4,229	5.6
2001	65,166	3,766	41.8	3,084	–27.1
2002	66,003	5,445	44.6	3,581	16.1
2003	66,795	7,007	28.7	4,698	31.2
2004	67,599	8,536	21.8	5,961	26.9
2005	68,435	9,844	15.3	7,304	22.5
2006	69,295	11,389	15.7	7,906	8.2
2007	70,158	12,550	10.2	9,656	22.1
2008	71,052	14,001	11.6	10,931	13.2
2009	72,039	13,870	–0.9	8,980	–17.8
2010	73,142	15,860	14.3	10,560	17.6
2011	74,224	18,788	18.5	11,205	6.1
2012	75,176	20,880	11.1	11,588	3.4
2013	76,148	23,766	13.8	12,480	7.7
2014	77,182	26,489	11.5	12,112	–2.9
2015	78,218	29,899	12.9	11,019	–9.0
2016	79,278	32,904	10.0	10,883	–1.2

Despite the prevailing economic situation in Turkey, overall economic relations with the Balkan countries increased significantly under the AKP governments. While the volume of trade between the Balkans and Turkey was around 3.5 billion US dollars in 2002, it exceeded 16 billion in 2016, having reached its peak in 2014 at 20.8 billion US dollars.[4] Turkey is an active partner for all Balkan countries in the sectors of tourism, textiles, mining, steel and energy. However, all this cooperation predated the AKP governments. These economic relations are the natural outputs of geographical proximity and mutual necessity, along with a common history. However, even though Turkey is an important economic partner for the Balkan countries, its position is not as significant as that of Germany, the USA, the UK, Russia and the EU. For instance, while in 2015 Germany's total export was around 1.3 million US dollars, Turkey's was limited to 143,883 US dollars.[5] In other words, even though Turkey and the Balkans have well-functioning economic relations based on certain advantages, Turkey does not stand as an irreplaceable actor for the Balkans. Still, if one sets out on a road trip from Ljubljana to Istanbul via Belgrade, it is highly likely that Turkish commercial trucks are one of the first things to catch the eye. The trucks, of course, are not exclusive to Turkey's trade with the Balkans, in that they represent Turkey's overall trade with European countries.

Turkey's investment and trade relations do not represent the entirety of its presence in the region. It also carries out many transnational activities in the Balkans. TİKA's investment and activities, the Yunus Emre Institute, the Diyanet and the YTB are significant to an understanding of what the Balkans means for Turkey and how the local actors see the activities of these transnational apparatuses, as part of Turkey's coercive ethno-nationalist Sunnification process.

TİKA is the second Turkish transnational state apparatus that became active in the region, after the Diyanet. As implied by its name and as described in its official framework of activities, TİKA plays similar roles to previously founded cooperation agencies such as the United States Agency for International Development (USAID), Deutsche Gesellschaft für Technische Zusammenarbeit (GTZ), the Japan International Cooperation Agency (JICA) and the Canadian International Development Agency (CIDA). Even though TİKA was founded in 1992, it was not very active, and its functions were limited to Central Asian Turkic states before the AKP period. Since 2002, AKP governments have opened more than forty new TİKA branch offices and Erdoğan has announced that TİKA's budget has increased more than twentyfold in the AKP period, reaching 317 million Turkish lira. Among the new branches, TİKA's Tirana and Skopje offices are the most active.

Even though, after the African countries, the Balkan Peninsula is the second most important target region for TİKA, Turkey has not succeeded in opening a branch office in Bulgaria. However, TİKA has been supporting some renovation works in that country. The Banyabaşı Mosque (Баня баши джамия) was renovated by TİKA between 2013 and 2014. The limited scope of activities and the absence of a TİKA branch office in Bulgaria, where there are hundreds of Ottoman monuments, was one of the questions I put to Süleyman Gökçe, the Turkish ambassador to Sofia. He noted that even though Turkey had been insisting on opening a TİKA office in Sofia, the Bulgarian administration thought that, as an EU country, EU funds should be sufficient to support its renovation projects. Ambassador Gökçe also noted that the Bulgarian state was afraid of possibly negative Bulgarian reactions to Turkish institutions, since most Bulgarian citizens thought Turkey's institutions are political, and potentially harmful.

Since the beginning of the AKP years, TİKA's increasing activities have served to demonstrate the successful implementation of soft power and public diplomacy. A number of scholarly works identify the Balkan region as a major focus of TİKA's activity in this millennium.[6] Some of the studies claim that TİKA has a friendly appearance in the host countries, because of its aid-oriented activities. For instance, in the article 'Turkey's role in the global development assistance community: The case of TİKA', co-authored by Rahman Nurdun, TİKA's former head and the current Undersecretary of the Turkish National Intelligence Agency (MİT), Hakan Fidan[7] notes that 'TİKA maintained its friendly relations with many bilateral and multilateral aid agencies through designing and implementing joint projects'.[8] Even though Fidan's work and most other studies highlight TİKA's soft power presence and friendly relations with both local actors and other aid agencies, the evidence from Bulgaria tells a very different story.

In Bulgaria, apart from the Diyanet's undersecretary, no Turkish state apparatus has an official presence, though the Turkish government and municipalities might be involved in aid activities upon the request of local actors. A senior official who worked at the Foreign Ministry of Bulgaria was asked about this situation in the first quarter of 2018:

> We [Bulgarian state] have two answers: one of them is very official while the other is less so, but both of them are correct. First of all, we do not need Turkey's support directly, because we are a member of the European Union and get support from them if we need. Secondly, since 2007 or 2008 we realised that these Turkish institutions are highly political, and they categorise people according to their religion and ethnicity. We do not want any more division in Bulgaria . . . but let me tell you that Davutoğlu wanted to

open TİKA and Yunus Emre offices here [in Sofia] but we did not give an affirmative response to him, since we have some problems with Turkey's agents here and these institutions might open new cases for us.

From this it may be inferred that the Bulgarian state does not perceive TİKA's activities and Turkey's other soft power instruments as structures that keep within the boundaries of their official job descriptions. Why then did the Bulgarian state accept the activities of the Diyanet in the late 1990s, but not give permission to TİKA and the others in 2000? Mihail Ivano was one of the political actors who established the first protocol between the Diyanet and the Bulgarian Grand Mufti's office, and a chief advisor to Zhelyu Zhelev, the first post-communist president of Bulgaria, between 1990 and 1997. He told me that twenty-five years ago they were comfortable to invite the Diyanet to Bulgaria, but now according to him, this was a mistake since the Diyanet is not a Turkish institution, it is Erdoğan's political instrument. These days, current political actors and bureaucrats do not make the mistake of inviting other pro-Erdoğanist political instruments to Bulgaria.

Ivano's view may sound overly mistrustful, but given that his predictions are based on the experiences of the other countries in the region, it becomes more understandable. One needs to remember that TİKA is not only active in construction or renovation in the Balkans. It has also been involved in education activities at various levels, providing vocational training courses and supplying basic healthcare support. Religion- and power-oriented discrimination within these activities has been observed by the authorities. For instance, one of the TİKA representatives in Albania emphasised that although Turkey has been offering free service to everyone via TİKA, the institution's only red line is the enemies of Turkey. Even though the representative did not mention who or what has been defining the concept 'enemies of Turkey', it is obvious that the Erdoğan administration is the only decision-maker on these critical issues in the new Turkey.

According to TİKA's official reports, Albania is a key country receiving a significant number of services from the institution. Moreover, throughout the AKP years, Albania's share in TİKA's total budget has been steadily increasing, from 1.25 per cent in 2009 to 3.3 per cent in 2018. With this budget TİKA has supported various projects, such as the restoration of the southern historical city of Gjirokastër, whose old town is a UNESCO World Heritage site. Yet until 2014 TİKA's most intense and visible activities remained the restoration of historical mosques and supporting the activities of the Muslim Community of Albania (Komuniteti Mysliman i Shqipërisë). For instance, the main building of the Muslim Community of Albania was constructed by TİKA with a grant of 300,000 euros. Yet after the election of Skënder Bruçaj as the chairman of the Community, TİKA's role in Albania changed, since the AKP sees Bruçaj as a member or sympathiser of the Gülen Movement. Actually, they are not totally wrong.

Figure 6.2   Headquarters of the Muslim Community of Albania. Photos by the author.

On 12 April 2017, I conducted an interview with Bruçaj. In response to a question about changes in the attitude of the Turkish state, Bruçaj responded as follows:

> All of the Turkish officers have been arguing that I am a Gülenist and serving the aims of the Gülen Movement. I have close relations with some of the people from the Movement, but they are personal relations. They are my friends. They also have very good relations with other socio-political figures in Albania. It is not a secret that when I was in Turkey for my university education in the late 1990s and early 2000s, I shared a home with some of the members of the Gülen Movement. But it is impossible for me to serve their demands, I am serving the Muslims of Albania as the top representative of this institution. I know the main reasons of the Turkish state's claims. They asked us to cut all of our official relations with the Gülen Movement. But I refused that since we have an independent structure. Yes, they [the Gülen Movement] are running some of our madrasas, and actually doing a good job. Why and how can I cancel their contract?

In Albania, there are seven madrasas and five of them are under the management of the Sema Foundation, which is the umbrella organisation of the Gülen Movement. One other madrasa has been run by another Turkish institution, which is called the Istanbul Foundation. It is under the control of the pro-AKP Aziz Mahmut Hüdai Foundation of Sheikh Osman Nuri Topbaş. The final madrasa is run by the Qatar Foundation and is for girls only. The supervision of all of these madrasas is performed by the Muslim Community of Albania. Bruçaj's very close relations with the Gülenists has affected many activities in the country, particularly those of TİKA, in an interesting way. In Albania, TİKA's activities and its budget share have been increasing since 2013, the year that marked the beginning of discriminatory attitudes. In this regard, Bruçaj went on to note that 'since the beginning of 2015, neither we nor the madrasas under the control of Sema Foundation have received any support from TİKA, but they have been doing construction and renovation of mosques all over Albania. Turkey only seems to serve the groups that have close relations with the AKP.'

According to TİKA's official reports, a significant majority of its activities in Albania are related to Muslim groups and Islamic monuments, which can be interpreted to reflect the domestic Sunnification of state identity in Turkey via state apparatuses. Moreover, TİKA has tried to construct new mosques in some areas where the impact of Islam is almost invisible among the locals. TİKA's activities in Albania have created three different views among the local socio-political elites. First of all, most Muslim communities, including Salafists and Wahhabis, have been sympathetic to TİKA, since it has been serving Islam by helping Muslim groups and renovating mosques. A second group of moderate Muslim groups and leading figures of the Muslim Community of Albania see TİKA's activities as the Islamic face of the AKP's Turkey, since the majority of its activities are related to Islam. These two perspectives together establish the third one, which is mainly argued by non-Muslim socio-political elites. This argument is that even though some of TİKA's activities are fundamentally important for Albania, they also pose a threat in terms of furthering divisions within the local communities and becoming an indirect support to some extremist Islamist groups. TİKA's current activities are hard to place in a context with well-defined boundaries. A major concern among the Albanian socio-political elites is the possibility of religion-oriented extremist movements that would destroy the peaceful environment in terms of the coexistence of religions. Therefore, Turkey's main criterion for aid as being friendly with the AKP has been raising suspicions in the context of providing (unintended) support for the extremist groups in the country.

Even though the socio-political context is similar to that of Albania, the perspectives of the North Macedonian elite are quite different regarding TİKA's presence and activities. TİKA's Skopje office was founded in 2006, and within a decade it managed to conclude more than 500 projects including building schools and hospitals and renovating old mosques. Furthermore, as a difference from the other TİKA branches, since 2013, when the Yunus Emre Institute was founded, TİKA has given Turkish-language courses and scholarships to successful students in eleven different regions of North Macedonia. As in the Albanian case, North Macedonia's share in TİKA's total budget has been increasing throughout the AKP period, from 2.33 per cent in 2009 to 4.4 per cent in 2017 and 4.3 per cent in 2018 and 2019. Despite TİKA's official documents, which state that the institution provides services evenly all over North Macedonia, it shows more visibility and impact in places with significant Muslim populations, such as Gostivari (Гостивар) and Tetova (Tetovë).

In North Macedonia, TİKA's red line is the same as in Albania and can be summarised as 'do not provide any service to the Gülen Movement and others who might be affiliated with them; and serve all other Muslim groups without question'. Furthermore, through all TİKA's activities the Turkish representatives have been warning the North Macedonian people regarding the danger of the Gülen Movement to a peaceful environment and to true Islam. The North Macedonian state is relatively less concerned regarding the unintentional support of extremist Islamic groups. For instance, the Reis-ul-ulema, the leader of the Islamic Religious Community of North Macedonia (Исламската Верска Заедница во Македонија), Sulejman Rexhepi, was very confident that all of the activities of TİKA and the Diyanet had been monitored by the local authorities and thus they would never attempt to do *wrong* things.

Indeed, Rexhepi's positive perspective represents the relatively general perception of North Macedonian Muslims. They have a strong liking for Turkey, and TİKA's presence is one of the main reasons for that. Even so, the state elite has been acting with some deliberation about TİKA's activities, since maintaining an equal distance from all Islamic groups is also a critical issue in North Macedonia. For instance, in late 2017, a key political actor who was in active duty in the presidential office in Skopje noted that 'supplying aid and service to some particular Muslim groups would be dangerous for us and the region. This is why we are observing TİKA's activities very closely.'

The Yunus Emre Institute is another transnational state apparatus that is active in the Balkan Peninsula under the AKP's new foreign policy approach. Like TİKA, it also functions like institutions of other countries, running cultural activities parallel to the UK's British Council and Sweden's Swedish Institute. Beyond being a replica institution, it was established to imitate some of the Gülen Movement's activities abroad, such as Turkish-language education and Turkish-Ottoman art courses.[9]

The Institute is one of the most influential state apparatuses, running more than forty branches from Japan to the United States, and has an annual budget of more than one hundred million Turkish lira. As an indicator of the importance attributed by Turkey to the region, the first branches of the Institute opened in the Balkans (Bosnia & Herzegovina and North Macedonia). In the opening ceremony of the Yunus Emre Institute's North Macedonia branch in Skopje, Ahmet Davutoğlu, then the prime minister, said, 'We would like to make a novel contribution to cultural exchange in the Balkans. Cultural relations between Turkey and North Macedonia will lead the way for a new and enlightened Balkans.'[10] While indicating the significance of the Balkans, Davutoğlu's wording, 'the new enlightenment', emphasises the hierarchical positioning that shapes Turkey's policy and discourse in the region. Nevertheless, even though Turkey made significant efforts to open a Yunus Emre Institute office in Sofia, the Bulgarian state did not allow it. When asked about the reason, the same senior official in the Bulgarian foreign ministry gave the same answer regarding the Bulgarian administration's political concerns about Turkish-originated transnational state apparatuses. Indeed, it would be unrealistic to argue that the Turkish authorities are not aware of these concerns of the political elites of the host countries. For instance, in a 2017 press interview Şeref Ateş, the current head of the Yunus Emre Institute, declared:

> there is a common belief that the Yunus Emre Institute is only about teaching Turkish, however, this isn't true. The Yunus Emre Institute is an institution that conducts Turkey's public diplomacy and other elements of what we call soft power . . . We believe that every culture, religion and ethnicity has the right to introduce its own values and interact with others, which is why we have united with countries that were excluded from the Western network . . . We are not an embassy or an institution that spreads propaganda about Turkey; we introduce Turkey as it is.[11]

Even though both Davutoğlu and Ateş used the phrases 'new enlightenment', 'the right to introduce one's own religion' and 'introducing Turkey as it is' with positive connotations, the activities of the Yunus Emre Institute have been perceived with some concern since 2013, when Turkey's coercive ethnonationalist Sunnification began. The Albanian case is an interesting example: the Albanian branch of the Yunus Emre Institute was established as one of the first branches abroad in 2009 and had two offices, one in Tirana and the other in Shodra. Both branches have been conducting activities that promote the Turkish language, culture and art, and eventually Turkey's visibility in Albania. In 2017, one of the senior figures in the Yunus Emre Institute's Tirana office stated that 'our main duty is to promote our cultural and historical values, but you should note that today's values are also important for us and therefore our second duty, which has an equal importance, is to express the current values of our countries'.

These sentences do not contain any religious elements and at first glance, the Institute's activities seem to be structured along a merely conservative and religious framework. However, Turkey's ethno-religious domestic transformation has affected the activities of Yunus Emre Institute in Albania. In the first quarter of 2017, I interviewed the former Minister of Tourism, Cultural Affairs, Youth and Sports (between 2009 and 2011), Ferdinand Xhaferraj, who signed the Yunus Emre Institute's acceptance agreement on behalf of the Albanian state. Xhaferraj argued that in almost all Turkey's activities via Yunus Emre you can see the effect of Turkish Islam under the cover of cultural activity. He also emphasised that the instrumentalisation of culture for religious aims and vice versa is not exactly what the Albanian state wants. Thus this shift has been creating a different perception of Turkey in the eyes of Albanian citizens.

Two points need to be stressed here: the importance of Turkish Islam for Albanian Muslims and the recent transformation of the image of Turkish Islam. In his article dated 2010, Raximi underlines that after the communist period and until the beginning of the 2000s, Arabic and north-east African Islamic organisations were dominant in the country. Yet most of the Albanian people found these organisations' understanding of Islam to be incompatible, and the imposition of the methodology of their doctrines less than appealing. In this situation, the influence of Turkish Islam became a 'course of treatment'.[12] But the coercive ethno-nationalist Sunnification in Turkish politics has changed this situation as well as the activities of Yunus Emre Institute. During a visit to a Salafi non-governmental organisation in 2017, the League of Imams of Albania (Lidhja e Hoxhallarëve të Shqipërisë), I observed that the Yunus Emre Institute and TİKA had been supplying scholarships to the promising 'sons' of the leading figures of the organisation. During the visit, a representative declared that 'it is so normal for us to establish collaboration with Turkey, at the end of the day, both Erdoğan and ourselves are serving the same religion, same God'. However, serving religion and the Ummah mentality has created the fear of a 'possible proliferation of religious extremism' among locals.[13] For instance, during my 2018 interview with a senior officer from the Department of Religion–State Toleration in the prime minister's office, the officer noted that 'in Albania, whoever disturbs the harmony will lose. Currently, I think, Turkey's ambitious arms have that potential, because they are passing their boundaries.'

In North Macedonia, the Skopje branch of the Yunus Emre Institute was established in 2010 and is one of the most influential branches in the Balkans. It has been organising seminars, teaching programmes and conferences on Turkish culture, language and art. Moreover, it has established various collaborations involving the provision of Turkish-language courses to high-ranking officials in the North Macedonian army. On 15 April 2017, Fuat Korkmaz, the head of the Yunus Emre Institute in Skopje, provided a framework for the mission of the institution and the position of religion within this mission:

> We are a part of the new proactive Turkish foreign policy of the AK Party. Our mission is quite different from official diplomats: we are touching the ordinary citizens and their future. We want to constitute Turkey's image which will continue throughout the generations . . . We are also fighting against the traitors of Turkey. Islam constitutes the core of our culture. We are not directly promoting Islam, but how can we differentiate Islam from Turkey and Turkish culture? However, we are not categorising people according to their religion or political views. For example, we organised an activity by Lake Ohrid where pianist Fazıl Say was one of the guests, you know he is an atheist and anti-Erdoğanist. Despite all this, he is an important value for Turkey.

Based on Korkmaz's explanations, one might argue that the Yunus Emre Institute is a fundamental and active player in the new Turkish foreign policy, which is dominated and represented by the religious identity and ethno-nationalist proponents, as a reflection of domestic changes in Turkey. Most Muslim groups and individuals in North Macedonia are pleased with the new situation, but the state elites have been approaching it with caution. The common point of view among them is that Turkish Islam is indeed preferable to Arab Islam, but this does not mean that they will shut their eyes to all activities of the Yunus Emre Institute. Beyond that, some civilian Muslim elites are also sceptical about the activities of the Institute in Skopje. On 16 April 2017, Ismail Bardhi, a prominent professor of religion studies in North Macedonia, noted that 'it would be a lie, if someone tells you that the Yunus Emre Institute does not work for and with Islam, but the question should be for which Islam: Muhammed's, North Macedonia's, or Erdoğan's?'

Regarding the issue of serving the Ummah and its reflection in the AKP's Balkan policy, it would be natural to assume that the Diyanet is the leading actor in this process. Yet the visibility of the Diyanet remains limited – or in other words, it stays within its official boundaries when compared to TİKA and the Yunus Emre Institute. However, serving the Ummah would not be problematic for the Diyanet since its official mission entails just this. Yet the transformation of the Turkish state's identity and power resources has also affected the Diyanet's missions in Bulgaria, Albania and North Macedonia. First of all, the Diyanet also partners with TİKA and the Yunus Emre Institute in their operations. For instance, the Diyanet sends and trains imams for the mosques reconstructed by TİKA and the Institute, and organises *iftar* dinners and cultural programmes for mosque communities.

This hegemony of the Diyanet comes from both Turkey's identity transformation and from the Diyanet's financial capacity. Yet Turkey's authoritarian drift since 2013, and its desire to enlarge its influence in other countries, have changed the perception of the Diyanet in the eyes of the Balkan elites. The Diyanet has begun to use its financial capacity as a tool of sanction on its counterpart institutions in the Balkans. Even though this has created a disturbance among official Muslim institutions and non-Muslim socio-political elites in these countries, they cannot react because of the possibility that the void the Diyanet would leave would be filled by Arab actors. That is, particularly after 2013, the Diyanet has become a lesser evil in the region.

In Bulgaria, the Diyanet has been officially supporting the Grand Mufti's Office with financial and other resources. In 2016, during my first field-study visit to his office, the current Grand Mufti Mustafa Hadzihi highlighted that the Bulgarian Grand Mufti's Office is systematically receiving around two million Bulgarian lev and material resources each year from the Turkish Diyanet. This financial support is very important since, according to financial staff in the Bulgarian Grand Mufti's Office, if the Turkish Diyanet cuts its financial support, they cannot even pay the salaries of imams. Therefore, the Bulgarian Muslim community, at least on an institutional basis, is very much dependent on Turkey, and this situation turns the Office almost into a 'colonised institution'. In this regard, some of the staff members in the Bulgarian Grand Mufti's Office admit that Turkish Diyanet looks down on them.

The Albanian case is the total opposite of the Bulgarian one. Because of the Gülenist reputation of the current chairman, the Diyanet renounced its financial support to the Albanian Muslim Community in 2014. Even though Turkey's Diyanet has been questioning who the representatives of the Muslims in Albania are, the chairman of the Albanian Muslim Community, Bruçaj, complained that the Diyanet had never seen them as its equivalent. It has acted as if they were an office of mufti of Turkey, which is very wrong. According to him, his community is older than the Diyanet and furthermore he, as the chairman of the Albanian Muslim Community, is not a state officer, as is the head of the Turkish Diyanet.

The interviews I conducted in the region indicate that the Turkish Diyanet has been supporting certain other Turkish Muslim groups, such as the Süleymancı community, in Albania, but neither Görmez nor the representatives of the Diyanet in Tirana declared any particular point on that issue. Yet the visibility of the Diyanet, as the engine of Turkey's efforts towards 'serving the Ummah', has been revealing itself in different ways. The building of the Great Mosque of Tirana, also called the Namazgâh Mosque (Xhamia e Madhe e Tiranës), is the best example of this. It was constructed by the Diyanet to be the biggest mosque in the Balkans. At its opening ceremony, Erdoğan proclaimed that 'in my heart there is no difference between my hometown Rize and Tirana, there is no difference for me to supply services to my own people and to my Albanian brothers'. Still, some members of the Albanian socio-political elite have been suspicious of the construction of the mosque, Erdoğan's sentiments and Diyanet activities. They interpret the expressions of Erdoğan as going beyond the limits of brotherhood and as manifesting a hegemonic and hierarchical attitude. Second, the local elite perceive the construction of a luxury, dominant house of worship as an act that would potentially be detrimental to the peaceful coexistence of different religions in the country. On 27 April 2017, social scientist and journalist Gjon Borıçı from the University of Tirana noted that 'it is nonsense to open a mosque here with bismillah and promote Diyanet as a leading actor . . . We have not seen any Italian president open a church or promote the Vatican . . . If someone has to do it, we have local Muslim politicians.'

Figure 6.3 Construction of the Great Mosque of Tirana/Namazgâh Mosque (Xhamia e Madhe e Tiranës). Photos by the author.

In comparison with TİKA and the Yunus Emre Institute, the Diyanet's position is quite modest in North Macedonia. In 2017, Murat Alkan, the Diyanet councillor in Skopje, underlined that the Diyanet is one of the most welcomed institutions in North Macedonia, with fourteen imams and one female preacher to give training to the imams of North Macedonia. As in the other case countries, the Diyanet is supplying non-financial resources to the mosques as well as free Quran courses, and is involved in aid activities. Alkan also notes that one of the main aims of the presence of the Diyanet is to protect Muslims' rights through the umbrella organisations of local Muslims. In this regard, most Muslim organisations appreciate the presence of the Turkish organisation in North Macedonia. Again, some local political actors have been observing its activities with cautious eyes, to prevent potential acts that might disturb the modest position of the Muslims in the country. The Diyanet played a more dormant role before the AKP period. It then started to construct its patterns of activity according to the policies of the AKP and aligned with corresponding changes in the identity of the Turkish state.

The last active transnational state apparatus originating in Turkey is the YTB, but this has a different structure compared to the others. Whereas the YTB was formed to serve the members of the Turkish diaspora in cultural, educational and economic fields, in the Balkans it has been serving only Muslims under the name of the kin policy. The main difference with the YTB is that it does not have any official branch or office in the Balkans and therefore it has been controlled from Ankara under close connection with the branches of other transnational apparatuses. In this respect, most of the local socio-political elites are not aware of the activities of the YTB and some of them have not even heard of it. Even though the government officials of the host countries are aware of YTB activities, they cannot apply any significant sanctions due to the lack of official YTB offices in their countries.

One of the most significant activities of the YTB is to organise the frequent Balkan Youth Forums (Balkan Gençlik Forumları), which agglomerate Muslim and/or Turkish youth from North Macedonia, Albania, Bulgaria, Serbia and Kosovo.[14] The question here should be: How does the YTB Ankara office find and select these Balkan youth, and what are the main criteria in this selection process? At this point, the other Turkish transnational state apparatuses, Turkey's civil society actors and religious communities become part of an effort to meet these youth in Ankara and Istanbul under the umbrella of the AKP's YTB. According to my field observations and from allusions made by state officials in the case country, among the significant criteria for selection at these meetings is sympathy with Turkey, the AKP and Erdoğan. Another significant activity of the YTB in the Balkans is Turkey Scholarships (*Türkiye Bursları*), which provide an opportunity for Balkan students to obtain a university education in Turkey with budget-based collaboration with TİKA and the Diyanet. For this scholarship, the importance and priority of Islam is the most salient point. Therefore, these students from Albania, Bulgaria and North Macedonia are enrolled only in the theology faculty of the pro-AKP İbni-Haldun University, in Istanbul.

Under the shadow of these observations and findings, the AKP has realised that Turkey's Western-oriented *laik* foreign policy has not been serving the new interests of Turkey, and so it aims to establish deeper relations with the Balkan countries, but particularly with the Muslims of these countries. Turkey has in fact been preferring to serve the Ummah, instead of expanding relations with all components of the Balkans, in spite of the fragile economic conditions prevailing in the region. Even though the socio-political elites of the host countries are pleased with these initiatives, they are at the same time suspicious. Hence, this mostly single-sided and religion-oriented investment approach is one of the significant indicators of how its preferences make Turkey an ambiguous power in the region.

Notes

1. Öniş, 'Beyond the 2001 financial crisis'.
2. Erinç and Ünüvar, 'An assessment of the Turkish economy in the AKP era', 12.
3. For details, please see https://www.theguardian.com/world/2018/aug/13/how-serious-is-turkeys-lira-crisis-and-what-are-the-implications, accessed 5 June 2020.
4. Ekinci, 'Türkiye–Balkan İlişkileri', 9.
5. Nuroğlu and Nuroğlu, 'Balkanlarda Almanya ve Türkiye', 13.
6. For some of these studies, please see Ibrahim, 'Soft power and public diplomacy in Turkey'; Atinay, 'Turkey's soft power'; Brljavac, 'Turkey entering the European Union'; Fidan, 'A work in progress'; Ipek, 'Ideas and change in foreign policy instruments'.

7. Hakan Fidan served as TİKA's head and then became head of the National Intelligence Organisation. This has created issues of confidence among policy-makers of the host countries *vis-à-vis* TİKA. The following sentence, as an extract from the fieldwork for this book, speaks volumes on that debate: 'If the current undersecretary of the National Intelligence Organisation is the previous head of TİKA, how can we trust TİKA to keep its activities within legal boundaries?'

8. Fidan and Nurdun, 'Turkey's role in the global development assistance community', 110.

9. The relationship between the Yunus Emre Institute and the Gülen Movement goes far beyond the Institute's replicating the Gülenists. The first head of the Yunus Emre Institute and many previous staff members were arrested after the 15 July coup attempt, accused of being members of the Gülen Movement. Furthermore, after the coup attempt Turkey's political elite prescribed that one of the duties of the Yunus Emre Institute was to fight against the Gülen Movement abroad.

10. Yunus Emre Bülteni no. 5 (May 2010, Ankara), 7.

11. See https://www.dailysabah.com/diplomacy/2017/07/24/yunus-emre-institute-head-ates-as-an-element-of-soft-power-our-aim-is-to-introduce-turkey-its-culture-to-the-world, accessed 3 June 2020.

12. For Raximi's article, please see www.balkaninsight.com/en/article/albanian-muslims-grapple-with-religious-identity, accessed 3 June 2020.

13. Ummah is a fundamental concept in Islam, expressing the essential unity and theoretical equality of Muslims from diverse cultural and geographical settings. In the Quran, Ummah designates people to whom God has sent a prophet, or people who are objects of a divine plan of salvation.

14. Ekşi, *Kamu Diplomasisi ve AK Parti Dönemi Türk Dış Politikası*, 349.

7

EXPORTATION OF DOMESTIC CONFLICTS

In May 2015, at the opening ceremony of the Namazgâh Mosque in Tirana, Erdoğan underlined that

> [I]n our country, we have been struggling against the parallel structure [the Gülen Movement]. This structure is a threat for our state and nation and therefore we consider it as a terrorist organisation. We are going to maintain our struggle with this structure both in our country and all around the world. I know that this organisation [the Gülen Movement] has some activities in Albania which is our sibling country, and I talked with my friend Edi Rama and I believe he will do the necessary things. I believe that none of my brothers in this country will give credit to this organisation. You might rest assured that Turkey, with its TİKA, Diyanet, Yunus Emre Institute, is strong enough to supply all the things that this organisation has been doing.

It is true that Albania is a country where the Gülen Movement is very strong in its organisational structure, institutional capacity and relations with the local socio-political elites. The movement has been active in education with the Sema Foundation since 1993. According to the 2018 figures, it has been running five madrasas, six secondary and high school complexes and two universities: Epoka and Beder. At the other end of the educational ladder, in Tirana there is also a big kindergarten called Meridian. Furthermore, the Movement has a media outlet, business associations and cultural centres. Even though the Gülen Movement is influential in Albanian socio-political life, Erdoğan explicitly asked both the president and prime minister of Albania to shut down all these institutions, at the diplomatic meetings accompanying the inauguration ceremony. The responses of the Albanian officials have yet to be made public, but the reaction of Ben Blushi, a member of the Socialist Party, was very clear and significant. On 15 May 2015, Blushi uttered these words from the rostrum of the Albanian Parliament:

> First of all, I would like to thank you, Turkish President, for Namazgâh Mosque which is very important for our Muslim community. Even though as a state we should construct it, we do not have enough resources for that. In this regard, I would like to thank you President Erdoğan for this important present. But, as far as I know, he wanted something quid pro quo for this mosque. Presents should be without any demand, but he demanded that we shut down the institutions of one particular organisation [the Gülen Movement], which he has been considering as a terrorist organisation . . . We do not witness any terrorist activity of this group, but Erdoğan demanded that because of his interests . . . I cannot accept this, and I am sure most of you [members of the parliament] cannot do so either . . . We will reject this demand, because we are not a colony which get decisions after a present . . . As far as I can understand, Erdoğan asked this because of his political journey . . . It is unacceptable . . . because we are not a part of that struggle.

This only is one particular example of the issue of exportation of domestic conflicts into the Balkans via transnational state apparatuses during the AKP period. The majority of such issues seem to be related to the Gülen Movement, indicating the AKP's major political crisis in Turkey. The struggles among Turkey's ideological groups have been making themselves evident in the Balkans. Yet as with most other issues, it is impossible to claim that the situation is identical or even similar in each Balkan country. The issues are handled in different ways depending on the positions of the political actors and the power relations in the host countries. As a last point, even though most of the issues are not directly related to religion, Turkey's identity turn towards coercive ethno-nationalist Sunnification has rendered religion a part of many issues in the exportation of domestic conflicts.

Bulgaria's demographic structure makes it different from the other case countries. The Bulgarian Muslims, who are ethnically Turkish, Pomak or Roma, constitute approximately 7 per cent of the overall population and Turkey considers them in terms of kinship (*soydaş*), which is distinct from and even stronger than religious brotherhood. Around four hundred thousand Bulgarian citizens live in Turkey, and six hundred thousand Bulgarian citizens have Turkish passports and the right to vote in general elections. Bulgarian Turks and Pomaks (and Roma) who have migrated to Turkey and clustered in big groups in Istanbul and neighbouring cities (especially Bursa) are becoming an issue that unites domestic politics with foreign policy.

Turkey plays the role of motherland for most Bulgarian Muslims, and some of them argue that 'we know that the motherland is just over there, even if we never go'. This makes better sense when considered in light of the fact that the Bulgarian Turks constitute the biggest extra-territorial ethnolinguistic Turkish minority, as an Ottoman residue. Therefore, while Turkey considers Bulgarian Muslims in terms of kinship, most of the Bulgarian Muslims see Turkey through the lens of *motherland*.[1] All this considered, it was not the Turkish state that initiated activities in Bulgaria first: it was the Gülen Movement, and currently the exportation of domestic conflicts is focused on the AKP's fight with the Gülen Movement. The AKP is trying to win the hearts and minds of Bulgarian Muslims against the presence and established status of the Movement.

The presence of the Gülen Movement in Bulgaria is not a subject that has been studied sufficiently, since it did not become an issue until the rift between the AKP and the Movement. As such, the academic literature does not provide much guidance on the historical formation of the Gülen Movement in Bulgaria. Therefore, I had to focus on conducting interviews with senior members of the Movement in Bulgaria. As a Turkish researcher, it was almost impossible for me to establish any contact with the members of the Movement, since they were concerned about attracting publicity to themselves as Gülenist representatives. At the Turkish embassy and the Diyanet, officials also avoided mentioning the name of the Movement or commenting on its activities. After a year of effort, the opportunity for an interview with a Gülen Movement representative arose and the interview was conducted in Sofia in the first months of 2017.

According to this representative, the Gülen Movement started its activities in 1993 after the collapse of the communist regime, with educational institutions. Through these institutions, it signed sponsorship agreements with the Grand Mufti's Office during the days of controversial Grand Mufti Nedim Gencev.[2] The Movement then started to support the Grand Mufti's Office financially and took partial control of the Momchilgrad, Shumen and Ruse İmam Hatip high schools. Alongside these support activities, the Movement established the *Zaman Weekly Newspaper*, published in Turkish and Bulgarian, as well as the religious journal *Ümit*, and ran the Bulgarian–Turkish Democracy Foundation until 1998. In that year, in the aftermath of the 28 February 1997 'post-modern' military coup process in Turkey, the activities of the Gülen Movement were stopped and/or frozen by the Bulgarian authorities in line with the demands of the Turkish authorities. The Diyanet took over the Movement's supportive role in the Grand Mufti's Office and İmam Hatip high schools. Yet the relative weakness of the Turkish economy prevented sustainable support and the Gülen Movement regained its former role in *de facto* ways. In this regard, the current Grand Mufti noted that 'the Turkish Diyanet was incapable of supplying our demands until 2002, so we received the support of the Movement'.

After the 'frozen period' between 1998 and 2002, the Gülen Movement recommenced its activities in various areas as the AKP came to power. They started running activities with the Grand Mufti's Office and after 2010, a secretary general was appointed to the Office who had close relations with the Gülen Movement. Beyond this, between 2008 and 2013 the members of the Movement obtained almost all the critical positions in the Office of the Grand Mufti. Notwithstanding, no official at that office could give satisfactory answers about how the members of the Movement were appointed to these positions. In fact, the 'unofficial coalition' between the Movement and the AKP provided these opportunities.

Beyond these activities, in 2011 the Gülen Movement managed to open two secondary and high school complexes under the name of *Drujba* (*dostluk* in Turkish, friendship in English). The bigger of these schools was established in the periphery of Sofia with a capacity of more than five hundred students. The other was located in Plovdiv, where the majority of the population is Turkish and Pomak Muslims, as a boarding school with a capacity of 120 students. According to Mihaglev, even though there was no direct support from the AKP government to the Gülen Movement in its activities in Bulgaria, the period between 2008 and 2013 can easily be called 'the golden age' of the Movement. The support of the Turkish embassy played an important role in solving any problems that arose. The golden age, though, ended right after the corruption investigations, which were publicly believed to have been carried out by members of the Gülen Movement in the judiciary and the police.

In 2017, Süleyman Gökçe, the Turkish ambassador to Sofia, highlighted that 'our friends in Bulgaria have realised the danger quite late. There are still many activities of this dangerous Movement in many areas. Yet the Bulgarian state has not understood the danger, in contravention to our suggestions.' However, according to the Gülen Movement representative, the Diyanet threatened the Grand Mufti's Office, via the embassy, to cut off financial support if it maintained relations with the Movement. Therewith, all pro-Gülen staff were dismissed from the Grand Mufti's Office as well as the Momchilgrad, Shumen and Ruse İmam Hatip high schools. All the staff of the Grand Mufti's Office withdrew their children from schools run by the Movement. This was a crucial point in the exportation of domestic conflicts via state apparatuses and the instrumentalisation of religion. Though no parent was willing to be interviewed in Sofia, some of those who had taken their children away from the Gülenist school in Plovdiv were interviewed. One interviewee[3] emphasised that they were happy with the education provided in the Drujba schools, which were run according to Bulgarian state regulations. They knew that some of the teachers were from Turkey and were members of the Gülen Movement. Yet he also stated that it was impossible for them to know that these people (that is, Gülenists) were terrorists, because they were all together with the staff of the Turkish Consulate. He claimed that the pro-Gülenist teachers are not in fact terrorists, but their seniors in Turkey and in the USA are harmful people for the Turkish nation and for Islam.

It is clear that until the 15 July 2016 coup attempt in Turkey, the issue of the exportation of domestic conflicts was limited to the representatives of the Gülen Movement, Turkey's Sofia Embassy, the Diyanet and Muslim communities of Bulgaria. The cooperation of the Embassy and the Diyanet removed the Movement from religion-based management areas. The method employed by the Turkish authorities indicates that Turkey preferred not to use the official diplomatic channels to reach its aim, but to instrumentalise the Diyanet.

However, the failed coup attempt has changed the perception of the Bulgarian authorities on the issue, alongside the methods of the Turkish side. Turkey's Sofia Embassy, as an official representative of the country, has come to the fore and asked the Bulgarian state to take the initiative regarding the danger of the Gülen Movement, which would be good for both Turkey and Bulgaria. On the night of the coup, Ambassador Gökçe took an open position against the coup attempt, and the Bulgarian government held an emergency meeting regarding this major issue of its neighbouring country on the following day. After the meeting with Gökçe, Bulgarian prime minister Boiko Borrissov noted that 'we always supported observing the laws and constitution of any country. There is a way to topple governments and that is through elections. Peace cannot be achieved through war and death.' Under these circumstances, the Bulgarian government repatriated more than seventy Gülenists to Turkey, only two of whom had Bulgarian residence, the rest being individuals who had tried to escape from Turkey as illegal migrants. In so doing, the Bulgarian state started to exercise influence on the Gülen Movement, using its regulative role. In this regard, the representative of the Gülen Movement in Bulgaria noted that inspectors had visited Drujba School in late July by order of the Bulgarian government, but could not find any discrepancy to justify cancelling the school's licence.

Yet Turkey's coercive ethno-nationalist Sunnification often transgressed the boundaries of diplomatic practice. Contrary to established diplomatic patterns in Turkey, the Diyanet was instrumentalised in the struggle with the Gülen Movement both in Turkey and abroad. In December 2016, many news agencies reported that the Diyanet had been involved in intelligence activities against members of the Gülen Movement in various countries. For instance, on 8 December 2016, *Cumhuriyet* published a detailed report claiming that Diyanet had been gathering intelligence via its imams in thirty-eight different countries and the imams were commissioned to report on pro-Gülenist individuals, businesses, foundations and other institutions. The activities of the Diyanet and the espionage operations of the Turkish imams in Sofia and Plovdiv, where the Gülenist schools operated, were mentioned twice in this report. Yet the problems of the Diyanet imams in Bulgaria predate the coup attempt. On 21 February 2016, the Bulgarian press and some Turkish media organs shared the news of Uğur Emiroğlu, the Diyanet's representative in Bulgaria, being declared *persona non-grata* for transgressing the limits of religious activities. Ambassador Gökçe addressed this issue during our interview, but he blurred over the question. Another interview was conducted with another senior official, who simply denied the accusations.

Because of its domestic political conflicts, its social diversity (mainly North Macedonian Orthodox and Albanian Muslims) and its economic structure being relatively dependent on Turkey, the case of North Macedonia remains unique. It is a country where Turkey exerts considerable influence via all its transnational state apparatuses: the Diyanet, TİKA, the Yunus Emre Institute, the Anadolu Agency (the state-run news agency), other pro-AKP cooperation agencies and transnational religious communities.

In North Macedonia it was very difficult to talk about the Gülen Movement, particularly because of the struggle between the Movement and the AKP since 2014. Yet ironically enough, a huge commercial state-run Halkbank sits on top of the building used by the General Directorate of Yahya Kemal Colleges, the headquarters of the Gülenist education network in North Macedonia.

Figure 7.1 The main office of the Gülen Movement under the name of the Yahya Kemal Education Centre and Halkbank advertisement. Photo by the author.

According to the representatives[4] of the Gülen Movement in Skopje, the Movement started its activities in North Macedonia in late 1992 and established the North Macedonian branch of the *Zaman Daily*, which has been active in three languages: Turkish, Albanian and North Macedonian. It then established the education network of Yahya Kemal Colleges in Skopje, Tetovo, Gostivari and Struga. The number of schools in the network reached six in 2013. The schools provide education in English and the Macedonian language to Albanian, Turkish, North Macedonian and Bosnian students. The Movement also runs two private language schools that are active in summer in Skopje and Gostivari under the umbrella of the Sedef Education Centre. Under the official name of the Tolerance Foundation it also runs two student dormitories in Skopje and Tetovo. Even though more than two decades of positive presence has ensured its credibility, its struggle with the AKP has damaged the image of the Gülen Movement in North Macedonia. The chief representative of the Movement in North Macedonia noted the following on 15 April 2017:

> After July 15, there is still huge sympathy among people towards us, but indeed there is a little change in the minds of people. Erdoğan is very strong here and is fighting with all his team: TİKA, Diyanet, Yunus Emre and other Islamic communities. Before he declared war on us, we were in a unique position. We are still in a unique position but Erdoğan has been trying to perplex the minds of people, particularly Muslim people, since he never understood what we are doing here. We are supplying a service to the people for the sake of God, and it is so hard for him to destroy this image.

This does seem to sum up the overall situation regarding the credibility of the Gülen Movement among the North Macedonian people. Yet the efforts of Turkey's transnational state apparatuses against the Movement have exercised a considerable impact on North Macedonian people, particularly the Muslims. In April 2017, a member of parliament from the Democratic Union for Integration Party (Демократска унија за интеграција), one of the biggest political parties in North Macedonia, declared that the Gülen Movement had been very active in North Macedonia for a very long time and not been involved in any illegal issues to date. Its schools were still active under the North Macedonian national laws, it had been paying taxes, it was not doing anything counter to the North Macedonian state–religion mentality, but according to him, the Turkish state had been asking the political elite to forcefully shut down Gülenist organisations. He underlined that this request from Turkey is a kind of hegemonic interference in the internal affairs of North Macedonia.

Not all the North Macedonian political elite, however, shares this point of view. There are those who do not interact with the activities of the Movement but benefit from the Turkish transnational state apparatuses. For instance, the ideas of a leading figure of the Turkish National Unity Movement (Türk Hareket Partisi, THP) are quite different. He declared that before the coup attempt in Turkey the North Macedonians were not aware of the dangerous structure of the Gülen Movement; according to him, if the Gülen Movement found an opportunity in North Macedonia, it might try to capture the state structure. He was also very grateful for the activities of Turkish-originated transnational state apparatuses in North Macedonia, since they had revealed the true face of the Gülen Movement.

These are samples of the differing views regarding the AKP and its struggle with the Gülen Movement in North Macedonia. Three elements play key roles in this situation. The first is Turkey's pressure on the North Macedonian authorities to clamp down on the Gülen Movement, and these authorities' less-than-adequate response to these demands, despite the fact that Turkey plays an important role in supporting the North Macedonian state in the international arena and is a major economic partner. The second element is the historical and emotional ties binding North Macedonia's Muslims with Turkey. The sympathy for Turkey felt by the Muslim part of Skopje and other Muslim majorities is so strong that the people will not tolerate anything against Turkey. Linked to this, the third element is that since 2007 and particularly after 2013, Turkish trans-national state apparatuses have been working even more intensely, particularly in cooperation with the Muslims of North Macedonia. The Turkish institutional structures – the Diyanet and its imams, TİKA with its projects, the YTB and the Yunus Emre Institute with its cultural activities – have been working closely with Muslim groups. Here, the defamation campaigns that the AKP has run have had a negative impact on public perception of the Gülen Movement. The foundations of Turkey's religious communities in North Macedonia are trying to replace Gülenist influences, in coordination with the AKP. Apart from these ethnically Turkish–Islamic communities, Turkey has started to support some local Islamic communities in order to consolidate its supporters in North Macedonia and establish a strong bloc against the Movement. The most visible of these communities are *Süleymancıs*[5] providing student housing, the Fettah Efendi Foundation[6] with its conversation (*Sohbet*) meetings for both male and female Muslims and the Mustafa Pasha Foundation[7] which offers scholarships and education activities.

Figure 7.2 Some examples of the local Islamic communities and ethnic Turkish communities that have been supporting the activities of the AKP. Photos by the author.

All these efforts aim not only at establishing a common enemy for the Muslim groups and the AKP, but also at consolidating a common political future based on a symbiotic relationship. Throughout the field studies that culminated in this book, I observed the intensity of Turkish influence on North Macedonian socio-political life, enacted through official state apparatuses and Sunni Muslim communities. Most Turkish-speaking Muslim North Macedonians follow Turkish politics closely and use the language that indicates how they position themselves within the political debates. The Turkish constitutional referendum held on 16 April 2017 rendered this influence highly visible in Skopje.

During the referendum process the 'Muslim part of Skopje' was full of the 'yes' flags of the AKP. Most of the Muslim individuals declared open support for the AKP and emphasised a belief in the referendum being an opportunity for the AKP and Erdoğan to defeat the guardianship mechanisms as well as Turkey's internal and external enemies, notably the Gülen Movement. The AKP's main discourse in the referendum process had been absorbed completely by the local people. Beyond that, in the streets of Skopje most ordinary Muslim North Macedonians declared that the referendum was a turning point for the future of the Islamic world. The victory of Erdoğan and his party was closely associated with the victory of Islam against its enemies. Throughout the interviews I conducted with representatives of the Turkish transnational state apparatuses there was an insistence that there had been no religious exploitation. However, some state officials of North Macedonia had different perspectives. For instance, a senior member of the North Macedonian foreign ministry felt that Turkey has been trying to establish a new kind of relationship with the Muslims in North Macedonia via instrumentalising Islam as a common value. Turkey's imams are important in this process, he said, but also TİKA is constructing mosques and supporting certain religious foundations, the Yunus Emre Institute is organising religious events – and in all of these activities there is also Erdoğanist propaganda. The instrumentalisation of religion by Turkish state apparatuses may be creating a political hinterland and enlarging the political influence of the AKP, but it is taken with caution by the North Macedonian political elites.

On the night of Turkey's 16 April 2017 constitutional referendum, the results were celebrated by Muslim North Macedonians on the streets of Skopje. Some streets were blocked by AKP supporters who shouted slogans valorising Erdoğan and the AKP. When asked about the reasons for these celebrations, a senior figure in the Macedonian Turkish Democratic Party (Makedonya Türk Demokratik Partisi, Демократска партија на Турците, TDP), who was also one of the leading figures in the demonstration, expressed the view that the referendum was a very important opportunity for all Muslims and Turks to display their power against enemies such as the Gülen Movement, both in Turkey and around the world. He argued that with the results of the referendum, Turkey would once again fly with passion and demonstrate its real power.

The Albanian case stands in contrast to the other case countries in terms of the exportation of domestic conflicts; indeed, each of the cases may be said to occupy one corner of a triangle of possible reactions. While the Bulgarian case can be described as giving such problems the boot with diplomatic solutions, the North Macedonian case might be characterised as turning a blind eye to any possible problems. The differences between the countries stem from their positions and capacities within the international system, their economic relations with Turkey, and Turkey's image in the eyes of their political elites. Bulgaria, as a member state of the EU, could visibly act against the exportation of Turkey's domestic conflicts via transnational state apparatuses. Relatively weak North Macedonia has, in contrast, been voicing its reactions in near-silent ways. Yet in face of all these differences one point is clear: that Turkey's recent foreign policy has been shaped by domestic political issues. Turkey's new religious identity has not only changed state behaviour but also transformed the visibility of its power in these countries. The difference in the Albanian case rests mostly on Albania's history, Turkey's limitations in using the proper channels and the impact of the Gülen Movement.

As noted previously, among the countries in the Balkan Peninsula, the Gülen Movement has an exceptionally strong position in Albania. There are three major reasons for this. First of all, the Movement has long experience in the country and has been active in education, the media and civil society. For more than two decades it has controlled almost three-quarters of religious education. This background gives it significant credibility among the socio-political elites of the Albanian state. Second, the children of some senior and junior politicians have been educated in Gülenist schools. This educational identity formation constitutes the backbone of the societal impact of the Gülen Movement in Albania and over the years the Movement has created deep relations with the state elite. During my fieldwork in the Albanian Muslim community, the Albanian foreign ministry and other state institutions, almost all of the interviewees spoke of the Gülen Movement in very positive terms.

The last point regards the Gülen Movement's 'moderatist' understanding of Islam. As noted previously, the Albanian state has sought to consolidate an environment of tolerance in the variety of religions, both in the state and in society, and to prevent the formation of extremist or radical groups in the country. Therefore, in the eyes of the state elite, the Movement is almost tailor-made for Albania. Most of the current and previous political figures and state elites underlined the importance of Islam in Albania as a Muslim-majority county, but at the same time emphasised the liberal socio-political atmosphere of the country. According to them, the great value of Albania is religious, cultural and ethnic harmony. They related that when, after the Cold War, some of the extreme Islamic communities tried to disturb their religion-oriented socio-political balance, the Gülen Movement under the guardianship of President Özal ran to their rescue. When in the 1990s Albania's capacity was not enough to sustain its support for all the desired societal mechanisms, the Gülen Movement covered some of the civic and religious education issues. The Gülenists have been working with the Albanian elite and population for over twenty years and are one of the most loyal groups concerning Albanians' understanding of religious tolerance. These Albanian socio-political elites are certainly aware of the problems that the Gülen Movement has had with Erdoğan. But at the same time, they are very strict about any interference in the internal affairs of Albania.

However, due to the intense influence of the Gülen Movement, it was not possible to get an objective point of view from the socio-political elites of Albania, most of whom have worked together with the Gülenists for a long time. Some former students of the Gülen schools currently occupy critical positions in the Albanian state. The positive impact of the Gülen Movement on Muslim elites has also affected perceptions of non-Muslim socio-political elite. Albanian perceptions of the AKP did not start out negative, but arrived at the current situation through the changes the party has recently undergone in the context of Turkish domestic politics. In this regard, most of the socio-political elites see certain Turkish-originated ideas, such as strategic depth, alongside the aggressive tone *vis-à-vis* the EU, increasing authoritarianism and an overdose of religion as the main reasons to lessen Turkey's influence and prestige in Albania. Indeed, these are widespread perceptions of the socio-political elites of Albania, and the popularity of such views owes a great deal to the Gülen Movement's impressive defence against the negative propaganda of the AKP. Here, the Albanian case presents the exact opposite of the cases of North Macedonia and Bulgaria, and the triangle of possible reactions visualised earlier must be stretched to accommodate this distance.

In North Macedonia and Bulgaria, as noted in the previous pages, Turkish state apparatuses and pro-AKP religious communities have managed to provide services where the host countries are deficient. In the Albanian case, the situation is different. Turkey has been trying to influence Albanian society via the same methods and state apparatuses, but the Gülen Movement does not leave much space to be filled by the AKP in the fields of education, religious service and cultural activities. Turkey also utilises TİKA effectively in Albania, but it falls short of uprooting the establishment of the Gülen Movement. Since 2015, I have observed that the Albanian state made some compromises with Turkey to decrease the stress engendered by this issue. For instance, in 2015 the Albanian Muslim community took over the management of H. Sheh Shamia madrasa in Shkodra from the Gülen Movement, and gave it to another Islamic community, which is popularly believed to receive financial support from the AKP government. However, in 2017 the Albanian state determined that one of the teachers of this madrasa was promoting the propaganda of radical Islamist groups in her courses. After a serious investigation, the Albanian state realised that the teacher also supported the AKP and Erdoğan, via her social media accounts. This issue has been used by the Gülen Movement as counter-propaganda against Erdoğan and the AKP. The members of the Gülen Movement have been accusing Erdoğan's Turkey of supporting radical Islamist groups to denigrate the activities of the Gülen Movement. Yet none of the state officials in Albania could cite any solid evidence regarding Turkey's direct and indirect support for Islamist groups in Albania.

This chapter has explicated how domestic and foreign policy changes in Turkey have been directly reflected in its policies in the three case countries. Policies on the Balkans have seen an escalation of priority in the eyes of Turkish diplomacy. In this framework, Turkey has utilised state institutions such as the Diyanet, TİKA and Yunus Emre Institute to maximise its influence on the region, alongside its official embassies. The result has been a more visible, active and challenging Turkish presence in different sectors and areas of the Balkans. Turkish authorities have also tried to export the country's major domestic conflict to the Balkans and all the apparatuses that are at the disposal of the AKP government have been deployed to uproot the Gülen Movement. However, the recent authoritarian drift and the turn towards coercive ethno-nationalist Sunnification in AKP policies have damaged perceptions of the AKP and Turkey in the Balkans. The recent isolationism in Turkey's foreign policy and its rising de-Europeanisation make the AKP's proposals harder to accept. Turkey's interventionist attitudes towards the domestic issues of the Balkans countries also render its image somewhat imperialist in the eyes of ordinary citizens.

Under these circumstances, I might put forward two main propositions. First, Turkey has not lost its power position in the Balkans, since it has a significant impact on the case countries in economic and political terms. However, it is hard to argue that Turkey still maintains its soft power via instrumentalisation of transnational apparatuses, since these have often violated their legal limits. Second, since the very beginning of the Republican period, Turkey has aimed to establish a certain level of stability in the Balkan Peninsula. Yet with its authoritarian transformation, Turkey has become a less than constructive actor in the region, exporting its domestic struggles via instrumentalisation of religion and transnational apparatuses.

This new role and Turkey's ensuing pattern of behaviour have been reciprocated in different ways depending on the case countries' domestic politics and their positions in the international system. The power and influence of the Gülen Movement is another factor in the reactions of the case countries, but the main determinant is the *response capacities* of the countries in question. In this regard, the Bulgarian state seems to have the greatest capacity to respond directly to the problems exported from Turkey. It is a member state of the EU, which could intervene to block some of Turkey's demands. On the other hand, the Bulgarian authorities are aware that without the Diyanet's financial support there may be serious issues among the country's Muslim population. Therefore, it has been trying to frame the issues in a delicate balance. The case of North Macedonia is quite different, since Muslims here feel themselves to be a part of Turkey and are deeply interested in its domestic politics. Notwithstanding, due to additional economic and diplomatic interests, the North Macedonian political elite opts not to regard Turkey as a problematic actor. In fact, because of its relatively weak economy, the North Macedonian state has positively welcomed the constructive activities of the Turkish state apparatuses within its borders. The Albanian case is the 'couch grass' among the case countries, and for two main reasons. First of all, the power and impact of the Gülen Movement is too strong for Turkish transnational apparatuses to break and this buffers any potential submission of Albanian political actors to Turkish demands. Second, the Albanian state does not allow any activity by Turkey that involves religious exploitation, and this limits Turkey's influence.

Notes

1. Okyay, *Diaspora-Making as a State-Led Project*.
2. Nedim Gencev is the last Grand Mufti appointed by the communist regime. He was known to have close relations with the regime and therefore he has never enjoyed significant credit among Bulgarian Muslims. For details, please see Eminov, *Turkish and Other Muslim Minorities in Bulgaria*, 64–7.
3. The interview was conducted on 12 April 2017, in Plovdiv. The interviewee was a regular community member of the Dzhumaya Mosque (Cuma Camii) and did not give permission to use his name in this study. The interview was conducted in a Turkish coffee shop, also called Dzhumaya. During most of the interview, the interviewee lowered his voice, because just six months earlier the Bulgarian state had accused Turkish imams in Bulgaria due to their 'intelligence' activities.
4. On 14 April 2017, I paid a visit to the General Directorate of Yahya Kemal Colleges and explained why I wanted to conduct an interview with representatives of the Gülen Movement. There were two middle-aged men, whom I later learned were the main representative of the Movement in the country, and the General Director of Yahya Kemal Colleges all over North Macedonia. They accepted the interview request and talked with me for four hours, explaining the historical journey of the Gülen Movement in Macedonia. They did not permit to me use their names, for security reasons. Beyond that, the main representative of the country warned me with these words: 'Skopje is a very small city as you know, and everybody knows everybody. In the other part of the city

[the Muslim-majority Albanian part] people do not even want to talk with us because of pressure from Turkey. If you see us in any area of the city, do not even say hello, because it will affect your interview schedule negatively. People could think that you are one of us and not want to talk to you.'

5. Süleymancıs (Süleymancılar) is one of the branches of the historical Nakşibendi Community. It was founded by Süleyman Hilmi Turan (1888–1959).

6. Founded in Skopje by Muderris Abdulfettah Rauf, known as Fettah Efendi (1910–63), who was an expert in all three major Muslim languages, Arabic, Ottoman-Turkish and Persian, as well as a renowned scholar.

7. A mosque community in Skopje, very active in the field of education.

8

INTERFERING IN THE INTERNAL
AFFAIRS OF HOST COUNTRIES

Opportunity structures in both domestic and international conditions have placed the AKP and Erdoğan in a hegemonic position in Turkey. When the party was first elected the government was in a readily mutable condition, but over time the AKP made use of opportunities and created new ones to consolidate itself in a position of power. In this way, crises have been turned into opportunities, through practices that are reminiscent of the exceptional leadership paradigm. The infusion of religious elements into discourse and policies, together with authoritarian practices, have changed the identity and behaviour patterns of the state. Turkey's new foreign policy approach incorporates the AKP's neo-Ottomanism, and manifests as a desire to intervene and if possible, become dominant in every aspect and avenue of societal life, both domestically and internationally. The AKP has foregrounded ethno-religious elements in line with the ideas of Davutoğlu as well as the dream of leadership of the Islamic Ummah long embraced by Erdoğan. Neo-Ottomanism as enacted by the AKP thus has four pillars: Sunni Islam, 'Turkishness', the desire to be dominant in Turkey and its neighbourhood, and consequential adventurism. Islam is exploited through all these pillars and on every occasion, as the AKP seeks to exercise influence, where possible through public diplomacy, that it carries out via transnational state apparatuses like TİKA, the Diyanet, Yunus Emre Institute and the YTB.

There is a popular conviction among the political elites of the Balkans that the Turkish state has been involving itself in the internal affairs of its neighbours by supporting new political parties and dividing existing ones, using the financial power and religion-oriented influence of its transnational apparatuses. Despite the fact that Turkey's domestic conflicts are exported in different ways to Bulgaria, North Macedonia and Albania, the effects of this exportation are similar. Most salient is the change in perceptions of Turkey in the eyes of the socio-political elites in the Balkans.

Süleyman Gökçe, the former Turkish ambassador in Sofia, expressed Turkey's normative duty to Bulgarian Muslims and Turks, focusing on Turkey's mediator role. According to him, Bulgarian Turks, Bulgarian Muslims and people of Turkey are as close as two coats of paint. Yet he also confessed that Bulgarian Muslims suffered a lot before the establishment of democracy in Bulgaria, and in those days Turkey was not very influential in protecting Bulgarian the Muslims. But now, he said, Turkey is much stronger and ready to go to bat for the needs of Muslims and Bulgarian Turks.

These needs do exist. After almost five centuries of Ottoman rule, Bulgaria gained independence in 1878 and Muslims became a minority in the country, alienated from critical positions of politics and the state system by the Orthodox Bulgarian majority.[1] Alongside that exclusion, Bulgarian Muslims have not been totally free to conduct their religious practices and use their mother tongue in much of the public space.[2] All these pressures and restrictions created a reaction among Muslim and Turkish Bulgarians against the communist regime, but the Bulgarian state managed to reduce the tension by establishing the Movement for Rights and Freedoms (Движение за права и свободи, Hak ve Özgürlükler Hareketi, HÖH) under the leadership of Ahmet Dogan (Ахмед Демир Доган).

Although the HÖH was officially established in 1990, it is commonly believed that Ahmet Dogan had started to organise the party in the early 1980s. When in 2007 the Bulgarian state revealed records of secret service staff and paid agents during the communist period, Dogan's name was listed among the paid agents of the Bulgarian State Committee for Security between 1974 and 1988. Dogan is also a social scientist who obtained his PhD with a dissertation entitled *Philosophical Analysis of the Principle of Symmetry*, which was also the core ideological grounding of the HÖH. Under Dogan's theory, the Turks (referring to all the Muslims in Bulgaria) would be able to live and participate in socio-political life and therefore could feel themselves as the equals of Bulgarians of other ethnic and religious backgrounds. This meant that Bulgarian Muslims would be integrated into the system, thereby forestalling the formation of separatist movements. It has been widely believed that Dogan's thinking and the HÖH were designed deep in the workings of the Bulgarian state, to preclude any kind of ethnic-based separation or mass protest. Most Bulgarian political elites and experts on contemporary Bulgarian politics argue that Dogan and his friends established their political party under the guidance of the Bulgarian state, and that this move on the part of the state enabled it to enjoy the best of both worlds. Not only did Dogan's political movement gather almost all Muslims and particularly Turks and Pomaks under its benign umbrella, it has also blocked potential involvement by the Turkish state, via instrumentalising the cause of protecting the rights of Turks and Muslims.

Even though from the very beginning of the HÖH certain other Muslim and Turkish luminaries, notably the former Grand Mufti Nedim Gencev, tried to devise new political structures for Muslims and Bulgarian Turks, such endeavours were less than successful. Thus, representing Bulgarian Muslims undivided, the HÖH managed to find a reasonable number of seats in the Bulgarian parliament, starting from the first democratic elections. Between 2001 and 2009, the party achieved a position in coalition governments and controlled some ministries such as the Ministry of Agriculture. Since 2009 the Bulgarian state has given the franchise to its citizens in the diaspora, the majority of whom live in Turkey, and the HÖH became the first party in the ballot boxes outside Bulgaria. Moreover, since 2009 the party has been gaining a small number of seats in the European Parliament.

Despite the HÖH's relatively successful election record and its respectable acceptance rate among both Bulgarian Muslims and some non-Muslim Bulgarians, since the early 2010s some former party members and members of parliament have aimed to establish a new political structure against the presence of the HÖH. Among them, the People's Party for Freedom and Dignity (*Narodna Partiya Svoboda i Dostoynstvo*) was founded by Korman Ismailov, a former HÖH member of parliament, in 2011, but did not pass the 4 per cent election threshold in 2013. During the establishment period of the party, some news agencies claimed that it received direct financial support from Turkey, and put forward Erdoğan's October 2010 visit as indicator of this support. In October 2010, Erdoğan paid a diplomatic visit to Sofia and met Korman Ismailov and other leading figures of the party but refused to meet Ahmet Dogan. Furthermore, also in 2010, Boyko Borissov openly warned Erdoğan with these words: 'No party intermediaries are necessary between Bulgaria and Turkey. I insist that our Turkish colleagues review their relations with certain circles in Bulgaria who present themselves as actors expressing the will of the Turkish state in Bulgaria.'[3] Four years later I was able to interview one of the founders of the People's Party for Freedom and Dignity, who addressed some of these issues:

> The establishment of the HÖH was a necessity to prevent possible tensions, extremism and long-lasting problems between two different ethno-religious groups. But, like everything else, it has a shelf life and I think it is over for a long time now. It is not responding to the main problems of Muslims, Turks, Pomaks and other minority groups in Bulgaria. We saw this problem a long time ago and tried to change the fate of the country's minority groups. We couldn't be totally successful, but we have woken up a sleeping structure . . . There are many rumours about our relations with Erdoğan, people were saying that we were getting direct and illegal money from Erdoğan and they also said we got money from Turkey's religious communities and municipalities . . . If we got that money, we would be very successful during the elections. Indeed, we got Turkey's support, but this was limited to the discursive level.

Even though the People's Party for Freedom and Dignity was not successful, it was the first signal regarding the division of the pro-Turkish HÖH and Turkey's direct and indirect intervention in the Bulgarian domestic political arena. Inside the HÖH, some leading figures started to argue that it had become Ahmet Dogan's personal party and had started to lose its inclusionary vision. Even though Dogan did not want to give up the chair of the party, he left it in favour of Lütfi Mestan because of intense opposition in January 2013. Dogan then constituted a new position for himself, that of honorary president. With Mestan's chairmanship, a new discussion started within the party ranks: Turkey's direct support of the HÖH under Mestan's rule. A close political comrade of Lütfi Mestan expressed the view that the main source for such claims was Ahmet Dogan, who aspired to occupy the presidency once again, and therefore all the noise was about party inner politics. But it is also true that, according to other close political comrades of Lütfi Mestan, before Mestan's term the HÖH had become an anti-AKP party. According to them this was wrong, since as a political party that aims to support the rights of Bulgarian Turks, it can't take such a position. It has to remain objective.

Despite the fact that Mestan managed to override these claims and all the intimidation he faced, in 2015 he was removed from his post by the central council and expelled from the party for what it considered an excessively pro-Turkish government stance following the downing of a Russian bomber jet by the Turkish Air Force.[4] He then promptly founded another pro-Turkish political party, Democrats for Responsibility, Solidarity and Tolerance (Демократи за отговорност, свобода и толерантност, DOST), and claims about the direct influence of the Turkish AKP reached an apex. A key reason for this perception was that in a propaganda film put out by the DOST, former Turkish ambassador Süleyman Gökçe appeared in one scene and spoke in favour of the DOST. Even though Gökçe denied such support in my interview with him, a senior party official with whom another interview was conducted was quite sure about it. Claims regarding Turkey's support to the DOST are not limited to this cameo appearance. More serious claims became widespread, involving the instrumentalisation of the Diyanet and its imams during the establishment period of DOST and before the 2017 elections. Even though the DOST obtained only 2.9 per cent of votes in the 2017 general parliamentary elections and did not gain any seats because of the 4 per cent election threshold, the furore and diplomatic crises that it created were bigger than its vote share.

On 21 February 2016, the Bulgarian press reported that Uğur Emiroğlu and three other Diyanet imams in Bulgaria had been declared 'persona non grata'. According to the official declaration, the activities of Emiroğlu and the other imams were incompatible with their diplomatic status. According to the allegations, these Diyanet officials had been putting pressure on Bulgarian Muslims to extend their support to the DOST, and were even involved in some illegal financial activities supporting the DOST. The issue then escalated to another level. On 16 March 2017, the Bulgarian foreign ministry recalled its ambassador in Ankara, Nadezhda Neynsky, for consultation on the activities of imams from Turkey in the Bulgarian domestic political arena. Even though the ambassador preferred not to talk directly on these issues, a senior official in the Bulgarian foreign ministry stressed that since 2014, almost every month they had been receiving complaints from local political elites regarding the activities of Turkish imams and their pro-Erdoğan discourse, mostly in Blagoevgrad, Targovishte and Razgrad where Turks and Pomaks are a majority. Therefore, he noted that there was solid evidence undergirding the Bulgarian state's actions.

Although the Turkish embassy has consistently denied all such accusations, the activities of imams and similar attempts served to tarnish the positive image of the Diyanet and of Turkey in Bulgaria. Furthermore, they decreased the impact of the DOST, according to some party officials. On 14 April 2017, I had the opportunity to conduct an interview with Hüseyin Hafizoglu, vice president of the DOST, at the new headquarters of the party.[5] According to Hafizoglu, the DOST was founded to meet a glaring need. The other political structures have not provided true and satisfactory responses to the needs of the Muslim, Turkish, Pomak minorities and the rest of the Bulgarian citizens – and what is more, these inadequate political structures know that the DOST will be successful. From his point of view, that is why the other political groups have started a smear campaign against them and against Turkey. They want to kill two birds with one stone, targeting the Diyanet as well as the DOST since the Diyanet is Turkey's only active tool in Bulgaria and the Bulgarian state no longer wants it there. In this positionality, the DOST supports the presence of the Diyanet in Bulgaria, seeing it as a necessary apparatus serving Bulgaria's Muslim communities.

Apart from the arguments of the Bulgarian state and press, there is no evidence to prove Turkey's direct support or the instrumentalisation of the Diyanet to promote the DOST. However, the founding of the DOST in the wake of the HÖH has already created division and debate between these two pro-Turkish political parties. According to some of the senior Bulgarian-Turkish political actors in Sofia, to divide the Turkish political structure in Bulgaria is a new tactic that Turkey is using on the Muslims of Bulgaria:

divide and conquer. And they expressed certainty that if Turkey was involved in the process it was inevitable that the Diyanet would be there, since it is Turkey's only tool in Bulgaria.

Unclear though it may be what Turkey's role was and what functions the Diyanet carried out during the establishment and promotion of the DOST, it is no secret that we are seeing new discussions on Turkey and religion among Bulgarians. For instance, during the April 2017 Turkish constitutional referendum, the HÖH openly supported the side opposing the AKP and publicised this support on its website. By contrast, the DOST supported the AKP's argument throughout the referendum process. DOST vice president Hafizoglu openly declared that even though as a political party DOST had not explicitly joined the election campaign for the referendum, they saw the new constitution as an opportunity for a big and powerful Turkey, and it would represent an achievement for them as well.

In light of these debates in Bulgaria, two conclusions can be drawn. First, Turkey's coercive ethno-nationalist Sunnification of the state identity has also affected the domestic politics of Bulgaria and deepened the polarisation between the pro-Turkish political parties. Second, the utilisation and exploitation of religion and religious actors in these processes have created distrust among Bulgarian state officials of Turkey and its transnational apparatuses.

The North Macedonian case is fundamentally different from the cases of Bulgaria and Albania primarily because of its economic dependence on Turkey and Turkey's support for North Macedonia. Beyond these factors, North Macedonia exhibits a fragmented political spectrum that spans from pro-North Macedonian to pro-Serbian parties. There are more than twenty political parties active in North Macedonian politics, three of which are pro-Turkish while another three are pro-Albanian and pro-Muslim.

Even though there is no substantial evidence for the AKP's support for particular political parties in North Macedonia other than popular claims, one might argue that it has been following a different strategy than that used in Bulgaria. The AKP has worked with both the old North Macedonian pro-Turkish political parties and the new pro-religious Albanian Muslim political parties. Even though the AKP has exercised a significant influence on all of the pro-Turkish and pro-Muslim/Albanian political parties, two of them can be foregrounded here: the Turkish Democratic Party (Демократска партија на Турците, TDP) and the newly emerged BESA Movement (Lëvizja Besa). Beyond that, another point can be argued: that there has been increasing visibility for Turkey in North Macedonia, which has generated different points of view. For starters, the non-Muslim North Macedonians are just enjoying the Turkish investment. By contrast, while Muslim North Macedonians and Albanians have been pleased to see Turkey make an appearance, in hushed voices they have been talking about some discomforts. Yet it is hard to hear these voices, because since late 2013 the TDP has been receiving support from the AKP and particularly Erdoğan in very visible ways. Even though the TDP is not a strong party, due to Erdoğan's patronage its impact is bigger than its vote percentage.

Dating from the early 1990s, the TDP is one of the oldest political parties in North Macedonia, and occasionally has had the distinction of being the tiniest political party in the coalition governments. Since 2013, it has been undertaking another function, that of organising public rallies to support Erdoğan and the AKP at critical junctures of Turkish politics. Starting from the 2013 Gezi Park protests and throughout the 17–25 December 2013 corruption scandal, the 15 July 2016 coup attempt and the 16 April 2017 constitutional referendum, the TDP has organised and led street rallies. Furthermore, it has been organising alternative programmes during Erdoğan's visits to North Macedonia through its civil society organisation, named the Turkey Support Platform of Macedonia (Makedonya Türkiye Destek Platformu, Platforma për mbështetjen e Turqisë). Yet representatives of the Platform point out that their support did not start with the AKP period. They define their role as providing unconditional support to Turkey, since they believe that without a strong Turkey in North Macedonia they will be in a very difficult situation. But, the very same representatives also argue that before Erdoğan, there was no political actor who had the will and capacity to take care of their problems in North Macedonia. Thus, supporting Erdoğan does not have much to do with loving him, it is about the future of the North Macedonian Turks, Albanians and all Muslims.

Figure 8.1 Poster for a pro-Erdoğan demonstration organised by the Turkey Support Platform of Macedonia. Photo by the author.

Most non-Muslim North Macedonian political elites believed that Erdoğan's Turkey not only provided support for the pro-Turkish political parties, but had also created a pro-Albanian and pro-Muslim political party, the BESA Movement. BESA was founded by a number of prominent Muslim Albanian–North Macedonian figures such as Zeqirija Ibrahim, Bilal Kasami, Afrim Gashi and Skënder Rexhepi in November 2014. Arguably, Albanians were the best channel through which to exert influence on North Macedonia through Islam, since they constitute the majority of Muslims in North Macedonian socio-political corridors. Even though there are two large Albanian parties, the Democratic Union for Integration (Демократска унија за интеграција) and the Democratic Party of Albanians (Демократска партија на Албанците) that are politically active in the country, their nationalist tendencies are too strong to support any foreign intervention or impact.

In these circumstances, following the foundation of BESA in 2014, most of the pro-Albanian political parties and some of the North Macedonian political groups claimed that BESA was founded with the support of Erdoğan and that its activities have been indirectly supported by particularly the Diyanet and other Turkish transnational state apparatuses. Furthermore, both the Gülenists and other anti-AKP influential groups in North Macedonia claimed that BESA was founded by Erdoğan both to serve his Islamist neo-Ottomanism aims and influence North Macedonian political life in direct ways. However, none of the officials I interviewed revealed any substantial evidence in support of these claims. Diyanet consultant Murat Alkan, in Skopje, declared such claims to be nonsense, unsupported by a shred of evidence. What is more, he pointed out, all of the Diyanet's activities are monitored by the North Macedonian state, by Ankara and by other state institutions. He insisted that their activities are not a part of politics.

There are fourteen Turkish imams who are on active duty in various mosques in North Macedonia. Even though I tried to talk to six of them, they refused to discuss politics, remaining within the boundaries of their official duties in North Macedonia. Yet I managed to conduct an interview with one of the leading figures of BESA in 2017, regarding his party's relations with Erdoğan. He categorically rejected these claims and declared them to be one of the biggest lies produced by their competitors and enemies of Turkey. He also underlined that Turkey is a very important country and that BESA has good relations with the Erdoğan administration, like every political party in North Macedonia; and he defined BESA's political aim as finding reasonable solutions to the fundamental problems of North Macedonia and defending the rights of minorities in North Macedonia, including the Albanians and Turks.

It is obvious that one of the fundamental issues in North Macedonia is ethno-religious discrimination against non-Christian citizens. Therefore, many Albanians, Turks and other Muslim groups have been demanding their rights in various ways, and throughout this process Turkey's external support seems to have been very important. At this point, it would be good to note that Albania stands out among the case countries in the small area of the Balkans because of the role and position of religion in politics, and because of its attitude *vis-à-vis* Turkey's increasingly interventionist policies. The harmony of various religions and religious groups in socio-political life is both a moral and constitutional norm in Albania. This is because of the historical background of Albania and its bitter past experiences regarding religious issues.

Albania has a rich spectrum of political parties and none of them positions itself against the secular nature of the state and the constitutional norm of religious harmony. In 2011 Tahir Muhedini and Shpëtim Idrizi founded the Party for Justice, Integration and Unity (Partia Drejtësi, Integrim dhe Unitet, PDIU), whose official aim is to protect the rights of ethnic Albanians (mostly Muslims) and support them in the international arena. Some religious declarations of the party's leading cadre created concerns about its anti-secular tendencies. Similar to the North Macedonian case, in Albania most of the socio-political elites argued that Erdoğan had been supporting the PDIU and sending financial support via Turkey's transnational apparatuses. However, again just like the North Macedonian case, none of them revealed any substantial evidence and the representatives of Turkey's transnational apparatuses regarded the claims as nonsense, like the Diyanet consultant Murat Alkan in Skopje. Despite concerted efforts to conduct an interview with PDIU representatives, I received no positive response. However, in April 2016, the Greek daily *Kathimerini* published an article claiming that Erdoğan's Turkey had been supporting the PDIU in its religious ambitions in Albania and in the Balkans generally. The article was based on the testimonies of political actors in the Albanian parliament whose names were not specified. Furthermore, *Kathimerini* quoted the leader of the Union for Human Rights, which represents the Greek Orthodox minority in Albania, who claimed that the PDIU buys votes using money obtained from Turkey: 'The only party representative who met with Erdoğan during his last visit to Tirana, was Shpëtim Idrizi of the PDIU'.[6]

In spite of the absence of substantial evidence of direct or indirect Turkish support of the PDIU, most of the Muftis, the Chairman of the Albanian Islamic Community, Turkish expert journalists and political actors in the field argue that Erdoğan has in fact been supporting the PDIU, and through this support has been trying to increase Turkey's influence on Sunni communities. Indeed, the negative propaganda of the Gülen Movement about the AKP has a significant influence on this perception. Relatively neutral socio-political actors are also concerned about a possible increase in political Islam and radical Islamic within society. On this point, certain members of the Albanian parliament note that under Erdoğan's rule Turkey has become a more religious country; further, that some groups have been encouraged by this, and perhaps the PDIU is one of these.

All in all, it may safely be concluded that Turkey's involvement in the political sphere of Albania via religion and transnational apparatuses is not as significant as is the case in Bulgaria and North Macedonia. Yet the spillover of Turkey's identity transformation is visible in the country and has been creating apprehension among some of the socio-political elites.

Notes

1. Brunnbauer, '"Everybody believes the state should do everything for them"'.
2. Eminov, 'Social construction of identities'.
3. For details, please see www.novinite.com/articles/112559/Bulgaria+PM+to+Erd ogan%3A+No+Ethnic+Parties+Needed+as+Mediators, accessed 3 June 2020.
4. On 24 November 2015, a Turkish Air Force F-16 fighter jet shot down a Russian military aircraft near the Syria–Turkey border. According to the Turkish authorities the Russian aircraft was in Turkish airspace without permission, but the Russian Defence Ministry denied this claim and insisted that the aircraft was in Syrian airspace. Erdoğan pointed out that Turkey had the right to defend its airspace and Russian President Putin insisted on his country's general claim. This issue created a diplomatic crisis between Russia and Turkey that lasted more than a year.
5. Some observations about my visit to DOST headquarters are worth mentioning. Inside the building, none of the Bulgarian flags hung alone, but were mounted together with the Turkish flag. Most of the painted slogans and leaflets were written in Turkish. Some of the stationery and promotional materials had been donated by Turkey's Bursa Municipality. Also gracing the walls were a couple of Atatürk photos. When asked about these, VP Hüseyin Hafizoglu gave a quite open and remarkable answer: 'Actually this is our temporary building; we will move to the permanent one, but the atmosphere will be the same. Since we are a pro-Turkish party and our hearts are in Turkey, we are proud to keep Turkey alive in Bulgaria.'
6. For the relevant part of the article, please see www.tiranaecho.com/latest-news/ kathimerini-article-linking-erdogan-to-the-cham-party-stirs-waters-between-greece-and-albania-again/, accessed 3 June 2020.

9

DESTABILISING THE SECULAR ENVIRONMENTS OF HOST COUNTRIES

The role of religion in the Balkans can be discussed from two different perspectives. The first considers the interwoven structure of religion with ethnic, social and political problems after the break-up of the Ottoman state and later in the aftermath of the Cold War. Muslims have become either demographic minorities in countries like Bulgaria and North Macedonia or, despite their demographic majority, have had problems with access to resources. Thus, religion-related issues, and often religion itself, have been articulated alongside other problems such as ethnic divisions, economic difficulties and issues of social integration. In this way, religion has become a determinant in socio-political polarisation and a central element in the development of ethnic and national identities in the Balkans.[1] The violent dissolution of the former Yugoslavia created a new phenomenon that merged nationalism with Islam and established a base for solidarity.[2] Even though the Muslims in Albania, North Macedonia and Bulgaria have different understandings of Islam and different ethnic identities, religion is a major factor that both divides and unites.

On the other hand, religion, and again particularly Islam, is also a source of concern for the Balkan societies even including their Muslim populations, because of its diverse and radical manifestations. Islam's secondary position in the region has rendered the issue more sensitive. In this fragile context, some Islamic groups from the Middle East tried to establish themselves and fill the

void created by the inadequacies in the state capacities of the 1990s. The paradigms they promoted were perceived as a threat because of their incompatibility with the traditional and multi-lingual, multi-ethnic and multi-religious
socio-political life in the region. There was increased concern among Balkan
elites that the presence of socio-economic problems might facilitate the recruit-
ment of youth into these radical organisations.

All the Balkan countries have tried to establish mainly secular systems,
and Bulgaria, North Macedonia and Albania have received institutional support from *laik* Turkey. Despite the fact that they exhibit different forms of
secularism, they all see it as a prerequisite for their social harmony. Under-
standably, the socio-political elites and policy-makers of these countries have
tried to eliminate factors they consider harmful to their society and state systems. Turkey's recent emphasis on religious issues is a trigger for the secular
systems of Bulgaria, North Macedonia and Albania. The transformation of
Turkey's state identity has constructed a different image of itself as an actor
with the capacity to destabilise their secular environments.

Alexander Oscar, the president of a socially active and visible Jewish
community (Shalom) in Sofia, told me, 'It seems that this new situation will
destroy our relations with some of the Muslim friends'. In an interview on
12 April 2017, he made these observations on Turkey's new role in Bulgaria
and its reflection on intra-community relations:

> We have great relations with the Muslims of Bulgaria. We have been participat-
> ing in each other's events and national days and collaborating in various issues
> to make Bulgaria free in terms of religion. But it is also true that the Bulgarian
> Muslims have been affected by Turkey. We have been observing that Turkey is
> in a transition period which we feel here every day. Religion and an aggressive
> political attitude have become the new characteristics of Turkey. As a friend of
> Turkey and the Bulgarian Muslims, it makes me so sad, since it seems that this
> new situation will affect our peace here.

Indeed, Oscar's view is not an exceptional perception of Turkey's new
role and its reflection on a predominantly Eastern Orthodox country with
significant Catholic and Muslim populations. Bulgaria is a constitutionally
secular country and religious freedom is guaranteed by the state. Yet there is
also an unwritten hierarchy between the religions, and one might claim that

Islam is not at the top of it. Until the beginning of the 2000s, the Denomi-nations Act (Zakon za veroizpovedanigata) of 1949 was the main legal docu-ment regulating religious freedom and state–religion relations. While Article 13 frames the regulation of religious issues in terms of the separation of religion from the state, Article 37 states that it is a major duty for the state to maintain tolerance and respect towards all religious groups as well as non-believers. Under the EU reform and harmonisation process, the Denomina-tions Act was transformed in 2002 and moved beyond the recognition of religious pluralism. It sought to represent more liberal values with an aim of establishing a more harmonious society.[3] Even though the Bulgarian state is neutral towards religions on paper, however, with side-regulations it has been supporting the Orthodox church and providing a relatively more privi-leged status to its adherents. In this context, Muslims of Bulgaria requested indirect support from Turkey, to level the playing field. This issue was clear in the words of the Grand Mufti Mustafa Hadzihi. According to Hadzihi, even though Muslims are not second-class citizens in Bulgaria, it is also true that they have historical wounds and it is possible to feel that these wounds are still open. At this point, he also noted that he sees Turkey as a protector.

From Hadzihi's words and those of others who echo him, it is obvious they are aware that Turkey has been utilising religion more in recent times. The increasing role of Islam in Turkey's relations with Bulgaria and Turkey's authori-tarian drift are also issues that are being followed closely. For instance, before the constitutional referendum of 2017, most of the prominent Bulgarian news-papers turned their attention to the regime and/or system change in Turkey and started to discuss its possible effects on Bulgaria.

Most interviews with members of the non-Muslim socio-political elite pro-pounded that the increasing authoritarianism in Turkey and its instrumentalisa-tion of Islam in foreign policy would not only affect relations between Bulgaria and Turkey, but would also bring harm to social harmony in Bulgarian society. Yet these interviewees' fundamental apprehension was about the possible revit-alisation of extremist groups as a consequence of the intense tone of Islam com-ing from Turkey. Further, most of them argued that they had been observing Turkey taking advantage of the extensive network of the Diyanet in Bulgaria. They also claimed that the socio-political faces of Islam had become more visible under Turkey's influence. Some even argued that Turkey's transformation has

Figure 9.1   Headlines of major Bulgarian newspapers during Turkey's constitutional referendum. Photos by the author.

affected its exportation capacity. It has been converted from a secular exporter to an Islamist one. This is dangerous for Bulgaria, since Bulgarian secularism is the guarantor of Bulgarian social peace.

The foreign policy preferences and the identity of Turkey, the role of the Diyanet, and the apprehensions of the Bulgarian elites regarding the possible deterioration of its secular environment are interrelated. That is, Sunnification, intertwined with authoritarianism and ethno-nationalist policy discourse, has transformed the activities of the Diyanet in Bulgaria and rendered Turkish forms of Islam more visible. This visibility has created concern among the non-Muslim political elite because of the possible social discord that may emanate from it. Yet most of the Muslim socio-political elite has a fundamentally different view, in that they believe it will not create seriously altered radical religious practices within the Muslim community of Bulgaria due to the moderate nature of Islam there. Indeed, under the lack of economic and democratic powers, Islam seems to be the only tool for Turkey regardless of legitimacy concerns. Yet some of the Bulgarian-Turkish political elite have declared that this policy of Erdoğan is very rational from the realpolitik perspective. They were also aware that Erdoğan has been using religion to create a new image for Turkey in the Balkans and Bulgaria. Furthermore, they noted that Erdoğan has been using a language replete with religious discourse in Turkey and in constructing the country's foreign relations. According to them, this would be problematic for the Netherlands and maybe for France, but it is the only way to be an active actor among the Muslims of Bulgaria, since being a Turk and a Muslim is the only integrative component for Bulgarian Muslims. They underlined that other methods have been tried by Turkey's previous governments and leaders, but from a historical perspective they know that whenever a leader uses religion in this region, he gets more credibility with the Muslims of Bulgaria.

The Bulgarian Muslims have a perspective that segregates Islam from politics. Beyond that, both the Bulgarian and Anatolian Muslims share a moderate understanding of Islam, but the distance between religion and politics is less in Anatolia and therefore a link between the two can be built more easily, with the possibility of turning it into a national ideology for Turkey. The nation-building process in Turkey has not created liberal democracies in a Western form. Control and management of religion have always been an important item on the agenda of governments, inclusively and exclusively. Islam, in

Turkey, carries a significant capacity for mobilisation, and the demarcation between Islam and politics becomes blurred, depending on the preferences of the government.[4] Thus, the AKP has gained unprecedented support from the religious communities of Turkey.

Rather differently, Bulgarian Muslims have been trying to make a bigger gap between Islam, politics and radicalism. A recent survey conducted among Muslims of Bulgaria indicated that an overwhelming 86 per cent majority consider religion as important in their life. Nevertheless, the number of those who do not comply with religious requirements remains high: 54 per cent do not conduct daily prayers; 41 per cent do not attend the mosque. The highest level of religiosity was observed among the people in deepest poverty, 99 per cent of whom said that religion is important in their lives. Almost 100 per cent define themselves as religious and 46 per cent are considered by others as deeply religious. According to the same survey, there is no evidence of radicalisation among Bulgarian Muslims, who overwhelmingly favoured a secular state. A small chunk (2.8 per cent) supports the ideas of the so-called Islamic State. Erdoğan emerged as the most well-known and accredited leader with 49 per cent approval, surpassing Obama, Putin and Merkel.[5]

Thus there seems to be no serious problem in Bulgaria regarding the destabilisation of its secular environment. Turkey's influence is therefore not regarded as a foreign intervention that might increase the level of radicalisation. However, some Muslim socio-political elites are worried about Turkey's increasing instrumentalisation of religion and its possible effects on the social stability of Bulgaria. For instance, some of the former members of the Bulgarian parliament have noted that Bulgarian Muslims are not considering Erdoğan as a repressive leader, but they see him as a religious Muslim leader. According to them, when you visit small Bulgarian-Turkish and Pomak villages it is very possible to see the changes in clothing, language and attitudes among young Muslims. They argued that young Bulgarian Muslims are sharper in alienating the non-Muslims and in accusing elite actors of socio-political and economic weaknesses. Furthermore, Erdoğan is always in their mouths.

These arguments have merit since the transformation is quite visible in some areas where Turks and Pomaks form a majority, such as Pazadjik, Plovdiv, Bachkobo, Dolen and Leshten. Indeed, these are also poor residential areas of Bulgaria. As a consequence, one might claim two points regarding religion as a debated issue and as an element destabilising the secular environment of Bulgaria via Turkey's impact. First, there is a high level of concern among the socio-political elites of Bulgaria about the possible ramifications of the transformation in Turkey's state identity for Bulgarian Muslims. Second, it seems that this concern will remain for the foreseeable future, since Turkey is likely to maintain its influence on Bulgarian Muslims under the authoritarian Sunnification of Turkey.

Throughout my fieldwork across North Macedonia, 'Sustain our beautiful religion' was a common slogan among the representatives of Turkish state apparatuses and religious communities. This sentiment was seen as the secondary and in some cases the primary duty of Turkish structures. For instance, one of the teachers in the Skopje branch of Yunus Emre Institute expressed the view that their primary mission was to endear the Turkish language, values and culture to North Macedonian citizens. For that reason, although religion is not directly related to their areas of activity, it is at the heart of their unwritten mission, since it is impossible to separate Islam and Turkish cultures.

Regarding 'sustaining the religion', representatives of Turkish state apparatuses have talked with some restraint, since the instrumentalisation of religion by Turkey is a controversial subject in the region. Yet some representatives of civilian religious communities declared their aims and the role of religion in this framework more openly. For instance, Sevba Abdula, the president of the Fettah Efendi Foundation, revealed an interesting picture. According to him, the Foundation's aim is to generalise good values and true knowledge among the young generations of the North Macedonian people. For him, Islam is the core of these good values and true knowledge, and it is pity that throughout the years and particularly during the Cold War period, the North Macedonian people have almost forgotten their religion. Since the Cold War they have started to learn, but it is problematic to learn religion without the corresponding culture and knowledge. Thus, the Fettah Efendi Foundation and many others have been trying to inculcate religion with culture and knowledge. The Fettah Efendi Foundation in particular makes use of the writings of prominent thinkers like Ahmet Davutoğlu, and a variety of scholars have given lectures to the young generation. At this point, Abdula noted that they want religion not to be confined to mosques. For them, religion should be outside the mosque and establish an eclectic structure within real life.

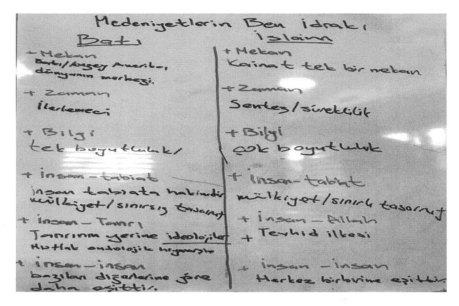

Figure 9.2 Notes from a public lecture at the Fettah Efendi Foundation in Skopje, explaining the difference between Western and Islamic civilisations, according to Davutoğlu's studies. Photo by the author.

Creating an eclectic structure integrating Islam in daily life invokes questions for North Macedonia because of its problems with religious pluralism and secularism. Even though North Macedonia is a country where the constitution and the Ohrid Agreement protect the multi-ethnic and multi-religious structure of society, it would be hard to claim that North Macedonian secularism does not create inequalities. There exists an implicit hierarchy among the three major religious components, the priority being given to Christian Orthodoxy, which represents the majority of the population. Also, after the Yugoslavia period, Western values and pluralism have become major elements in defining North Macedonian secularism because the country wanted to be a part of the 'Western club'. Therefore, even though Orthodox Christianity seems to have the greatest privilege, the state system has been careful to observe religious pluralism in its legislation.

Despite the efforts of North Macedonian authorities to establish a harmonious structure uniting various religious groups, the intertwining of religion and nationalism does allow stability to be consolidated in North Macedonia. In its societal hierarchy, the North Macedonian Orthodox church forms the first group and the Ohrid Archbishopric is the second. The third group encompasses other religious communities: Islamic communities, the Catholic church, the Evangelical Methodist church and the Jewish community. The state guarantees freedom of religion and allows its citizens to practise their religion freely, either alone or in community with others.[6] The Association of North Macedonian Muslims, also known as Dar al-Ifta, plays an important role in sustaining the position of Islam, including its legal manifestations and practices. This Islamic institution manages the affairs of North Macedonian Muslims and defends their rights as citizens of North Macedonia. Turkey's Diyanet is a permanent sponsor of the Association, but its activities are not sufficient to overcome the historically established inequalities between Muslims and others.

The inequalities are related to two issues: the state's unwritten bias towards Christians (mostly Orthodox North Macedonians) and the socio-economic weakness of the Muslims (mostly Albanians and Sunni Turks). In this regard, even though the constitution and the Ohrid Agreement presuppose a balanced representation for all ethno-religious groups in politics, there has not been much realisation of this presupposition in daily life. That is, the Ohrid Agreement has put an end to the ethno-religious conflict in the country but has not created full equality between Albanians and North Macedonians or Muslims and Christians.[7] Thus any external religious intervention or support might shift the balance towards conflict. The socio-economic conditions of the Muslims in North Macedonia are in great need of improvement, but North Macedonia's current economic capacity is not strong enough to take the initiative alone. In this context, it is highly relevant that Turkey and its transnational apparatuses are playing an active role in mostly Muslim areas. Even though the North Macedonian Muslims are almost equally distributed between rural and urban areas, they constitute the poorest segments of society. The largest numbers of Muslims are situated in the capital Skopje, followed by the cities of Kumanovo, Tetovo, Gostivar, Kicevo, Debar, Resen, Struga, and Ohrid.

A combination of historical conflicts and existing inequalities between Muslim and non-Muslim groups in politics, society and the economy have created a dilemma. On the one hand, the North Macedonian state, with the support of the EU and other Western powers, has been trying to maintain its socio-political stability.[8] On the other hand the North Macedonian state has been accepting direct and indirect support to improve opportunities for the country's Muslims, and Turkey is a leading supporter. Both Muslim and non-Muslim socio-political elites, however, have been worried about Turkey's increasingly Islamist tone during these support activities, since it has the capacity to damage the already minimal level of socio-political stability. In this regard, some of the leading public figures among the North Macedonian Muslims have underlined that since the beginning of the 2010s Turkey has developed a new motto: 'We will sustain Islam in North Macedonia and generally in the Balkans.' To this, they question: 'Which Islam?' As an answer, these people expressed the view that Turkey's institutions have been organising *iftar* dinners and other activities that unite Muslims, but just for a day. The rest of the promotion activities and discourses employed by Turkey's imams are not suitable for North Macedonia and the Balkans. Furthermore, religious and Western values have to be compatible, but Turkey's discourse has been moving away from the West. In this regard, it is impossible for Turkey to catch 'reasonable' Muslims, but possible for them to consolidate some of the young groups and radicals. For these local leaders, this is without question very dangerous for North Macedonia, since one single spark would be enough to ignite the entire region. They have publicly expressed concerns regarding Turkey's increasing Islamist interventions aimed at the wider Muslim communities. Most of the socio-political elite, whether Muslim or not, share the same ideas at different levels.

Here, we note that Turkey plays a dual role in North Macedonia, as both an external and an internal actor. Whereas Turkey is an external actor on paper, it is also an internal actor in two ways. First of all, in North Macedonia, Turkey has been represented by five different legal transnational apparatuses (the Diyanet, TİKA, the Anadolu Agency, the Yunus Emre Institute and the YTB), all which have been active in various sectors and adopt religious discourse in their activities. Furthermore, Turkey has been active in North Macedonia with more than twenty organisations, associations and foundations, with as much influence as an internal actor. Second, Turkey is not an ordinary foreign country in the minds of North Macedonian Muslims. The level of engagement in domestic political issues is very high and most Muslim Macedonians take sides and pursue daily political issues in Turkey as if they directly affected their lives. Thus, Turkey's domestic political transformations and the increasing role of religion in

the domestic political arena have long been affecting the social configuration and secular system of North Macedonia.

Although hardly any of the senior staff members of the Islamic Religious
Community of North Macedonia (IRC) or close colleagues at Reis-ul-ulema
in North Macedonia see any possible danger to the fragile secular environment of North Macedonia from Turkey's increasing religious activism, non-
Muslim socio-political elites hold the diametrically opposite position. The
obvious comfort of IRC authorities must then be related to their organic
relations with Turkey's Diyanet. These relations are so intense that the community has been adapting itself to the policies of Turkey, which seems to be
the only donor to mainstream Muslims in North Macedonia. For instance,
in front of all other Muslim organisations in the Balkan countries during the
Islamic Assembly Summit of Euro-Asia, which was held in Istanbul in 2016,
the head of the Islamic Religious Community of North Macedonia declared
the Gülen Movement to be a terrorist organisation for North Macedonian
Muslims. In March 2016, the rebuilding of the Burmali Mosque in the centre of Skopje turned into a public debate between the Muslims of North
Macedonia and the North Macedonian state. During the discussions, Sulejman Rexhepi, the head of the Community of Macedonia, declared that his
institution did not need any support from the Macedonian state, since the
Turkish government would take the initiative to rebuild the historic mosque.[9]
Yet some state elites observe this harmonious cooperation between the Community and the Turkish state as a dangerous element in North Macedonian
society's domestic balance. In this regard, a senior staff member in the office
of the North Macedonian prime minister and a close ally of the former prime
minister, Zoran Zaev, underlined that Turkey is a very close partner of North
Macedonia and therefore it would be quite difficult for them to cut ties with
Turkey. But he also added that this does not mean they are happy with all
Turkey's activities in North Macedonia. He clarified that support and collaboration on some fundamental issues – infrastructure, education, energy
and the various needs of North Macedonian Muslims – are very important
and make them very happy, but currently all roads lead to religion and this is
quite problematic for them. He boldly noted, that in all probability, Turkey
as a foreign country has to keep its relations in a diplomatic framework and
within certain sectors. Currently Turkey has been using religion as a tool, and

this could lead to a destruction of the social balance between Muslims and non-Muslims in North Macedonia.

Like the case of Bulgaria, an evaluation of my interviews in North Macedonia demonstrates that there has been a visible transformation regarding Turkey's increasing instrumentalisation of religion in the eyes of the socio-political elites. This transformation is not an isolated phenomenon, and is based on the positionality of these elites. While most official representatives of the Muslim communities seem satisfied with Turkey's new role in North Macedonia, some Muslim and most non-Muslim members of the socio-political elite are concerned about the increase of Turkish-originated religiosity because of its possible effects on the already fragile social balance in North Macedonia:

> I am not a social scientist and therefore maybe I do not know the proper terminology, but what you called secularism or religious pluralism is the backbone of the Albanian state and society. Furthermore, as a person who is a part of this society, I can tell you that the Albanian state mentality learns a lot from its history which is full of religious extremism and dictatorship. Therefore, I am dead sure that the Albanian state will never allow any external intervention against its religious pluralism . . . I cannot tell you that Turkey is a locomotive of religious extremism but I can easily tell you that whoever tries to destabilise our secular structure, it will be dismissed from Albania.

These words were uttered by Skënder Bruçaj, the head of the Muslim Community of Albania, and the leading organiser of a nationwide conference tour entitled 'On the Prevention of Violent Extremism and Radicalism and Promotion of Democratic Values and Civil Engagement' in 2016, in collaboration with the US embassy in Albania. The same year was named the year of 'de-radicalisation'. A special team from the Albanian government, the US embassy, other Western European embassies and some NGOs organised a number of events to fight the possible participation of Albanian Muslims in radical groups supporting the Syrian conflict.[10] Yet neither the Turkish embassy nor any other Turkish transnational apparatus wanted to play an active role in this initiative.

Albania is a Muslim-majority country with a secular constitution and pluralist legal regulations on religious matters.[11] Within this legal structure, the Albanian state officially defines itself as religiously neutral and tries to keep all religious groups at peace under the umbrella of the state. All religious communities enjoy equal rights within the borders of Albania and the constitution extends freedom of religion to all citizens. Therefore, both the predominant religious communities – Muslims, Christians and Jews – and other relatively small groups have had an equal degree of official recognition and social status, in an established structure, throughout Albanian history. Furthermore, religious communities have the right to hold their own property under existing legal regulations. Indeed, all the legal regulations come from a historical background. After the long Ottoman rule, the short period of independence and the Italian intervention of 1939 provided Albania with both traumatic experiences and a multi-religious population. Yet the main determinant was the period between 1945 and 1990, under the repressive communist regime that limited all religious activities until 1965 and afterwards defined the country as officially atheist. The system then banned all religious institutions.[12] However, the downfall of the communist regime and the rapid liberalisation process has transformed religion–state–society relations, and umbrella institutions have regained their impact. On the other hand, this liberalisation process created an open market for religious issues and rendered Albanian society vulnerable to extremist movements.[13] Under these circumstances, the Albanian state has been conducting a war on two fronts to protect its secular nature and to exterminate radical groups. In this context, Turkey's new role and image is something worth mentioning.

In the Albanian capital Tirana, an expert from the Department of Religion–State Toleration in the Prime Minister's office underlined the importance of secularism and peaceful religious pluralism for the Albanian people. He drew attention to Articles 10, 18 and 24, which regulate the relations between religion, state and society and frame the multi-religious structure and religious pluralism of the Albanian state. According to him, the Albanian state depends upon these articles to keep this multi-religious society together. These articles also encompass the historical heritage of the Albanian state and enact how a nation takes lessons from its past. According to him Turkey is not directly harmful to the secular structure of Albania, but it is no longer a guarantor of it. In the 1990s, Turkey and the Gülen Movement acted as external guardians of the modest mainstream Muslim structures of Albania, but in his eyes the current situation is not the same. He noted that particularly after the war between the AKP and Gülen, the AKP's discourse changed to a more Islamist one. He also claimed that the pro-Ikhwan Ardhmëria Foundation and its members have been getting support from the Erdoğan administration, although he could not put forward any evidence for this claim. Nonetheless, it is clear that there is a duality, in that whereas the Albanian state has been trying to incorporate such radical groups into Albanian multi-religious society, Erdoğan's Turkey has been encouraging them otherwise.

Even though the Turkish ambassador to Tirana and TİKA's representatives, the Diyanet and Yunus Emre Institute in Tirana, have rejected claims regarding Turkey's direct or indirect effect on the desecularising of Albania and support for radical Muslim groups, a picture can be compiled from small pieces of information. Some of the interviewees in my fieldwork disclosed official websites and bulletins of Turkish transnational apparatus. For instance, in 2014 TİKA announced that it supported the ALSAR Foundation (Alternativa e së Ardhmes – Alternative for the Future), which is regarded as an extreme group, during the Ramadan period and supplied their *iftar* dinners. In another example, the ALSAR Foundation has been providing scholarships to Muslim students in collaboration with TİKA, the Yunus Emre Institute and other Turkish-Islamic structures such as the Foundation for Human Rights and Freedoms and Humanitarian Relief (İnsani Yardım Vakfı, İHH).[14]

Some members of the Albanian socio-political elite are troubled by Turkey's increasingly Islamist foreign policy under the doctrine of neo-Ottomanism, which they do not see as a secular and therefore a suitable policy for Albania. Beyond that, interviewees from various political perspectives argued that the AKP had upset the balance of the fragile relations between democracy and religion and is currently trying to export its religion-based desires as incontestable truth – which is not compatible with the Albanian reality. In 2018, Mentor Kikia, a prominent journalist, Turkey expert and general manager of Top News, indicated that even though Turkey cannot destroy Albanian secularism, some of Turkey's recent policies run counter to the Albanian understanding of religion–society–state relations and have been creating undesirable sentiments among some of the Muslim groups. According to him, since the beginning of 2012–13, Turkey has not been a very favourable example to and partner of the

Albanian state against radical Islam, therefore the Albanian state and some of its Muslims have started to be sceptical about Turkey's activities. From Kikia's point of view there are several reasons for this scepticism. First of all, most of the Albanian Muslims believe that Erdoğan constructed the big mosque to establish his hegemony over them, and, secondly, the mosques constructed by TİKA and the Diyanet are becoming more and more garish, which is not compatible with the Albanian heritage. Lastly, there has been a power competition among the various religious communities in Albania, and Turkey had previously managed to stay outside this competition. Recently, however, it is becoming a part of the game by supporting some Wahhabi groups.

At first glance, Kikia's claims seem exaggerated, but they are in line with those of most other interviewees. For instance, Lutfi Dervisi, the Executive Director of Transparency International in Albania since 2008 and a Turkey expert, was interviewed on the same day as Kikia and argued that while Albania is becoming a more secular state, Turkey is becoming a more religious one. According to Dervisi, previously Turkey was a respected country among moderate Muslims. Recently however, there are many Turkey and Erdoğan fans among radical groups in Albania. Indeed, the claim about Turkey's relations with radical Islamist groups was echoed in some other interviews. Yet in Albania, as in the other case countries, it is almost impossible to find solid evidence regarding direct Turkish relations with radical groups, but one point is obvious: Turkey's new role goes far beyond being a sponsor of Islam abroad and involves extending its prestige and power, as claimed by the *Economist Europe* edition of 21 January 2016.

In May 2016 I visited Kombinat Mosque in Tirana, which is affiliated with Salafis. Most members of the mosque community declared their sympathies for Erdoğan's pro-Islamist discourse. The feelings of some members went far beyond sympathy. Many interviewees recommended that I really must visit the Recep Tayyip Erdoğan Pizza Restaurant in Durrës. In April 2017 the visit took place, to reveal that the owner of the pizza restaurant was a Salafi from Egypt. In response to the obvious question of why he had named the restaurant after Erdoğan, the owner said, 'I like him very much . . . You know he is wearing a Western tie but supporting Islam all over the world. May God help him; he is the only leader who will raise the flag of Islam.'

Figure 9.3 The Pizza Restaurant in Durrës, Albania. Photo by the author.

The sympathy for Erdoğan's Turkey among some pro-Wahhabi and pro-Salafi groups seems enough to create concern at various levels. The conflict between the Gülen Movement and the AKP has also affected Turkey's new pro-religious policies in Albania. According to Gjon Borıçı, a Turkey expert in the private Albania University, 'everything was very good before the 2010s, but after that Turkey and its domestic problems have become Albania's issues'. According to this interviewee, Turkey has been trying to be the leading figure among Sunni Muslim groups in Albania, but this is impossible under the Albanian conditions. Borıçı noted that Erdoğan's problem with the Gülen Movement changed everything because Erdoğan thought he could easily take the Albanian state on his side, but this is not what happened. According to Borıçı, Erdoğan offered a couple of billion dollars to take control of the pro-Gülen schools but the Albanian state has not ceded an inch to that offer. After that, Erdoğan and his agents started to establish relations in line with the advice of Sabri Demir.[15]

Representatives of the Gülen Movement who were quite negative about Turkey's activities against the secular environment of Albania had already mentioned Sabri Demir's relations with various Islamic groups on behalf of Erdoğan. Gülenist propaganda regarding Turkey's desecularisation activities exerts a strong influence on the Albanian socio-political elite. For instance, one of the representatives of the Gülen Movement in Albania claimed that Erdoğan had been constructing relations with Islamist groups both to establish hegemony among the Muslims and to minimise the Gülen Movement's positive impact on Albania.

Sabri Demir, in this regard, has been acting as the primary representative of Erdoğan. In late 2017, a well-known professor of political science and a former member of the Albanian parliament claimed that Erdoğan's Turkey had invested heavily in Albania and in the Balkans more generally. Turkey invested in the fields of politics, the economy and the military, trying to influence state policies. Then Erdoğan realised that these were not the key avenues to becoming an influential actor in the Balkans. He began to use Islam as a political tool and act like the leader of the Sunni-Islamic community, rather than a president. To this end he started to support pro-religious political parties and instrumentalise the Diyanet and other arms to create a new Muslim Turkey. He also tried to establish Erdoğanism among some of the Wahhabi and Salafi groups via financial influence, but according to the professor this is not a proper political methodology for creating a positive image, because by becoming more and more pro-Islamic Turkey has been losing the trust of the majority of Albanian Muslims.

Even though there are no surveys scrutinising the level of trust among Albanian citizens for Erdoğan's Turkey, one might claim that there is a direct relationship between Islamisation–authoritarianism and trust in the eyes of the Albanian people and of the state. The main reason here is that the Albanian state has been aiming to be a permanent member of the 'Western club', and the authorities are very much aware that desecularisation and backsliding from the values of contemporary democracy would affect this aim negatively. They have not reacted favourably to any external impact with a potential to disturb their goal. In 2017, one of the advisors to the Albanian prime minister, Edi Rama, noted these points:

> We have two unwritten and unspoken policies regarding Turkey. One is to keep the relations with Turkey in a very good way, because Turkey is a friend in economic, strategic and historical ways and no one can replace it. Second, there is a need to monitor some of the activities of Turkey both in Albania and the overall Balkans because it seems that sometimes they stray from the formal political roads. Turkey has started to establish relations with some political parties, and Islamic groups, but we do not think that this is a successful strategy. Furthermore, using religion is also an unsuccessful way in the Balkans since Turkey is an external actor and does not know the region's equilibriums.

Thus, the Albanian socio-political elite relies upon the resilience of the constitution's secular structure, lessons from history and the multi-religious social environment, and do not regard Turkey's negative impact as a serious matter. The remarks of the Bektashi Grandfather Hajji Baba Mondi during our interview summarise Turkey's situation in the eyes of most socio-political elites: 'If Turkey continues its pro-Sunni politics like this, it could be a fly in the ointment for the Albanian state, but I am sure the Albanian state will not allow this fly to sting it.'

All in all, a careful evaluation of the interviews reveals that Turkey's domestic political transformation directly reflects its foreign policy behaviour in the Balkans, bringing about four different situations: a visible increase in investment as a service to the Ummah; the exportation of domestic conflicts via formal and informal transnational apparatuses; involvement in the domestic politics of other countries for the purpose of enlarging its spheres of influence; and attempts to destabilise the secular environments of the host countries. These four situations are unprecedented in that Turkey had not shown such behaviour patterns in its foreign policy implementation before the second decade of the 2000s. On the contrary, from the early 1990s to the beginning of the 2010s Turkey was predominantly considered as a Muslim-majority *laik* country that would be a good role model for the three Balkan countries studied in this work. Yet Turkey's domestic transformations have been strongly transmitted to these countries through the activities of its transnational apparatuses.

Each case country has its own dynamics and therefore the issues show a rich variety. However, one specific issue can be regarded as a major determinant for all three countries: the reflection of the conflict between the Gülen Movement and the AKP on the Balkans. The falling out between the two former allies has been visible in these countries since 2013, yet its effects have been underestimated in most scholarly debate in the contemporary literature. The aborted coup of 15 July 2016 provoked some scholars to reflect on the multi-layered aspects of the AKP–Gülen schism and its reflections on the Balkan Peninsula. The fieldwork that was conducted for this book reveals that the impact of the rift is felt far beyond its natural territory because of the parties' huge spheres of influence in the region.

As a last point, even though various common elements appear in the reflection of Turkey's new foreign policy in the three case countries, the cases show meaningful differences. These differences stem from their economic strength, their multi-layered relations with Turkey and their positions in the international system. One crucial point is however shared between the three cases: Turkey's religion-oriented and authoritarian domestic political change has manifested as a coercive ethno-nationalist Sunnification of its Balkan policy, and this has transformed Turkey's position in the eyes of the Balkan socio-political elites, from the soft power it has been, to the ambiguous and uncertain one it is becoming.

Notes

1. Merdjanova, *Rediscovering the Umma*.
2. Henig and Bielenin-Lenczowska, 'Recasting anthropological perspectives'.
3. Petkoff, 'Church–state relations under the Bulgarian Denominations Act 2002'.
4. Cesari, *The Awakening of Muslim Democracy*.
5. For the full survey and findings, please see http://evet.bg/sites/default/files/images/Kurzfassung%20der%20Studie_0.pdf, accessed 3 June 2020.
6. Spasenovski, 'Religious diversity'.
7. Goga, 'The dimensions of a conflict', 16.
8. Ilievski and Talesk, 'Was the EU's role in conflict management in Macedonia a success?'.
9. Ali, 'Macedonia', 442–3.
10. Jazexhi, 'Albania'.
11. Endresen, 'The nation and the nun'.
12. Young, 'Religion and society in present-day Albania'.
13. Elbasani and Somer, 'Muslim secularisms in the European context'.
14. İHH was established in 1992 when a group of individuals came together to provide humanitarian relief to those affected by the war in Bosnia. The group later redirected its efforts to the war in Chechnya, and was officially founded and registered as an NGO in Istanbul in 1995. In 1999, the group's bank accounts were frozen by the Turkish government because it had supposedly neglected to register its fundraising campaigns with the government, and its anti-secular discourse. It became very active during the AKP period; it was one of the main actors in the Mavi Marmara flotilla issue with Israel. Regarding the İHH's ideological orientation, the majority of experts and scholars share the idea that it has a direct link with Islamist and extremist groups.
15. Sabri Demir has been the advisor to Erdoğan for the Balkan countries since 2009. He is a Macedonian Albanian who was born in Skopje and has lived in Tirana, Bosnia, Istanbul and the Syrian capital Damascus. He speaks almost all the Balkan languages as well as Arabic, and therefore can communicate with all the groups in the Balkan countries on behalf of Erdoğan.

CONCLUSION
THE NEW TURKEY IN THE BALKANS:
AN AMBIGUOUS ACTOR?

Since July 2018 the AKP has seized yet another electoral victory with its coalition partner, the MHP.[1] Observers evaluated the election as 'partly free, yet not fair'. And the results indicated that appreciating the transformation of state identity in Turkey are right-wing, conservative, Islamist and nationalist voters who are ready and willing to proceed further with the new power structure that relies on a coercive nationalist-conservative and Islamist bloc. The votes of Turkish citizens living in the diaspora, particularly in Europe, were decisive for Erdoğan. And he thus sought to organise election rallies targeting these populations. Germany and other states hosting large minorities of Turkish citizens refused his entry due to his Islamist-nationalist and, therefore, anti-Western stance. Election activities then shifted to the Balkans, demonstrating the success of Erdoğan's Turkey at transmitting domestic debates to the Peninsula.

Turkey has begun to encapsulate a 'power' transcending its own borders, not only through the exploitation of its transnational state apparatuses that this book has illuminated in detail but also through state-sponsored 'civil society organisations'. The Union of European Turkish Democrats (Avrupalı Türk Demokratlar Birliği, UETD), founded in 2004 in such a context, commenced propaganda activities in Western European countries as a reaching arm of the AKP. Since European countries prohibited Erdoğan from organising election rallies in their borders, the UETD organised its 6th Ordinary General Assembly in Sarajevo and invited Erdoğan as a speaker. Bosnia Herzegovinan President Balkir Izetbegović also attended the meeting, but the Balkan nations and people did not look kindly upon Erdoğan's focus on internal political struggles and his accentuation of Ottoman–Islamic elements. This is an example of the entanglement of domestic and international policies in Turkey, the divergent perspectives of different actors in the Balkans on the exportation of domestic issues and the domination of Turkey's coercive, ethno-nationalist Sunnification in all these processes.

In 2018, Albanian scholar, Xhemal Ahmeti produced a report for the Albanian government entitled 'Emancipating Albanian Culture from Turkish Effects'.[2] In publicised sections of the report, Ahmeti refers to Erdoğan as one of the strongest players in Albania after the Albanian government itself. Some actors, the report claims, are at the precise centre of socio-political debates in Albania and are known to be affiliated with Erdoğan. Ahmeti recommends that the Albanian government take concrete steps to defend itself against Erdoğanism and Salafist movements. The report proceeds to argue that authoritative individuals aligned with Erdoğan seep into mosque congregations, non-governmental organisations and political parties in Balkan countries and manipulate religion for the purposes they pursue.

The interviews conducted for this book indicate that such claims are intensifying in the Balkans. Turkey's infant religious policy cannot simply be reduced to an element of soft power or public diplomacy. Even with the use of Mandaville and Hamid's definitions of religious soft power – as we mentioned in the introduction – it is difficult to suggest directly that Turkey is a religious soft power. The fundamental reason for this is the uncertainty of the exact areas of dominance and fields of influence of the transnational state apparatus that has Turkey functionalised using religious values beyond its own borders. Moreover, Turkey supplies these instruments with authority by applying economic sanctions or delivering aid when deemed necessary – a crucial indicator of the impossibility of defining Turkish policy as soft power. However, all the discussions held along the axis of religion, identity and domestic politics have different faces, particularly in the Balkans. And these differences originate both from Turkey's constant evolution and the region's ethnic, political and religious diversity. Some emergent points highlight the danger of generalisation in this context. Turkey's policies under AKP rule extract varying outcomes from different actors in the region. Some groups are pleased with Turkey's religiously fuelled approach, while others are seriously perturbed. I therefore prefer to define Turkey as an *ambiguous* actor that has been instrumentalising its power and impact resources in hybrid ways.

Despite the argument that Turkey's nascent religion-based policy and activities could be categorised within the concept of public diplomacy, this policy preference is multifaceted and entails numerous problematic elements, such as the exportation of domestic conflicts, which inarguably exceed the definition of public diplomacy. Furthermore, Turkey's religion-based transformation, it seems, has effected different results on different actors in different countries.

In 2018, another result of this policy appeared in Austria, where the nationalist and conservative government decided to shut down seven mosques and to deport sixty imams financed by the Diyanet and their families. In justifying his decision, Austrian prime minister Sebastian Kurz underscored his government's concerns about burgeoning political Islam and radicalisation in his country. Erdoğan proceeded to portray this decision as the preliminary steps leading to a crusade. The most relevant issue for this study within the broader debate about the Austrian decision is that the activities of the Diyanet are not regarded as existing within the framework of moderate Islam. Erdoğan's reference to crusades reflects the employment of ethno-religious elements first in the domestic realm and then, in a boomerang-like fashion, in Turkey's foreign policy. Austria's reaction creates a benchmark for countries like Albania that aspire to become members of the EU.

We can proceed even further than the Balkans to see these outcomes. For example, Erdoğan's visit to the White House on 13 November 2019 spawned chaotic days never before seen in the history of Turkish–American relations due to Turkey's reactive foreign policy, not predicated on any obvious preliminary strategy produced by the evolving state identity. No doubt influential in this were Trump's incomprehensible policies, not the least of which being his approach to Syria. But after the Trump–Erdoğan meeting, which proceeded as if everything was normal behind the scenes, Erdoğan was unable to find the opportunity to explain himself at any think tank or university in Washington, DC. This was indubitably a consequence of Turkey's relative lack of self-confidence and lack of recognition for its new identity. Erdoğan was thus forced to speak to a group comprising only Turks at a new Diyanet mosque complex located in Maryland. Only a few Turkish members of the press corps observed the event, and it did not reach the global news agenda. However, circumstances materialising in the Balkans, where Turkey is a more exclusive actor and where Islam is decidedly more determinant, do not – or cannot – remain off the agenda. Religion, identity and institutions are salient for Turkey and the Balkans.

With fieldwork including more than 120 interviews in Bulgaria, North Macedonia, Albania and Turkey, I have tried to explain how the utilisation of religion has altered policy making, state identity, and power resources and structures in Turkey and how these changes reflect on the Balkan Peninsula through transnational state apparatuses and leaders' discourses. The fieldwork and observations verify some of the claims in this book's introduction, relating mostly to the existing literature and theoretical framework. As I embarked on this journey, I presumed that issues pertaining to the AKP's new Turkey would be indisputable, but I discovered instead more complicated and multifaceted issues, all of which would prompt different answers to the questions on my mind.

However, based on fieldwork, observations and my own personal judgement, I can clearly explicate three points, setting out from the Turkey–Balkans example regarding a point that Jeffrey Haynes underlined numerous times in a concealed manner but was relatively undiscussed. First, the phenomenon known as religious soft power does not and cannot remain soft to the extent necessary, or is intended to be presented when states enter the purview of the issue, because state configuration employs economic and other sanctions in the name of power through instruments that utilise religion. This situation suggests that states cannot use religion as a one-dimensional soft power. Second, religion or the extremist instrumentalisation of religion as a means of oppression at the hands of a political regime can prompt changes in the state identity. These changes can spread rapidly and alter the behaviour formation of states due to their consideration for foreign policy. This is inarguably influential on topics such as the leader, state system, institutional capacity, and areas of influence. Finally, we see once again that the changing identities of states do not relate merely to domestic policy. Fundamentally, the external perception of states by groups and their definitions through the lens of identity is exceedingly convoluted. And this complexity pushes us to deduce and ponder the Turkey–Balkans snare of religion, identity, power and politics. I can at least state that what I encountered during my fieldwork pulled me to this point.

Our world is neither completely secular nor completely religious, with reference to the *post-secular world* of Habermas, who claims that religion in modern society has become democratised and commercialised with massive religious institutions and a significant magnification of religious tourism. In this new world, the religious interacts with the secular through consensus, conflict and competition.[3] In the case of Turkey, Islam has been politicised, it interacts with nationalism and it has become the main agent in the transformation of state identity. In other words, religion, which has always rested at the heart of politics, recently became more visible, assertive and transnational. This observation corresponds with Turner's claim that religion is once again becoming politicised. The separation of state from religion becomes more blurred, and religion combines elements of soft identity, instrument and purpose within itself.[4] The connotation of religion here suggests more than a system of faith. Rather, religion encapsulates a system of behaviour that may find use as a tool of justification. This makes interaction more frequent between the religious and secular, and engenders both new challenges and new opportunities. Religion, with its identity-related influence and capacity to become a political instrument, manifests as a power resource that different agents – including the state – can employ. For Turkey, the multi-layered and multi-sided conflict between religion and *laiklik* dates to Ottoman times and includes the Balkan region. Therefore, the history of Turkey and the Balkans cannot be fully understood without taking the determinant role of religion into account. In the AKP period, the influence of religion in politics and *vice versa* has peaked and this situation is reflected on the Balkans. Remaining on this issue are the questions of how Turkey has become influential in the Balkans through religion despite its previously *laik* nature, and how do local elites in the Balkans perceive this novel approach?

Turkey has been invited and indeed welcomed into Bulgaria, North Macedonia and Albania because of its *laik* state identity and through the Diyanet. Since state identity and transformation represent the nucleus of this book, constructivist theory becomes highly relevant with its explicatory power on such issues. According to the general and main vessel of constructivism, identity is important, because it defines the perceptions of interests, threats and universal political preferences. Religion is a major element in the constitution of identity. Unlike realists, who argue that systemic conditions determine the interests of states, and liberals, who believe that competition between different interest groups determine interests, constructivists argue that identity shapes the interests of a state and that states act to achieve the recognition of their identities. However, as Wendt stated, identities are subject to change and can manifest themselves in different forms based on spatial and temporal circumstances. Constructivists emphasise interstate relations as a major reason for a modification in state identities. However, the Turkish case indicates the diverse malleability of identities. The change that Turkey experienced and its impact on these three Balkan countries highlights novel ideas about state identity, societies' perceptions, power formation and the position of religion. The Turkish case, especially as it pertains to Balkan countries, indicates that state identities can evolve after domestic struggles and that the change impacts certain regions more certainly and swiftly.

It is of course still early to declare any political actor in Turkey permanently victorious, so the analyses in this study frame a certain era beginning roughly at the turn of the millennium. Recognising the winner has become more uncertain due to developments in 2019–20. The Erdoğan regime twice lost the Istanbul Metropolitan Municipality election in 2019 to relatively new political actor Ekrem İmamoğlu, who was the candidate for the CHP–IYI party coalition and who won thanks to support he received from the Kurds. Additionally, crucial provinces such as Ankara and Bolu slipped through the hands of the AKP. One of the most salient underlying reasons for this loss is no doubt the economy, but we must refrain from complete certainty over whether this loss was grave. Ultimately, all candidates who defeated Erdoğan or his municipal mayoral candidates used both religion and nationality at least as much as the AKP. More precisely, they were impelled to believe this wholeheartedly, because they too were forced to evolve with the state structure identity in which they sought to exist. İmamoğlu, who read prayers at mosques throughout his campaign in exuberant displays, was forced to support Turkey's Northern Syria operation during the months of October and November 2019 despite the operation's connotations for the Kurds from whom he had received support. İmamoğlu also read the Quran in his mayoral office, while the CHP municipal mayor who won Bolu held the handover ceremony as a religious service. All of this points to Erdoğan's pervading even the places where the AKP lost, because they forced the transformation of the state identity under the prevailing circumstances. Therefore I claim here that, under the leadership of *the AKP's Erdoğan and Erdoğan's AKP*, the Turkish state identity has experienced a coercive, ethno-nationalist Sunnification transformation. But this is not the first instance of such dramatic transformation in Ottoman Turkish history, nor is a reshuffling of the cards likely any sooner that many analysts predict. The reality of uncertainty in Turkish politics and its effects on the Balkans lies in the long-term success of the AKP in power positions. In the history of the Republic, conservative parties – though not Islamist like the AKP – have often formed governments, but none have maintained power positions long enough to alter the orientation and identity of the state.

Three things stand out for the AKP in obtaining and maintaining power. The exploitation of socio-political crises is a major determinant through which the party has consolidated its power, feeling no hesitation when violating the law. President Erdoğan has used states of exception and extraordinary critical junctions to create remarkable and therefore hegemonic leadership. Second, the utilisation of religion and the role of ethno-nationalist notions as levels of discourse and policy making have rendered the party unrivalled in political competition, and Erdoğan has successfully portrayed this as a war of civilisation. Lastly, changes have been inflicted upon the state structure to unify party leadership with that of the state. This combination signifies a major change in domestic politics that also reflects on foreign policy, specifically in the Balkans, for the reasons this book mentions.

Playing a vital role in the impact of this change on the Balkans and the exportation of domestic politics to the region are Turkey's transnational state apparatuses. The Diyanet, an apparatus of premiere importance, is an institution specific to Turkish *laiklik*. Sandal argues that a religious institution acts, through its clergy as an epistemic community, providing expertise that informs and even programmes a political agenda for a certain interest group or body of adherents.[5] This framework and understanding must be customised and applied to the intricate relationship between the state and religion and to the role of the Diyanet in this relationship. Furthermore, it must be verified in Turkey's relations with the Balkans under periods of AKP hegemony. The Diyanet's complete dependence on state policies and the extreme absence of institutional or ideological autonomy precipitate its quick adaptation to changing policy preferences. It would be unrealistic to assert that the Diyanet has its own intellect or to burden it with an *ulema* role. Such a suggestion would be especially impossible in the AKP era. The AKP's adept utilisation of the institution stands as an example of the Althusserian argument that even revolutionary changes retain state apparatuses deemed useful and functional. On the other hand, it clashes with the traditional constructivist claim that states create new institutions as they change identity. The Diyanet entered the Balkans in the early 1990s as a representative of moderate Islam. However, it has since morphed into a transnational state apparatus that utilises and exploits religion for political purposes. Furthermore, the AKP has simply utilised existing institutions rather than generating new ones. New institutions like TİKA, Yunus Emre Institutes and the YTB act as *exterior guards and representatives* of the AKP. The recent descent into religious authoritarianism in Turkey downgraded the credibility of all these institutions, new and old, in the eyes of most socio-political elites in the region.

Turkey's transformation from an intermediator with historic roots to an *ambiguous, uncertain and unpredictable power* is important. Citations of the AKP as an example of the coexistence of Islam and democracy were frequent during the first decade of the party, allowing it to act as a 'soft power' during these years. It thrust us towards the fallacy that states can use religious soft power. But it soon started to enforce ethno-nationalist Sunnification, imitating some Kemalist methodologies of the first decades of the Republic. Turkey has failed to sustain its *laik* stance in terms of state–religion relations, as Haynes argues. To the contrary, it has leaned towards the use of religious elements in excessive doses, violating legal and moral boundaries and forcing its worldview onto others.

The impact of Turkey's state identity changes on three Balkan countries – Bulgaria, Albania and North Macedonia – varied depending on internal dynamics, international positions, levels of economic development and demographic structures. Bulgaria, as an EU member state, prohibits any foreign organisation other than the Diyanet, and tries to limit Turkey's influence over its Turkish minority.[6] The policies that Turkey defines as public diplomacy or soft power do not get the same reaction from all groups and actors. North Macedonia, with its relatively weak economy and assumed dependence on Turkey, has cleared a space for Turkey's religion-oriented policies, with reluctant acceptance. The North Macedonian Muslim elite uses Turkish influence as a source of justification for their policies. The non-Muslim elite, however, is seriously concerned about Islam-based intervention by a third country. Albania exhibits a completely different situation. The AKP retains access to few minor and relatively radical groups and disturbs both Muslim and non-Muslim elites. All three countries, however, present a common behaviour of avoiding confrontation with Turkey, mostly because of the investments that accompany the AKP's policies of penetration and hegemony building.

The cumulative reflection of all this complicates the notion of defining Turkey's new policy preferences in the context of public diplomacy and the influential use of religion within the boundaries of the concept of soft power. Because specific groups seem to be targeted in the host countries rather in than the whole society, the consent that this new policy creates relates strongly to the sense of belonging and the behaviour and beliefs of individuals. These policies cannot be defined, then, simply in the religion–soft power framework because economic incentives and sanctions are used alongside religion. Beyond that, it is difficult to claim that Turkey is a sharp power with its authoritarian practices and its inability to accomplish its objectives. Collectively, the fact that Turkey is an unpredictable, uncertain and ambiguous power is reflected in its new identity in the Balkans.

The Balkans is the first region in which this new power and identity formation appears. Turkey has some established domestic problems with certain identity groups such as the Kurds.[7] And these domestic issues have spread to European countries with significant Turkish populations, such as Germany, France, Sweden and the Netherlands. Something similar is currently taking place in the Balkans with another group: the Gülen Movement.[8] The pursuit by both the Gülenists and the AKP of legitimacy through religion, particularly in the Balkans, has inflamed the conflict between them on a level of religious discourse, especially in places where the Gülen Movement is well established. This seems to be the choice of the AKP, which utilises transnational state apparatuses on a religious basis in these places because it considers this the most effective means of discrediting the movement for conservative, nationalist Muslims – the AKP's natural audience. The party wants to create a more nationalistic, altruistic and eventually truer image in terms of the essence of Islam. To this effect, the AKP has given a platform to coercive ethno-nationalist and Islamist elements and established relations with previously ostracised groups that are potentially problematic for the peace and stability of the Balkans.

However, claims that the Gülen Movement dominates the Balkans, or that the AKP is dominant in these countries while the Gülen Movement occupies that role elsewhere, are unsupported. Power balances can change in an incomprehensible manner at unexpected times. The most interesting example of these changes is perhaps North Macedonia. I noticed in my field study in 2015 and 2016 that most Turkish speakers among the younger generation in Skopje gained command of their languages at Gülen Movement schools. In those years, the Gülen Movement occupied a relatively respectable position in the North Macedonian state and among Muslims. However, Gülenists were squeezed into a corner in North Macedonia in 2017–18 and were unable to establish direct relations with either the state or the Muslim community. Remember, I had to conduct my interviews confidentially. In January 2019, I encountered an intriguing scene in central Skopje. The Maarif Foundation, which the AKP established to forestall Gülen schools, opened an office in place of Gülen Movement schools – the headquarters of the Yahya Kemal Colleges and Gülenists' most important meeting centre. Although the Gülen Movement was influential in North Macedonia, various photographs express significant meaning for both North Macedonia and the Balkans.

Figure C.1   Replacement of the headquarters of the Gülenist Yahya Kemal Colleges with the AKP's Maarif Foundation

Additionally, it is essential to underline that academic studies and research usually divide the Balkans into East and West. This division seems less than convincing in this geography of frequent ethnic, linguistic, religious and cultural overlaps and transitions. However, the nation-building processes that commenced in the early 1990s created independent political units that focused on differences, that were characteristic of the period. Turkey does not consider these differences in its policies – an approach that appears to originate from its historical role in the region – which means that since losing the region in the early twentieth century it sees the Balkans as a monolith, with the exception of Greece and Bulgaria.

During the AKP period, Turkey abandoned this approach due to the coercive ethno-nationalist Sunnification of the state's identity and its reflection on foreign policy, and because it started addressing Muslim groups through state apparatuses and government-oriented non-governmental organisations (GONGOs). A comprehensive analysis of Turkey's policies towards the Balkans indicates that the incipient elite in Ankara tends to believe that countries and local groups share the Balkan idealisation in the Turkish capital. This idealisation and the subsequent strategies are not extrinsic to the transformation that Turkey has experienced. Turkey is selectively constructing its modern approach on the foundations of the Ottoman legacy, and views certain Muslims in the region as *more Ottoman* than others, anointing them its natural and historical interlocutors. Turkey therefore does not hesitate to intervene in domestic politics, creating a permanent influence through elements of culture, language, religion and economics. To suggest that Turkey's new policies are entirely ineffective would contradict findings that have emerged from two years of fieldwork. However, the effect is polarised; while some places and groups – mostly conservative Muslims – welcome its influence, others regard it with caution and concern. Turkey has a Balkan idealisation rather than a calculated and internally consistent policy. And this idealisation magnifies policy-makers' perceptions of the influence Turkey boasts in the region, and they believe that most Muslims in the region consider Turkey a guardian. The contentious notion of the 'clash of civilisations', which Ahmet Davutoğlu and other minor architects of Turkish foreign policy promulgated, appears internalised within a dire paradox. Whether this embodies a historical illusion or hidden potential has yet to become apparent. Another shortcoming of this idealisation is that it downgrades other actors in the region, including Serbia, Austria, Russia, Germany and the United States.

This book has, then, studied the use of Islam by the hegemonic and authoritarian governments of the AKP to transform the state's identity, exploiting domestic conflicts and creating states of exception out of them. It has sought to investigate perceptions of Turkey by Bulgarian, Albanian and North Macedonian socio-political elites in the context of the domestic transformation that Turkey has experienced in the new millennium. Such perceptions of Turkey warrant further research in other parts of the region and the world, especially in the Middle East and the Caucasus as neighbouring regions of Turkey, the EU and the United States and Russia as countries of strategic importance. Furthermore, similar changes in Morocco, Iran and Egypt merit additional study in comparison with Turkey and this book's arguments and findings.

Notes

1. Before the election, some prominent members of the MHP formed another nationalist party in Turkey: the IYI Party (Good Party). Its current leader, Meral Akşener, established the party on 25 October 2017, and it pursues a centrist political ideology, emphasising the restoration of the parliamentary system.
2. Please see https://www.theglobalist.com/albania-balkans-recept-tayyip-erdogan-european-union/, accessed 18 June 2020.
3. Habermas, 'Notes on post-secular society'.
4. Turner, *The Religious and the Political*.
5. Sandal, 'Religious actors as epistemic communities'.
6. Öztürk, 'The ambivalent nature of the relations between Bulgaria and Turkey'.
7. Baser, *Diasporas and Homeland Conflicts*.
8. Öztürk and Taş, 'The repertoire of extraterritorial repression'.

BIBLIOGRAPHY

Agamben, Giorgio, *State of Exception* (Chicago: University of Chicago Press, 2005).

Ahmad, Feroz, *The Making of Modern Turkey* (London: Routledge, 1993).

Akça, İsmet and Evren Balta Paker, 'Beyond military tutelage: Analyzing civil–military relations under the Justice and Development Party', in Sokullu Canan Ebru (ed.), *Debating Security in Turkey: Challenges and Changes in the Twenty-First Century* (Lanham: Lexington Books, 2012).

Akkoyunlu, Karabekir, *The Rise and Fall of the Hybrid Regime: Guardianship and Democracy in Iran and Turkey*, Dissertation, London School of Economics and Political Science, 2014.

Aktar, Ayhan, *Varlık vergisi ve 'Türkleştirme' politikaları* (Istanbul: İletişim Yayınları, 2000).

Ali, Muhammed, 'Macedonia', in Oliver Scharbrodt, Samim Akgönül, Ahmet Alibasic, Jorgen S. Nielsen and Egdünas Racious (eds), *Yearbook of Muslims in Europe*, Volume 9 (Leiden: Brill, 2017).

Aras, Bülent, 'The Davutoğlu era in Turkish foreign policy', *Insight Turkey*, 11, no. 3 (2009): 127–42.

Aras, Bülent and Aylin Gorener, 'National role conceptions and foreign policy orientation: The ideational bases of the Justice and Development Party's foreign policy activism in the Middle East', *Journal of Balkan and Near Eastern Studies*, 12, no. 1 (2010): 73–92.

Arat, Yeşim, 'Violence, resistance, and Gezi park', *International Journal of Middle East Studies*, 45, no. 4 (2013): 807–9.

Arendt, Hannah, *The Human Condition* (Chicago: University of Chicago Press, 2013).

Atinay, Hakan, 'Turkey's soft power: An unpolished gem or an elusive mirage?' *Insight Turkey*, 10, no. 2 (2008): 55–66.

Baser, Bahar, *Diasporas and Homeland Conflicts: A Comparative Perspective* (London: Ashgate Publishing, 2015).

Baser, Bahar and Ahmet Erdi Öztürk (eds), *Authoritarian Politics in Turkey: Elections, Resistance and the AKP* (London: I. B. Tauris, 2017).

Baser, Bahar and Ahmet Erdi Öztürk, 'In lieu of an introduction: Is it curtains for Turkish democracy?' in Bahar Baser and Ahmet Erdi Öztürk (eds), *Authoritarian Politics in Turkey: Elections, Resistance and the AKP* (London: I. B. Tauris).

Baser, Bahar and Mari Toivanen, 'Politicized and depoliticized ethnicities, power relations and temporality: Insights to outsider research from comparative and transnational fieldwork', *Ethnic and Racial Studies*, 41, no, 11 (2018): 2067–84.

Baser, Bahar, Samim Akgönül and Ahmet Erdi Öztürk, '"Academics for Peace" in Turkey: A case of criminalising dissent and critical thought via counterterrorism policy', *Critical Studies on Terrorism*, 10, no. 2 (2017): 274–96.

Bates, Gill and Yanzhong Huang, 'Sources and limits of Chinese "soft power"', *Survival*, 48, no. 2 (2006): 17–36.

Ben-Porat, Guy, *Between State and Synagogue: The Secularisation of Contemporary Israel* (New York: Cambridge University Press, 2013).

Berenskoetter, Felix, 'Thinking about power', in Felix Berenskoetter and J. M. Williams (eds), *Power in World Politics* (London: Routledge, 2007).

Berger, Peter, 'A bleak outlook is seen for religion', *New York Times*, 25 April 1968.

Berger, Peter, 'Secularism in retreat', *The National Interest*, no. 46 (Winter 1996/7): 3–12.

Bourdieu, Pierre, 'Symbolic power', *Critique of Anthropology*, 4, no. 13–14 (1979): 79.

Bozdaglioglu, Yücel, *Turkish Foreign Policy and Turkish Identity: A Constructivist Approach* (London: Routledge, 2004).

Brljavac, Bedrudin, 'Turkey entering the European Union through the Balkan doors: In the style of a great power?' *Zbornik radova Pravnog fakulteta u Splitu*, 48, no. 3 (2011): 521–31.

Bruce, Benjamin, *Governing Islam Abroad: Turkish and Moroccan Muslims in Western Europe* (London: Palgrave Macmillan, 2019).

Brunnbauer, Ulf, '"Everybody believes the state should do everything for them": An essay on state–society relations in communist Bulgaria', *Divination*, 31, no. 1 (2010): 171–80.

Büyük, Hamdi Fırat and Ahmet Erdi Öztürk, 'The role of leadership networks in Turkey–Balkan relations in the AKP era', *Turkish Policy Quarterly*, 18, no. 3 (2019): 119–27.

Çarkoglu, Ali, 'Turkey's November 2002 elections: A new beginning?' *Middle East Review of International Affairs*, 6, no. 4 (2002): 30–41.

Carling, Jørgen, Marta Bivand Erdal and Rohan Ezzati, 'Beyond the insider–outsider divide in migration research', *Migration Studies*, 2, no. 1 (2014): 50.

Carroll, Thomas Patrick, 'Turkey's Justice and Development Party: A model for democratic Islam?' *Middle East Intelligence Bulletin*, 6, no. 6–7 (2004): 6.

Case, Fareed, 'The rise of illiberal democracy', *Foreign Affairs*, 76, no. 6 (1997): 22–43.

Case, William, 'Semi-democracy in Malaysia: Withstanding the pressures for regime change', *Pacific Affairs*, 66, no. 2 (1993): 183–205.

Çemrek, Murat, *Özal's Politics with Special Reference to Religion*, Dissertation, Bilkent University, 1997.

Cesari, Jocelyne, *The Awakening of Muslim Democracy: Religion, Modernity, and the State* (New York: Cambridge University Press, 2014).

Cesari, Jocelyne and Jonathan Fox, 'Institutional relations rather than clashes of civilizations: When and how is religion compatible with democracy?' *International Political Sociology*, 10, no. 3 (2016): 241–57.

Checkel, Jeffrey T., 'The constructivist turn in international relations theory', *World Politics*, 50, no. 2 (1998): 324–48.

Christofis, Nikos, Bahar Baser, and Ahmet Erdi Öztürk, 'The view from next door: Greek–Turkish relations after the coup attempt in Turkey', *International Spectator*, 54, no. 2 (2019): 67–86.

Cinar, Kursat, 'Local determinants of an emerging electoral hegemony: The case of Justice and Development Party (AKP) in Turkey', *Democratization*, 23, no. 7 (2016): 1216–35.

Cizre-Sakallioglu, Umit and Yeldan Yeldan, 'Politics, society and financial liberalization: Turkey in the 1990s', *Development and Change*, 31, no. 2 (2000): 496.

Çınar, Menderes, 'The electoral success of the AKP: Cause for hope and despair', *Insight Turkey*, 13, no. 4 (2011): 107–12.

Çıtak, Zana, 'Between "Turkish Islam" and "French Islam": The role of the Diyanet in the Conseil Français du Culte Musulman', *Journal of Ethnic and Migration Studies*, 36, no. 4 (2010): 611–22.

Cornell, Svante E., 'What drives Turkish foreign policy?' *Middle East Quarterly*, 19, no. 1 (2012): 13–24.

Coşkun, Bezen Balamir, Salih Doğan and Mustafa Demir, 'Foreign policy as a legitimation strategy for the AKP's hegemonic project of the "New Turkey"', in Bahar Baser and Ahmet Erdi Öztürk (eds), *Authoritarian Politics in Turkey: Election, Resistance and the AKP* (London: I. B. Tauris, 2017).

Dahl, Robert A., 'The concept of power', *Systems Research and Behavioral Science*, 2, no. 3 (1957): 202–3.

Danforth, Nicholas, 'Ideology and pragmatism in Turkish foreign policy: From Atatürk to the AKP', *Turkish Policy Quarterly*, 7, no. 3 (2008): 83–95.

Davutoğlu, Ahmet, 'Turkey's foreign policy vision: An assessment of 2007', *Insight Turkey*, 10, no. 1 (2008): 77–96.

Davutoğlu, Ahmet, *Stratejik derinlik: Türkiye'nin uluslararası konumu* (Istanbul: Küre Yayınları, 2010).

Denzin, Norman K., 'The reflexive interview and a performative social science', *Qualitative Research*, 1, no. 1 (2001): 32.

Diamond, Larry and Leonardo Morlino (eds), *Assessing the Quality of Democracy* (Baltimore, MD: Johns Hopkins University Press, 2005).

Doğan, Sevinç, *Mahalledeki AKP: Parti İşleyişi, Taban Mobilizasyonu ve Siyasal Yabancılaşma* (Istanbul: İletişim Yayınları, 2016).

Ekinci, Mehmet Uğur, 'Türkiye–Balkan İlişkileri', *SETA Analiz*, no. 204 (May 2017).

Ekşi, Muharrem, *Kamu Diplomasisi ve AK Parti Dönemi Türk Dış Politikası* (Ankara: Siyasal Kitapevi, 2018).

Elbasani, Arolda and Murat Somer, 'Muslim secularisms in the European context', in Michael Rectenwald, Rochelle Almeida and George Levine (eds), *Global Secularisms in a Post-Secular Age* (Boston: De Gruyter, 2015): 171–88.

Elicin, Yeseren, 'Neoliberal transformation of the Turkish city through the Urban Transformation Act', *Habitat International*, 41, no. 1 (2014): 150–5.

Ellis, Stephen and Gerrie Ter Haar, 'Religion and politics in sub-Saharan Africa', *Journal of Modern African Studies*, 36, no. 2 (1998): 175–201.

Eminov, Ali, 'Social construction of identities: Pomaks in Bulgaria', *Journal on Ethnopolitics and Minority Issues in Europe*, 6, no. 2 (2007): 1–25.

Eminov, Ali, *Turkish and Other Muslim Minorities in Bulgaria* (New York: Routledge, 1997).

Endresen, Cecilie, 'The nation and the nun: Mother Teresa, Albania's Muslim majority and the secular state', *Islam and Christian–Muslim Relations*, 26, no. 1 (2015): 53–74.

Erinç, Yeldan A. and Burcu Ünüvar, 'An assessment of the Turkish economy in the AKP era', *Research and Policy on Turkey*, 1, no. 1 (2016): 11–28.

Esen, Berk and Şebnem Gümüşçü, 'A small yes for presidentialism: The Turkish constitutional referendum of April 2017', *South European Society and Politics*, 22, no. 3 (2017): 303–26.

Fidan, Hakan, 'A work in progress: The new Turkish foreign policy', *Middle East Policy*, 20, no. 1 (2013): 91–6.

Fidan, Hakan and Rahman Nurdun, 'Turkey's role in the global development assistance community: The case of TİKA (Turkish International Cooperation and Development Agency)', *Journal of Southern Europe and the Balkans*, 10, no. 1 (2008): 93–111.

Fox, Jonathan, 'Paradigm lost: Huntington's unfulfilled clash of civilizations prediction into the 21st century', *International Politics*, 42, no. 4 (2005): 428–57.

Fox, Jonathan, *Political Secularism, Religion and the State: A Time Series Analysis of Worldwide Data* (New York: Cambridge University Press, 2015).

Fukuyama, Francis, 'The end of history?' *The National Interest*, 16, no. 1 (1989): 3–18.

Göçek, Fatma Müge, *The Transformation of Turkey: Redefining State and Society from the Ottoman Empire to the Modern Era* (London: I. B. Tauris, 2011).

Goga, Aida, 'The dimensions of a conflict: The case of Macedonia', *Mediterranean Journal of Social Sciences*, 4, no. 10 (2013): 16–21.

Görener, Aylin Ş. and Meltem Ş. Ucal, 'The personality and leadership style of Recep Tayyip Erdoğan: Implications for Turkish foreign policy', *Turkish Studies*, 12, no. 3 (2011): 357–81.

Gramsci, Antonio, *Further Selections from the Prison Notebooks* (Minneapolis: University of Minnesota Press, 1995).

Güçlü, Yücel, 'Turkey's entrance into the League of Nations', *Middle Eastern Studies*, 39, no. 1 (2003): 199.

Gülalp, Haldun, 'Globalization and political Islam: The social bases of Turkey's Welfare Party', *International Journal of Middle East Studies*, 33, no. 3 (2001): 433–48.

Gurses, Mehmet, *Anatomy of a Civil War* (Ann Arbor: University of Michigan Press, 2018).

Habermas, Jürgen, 'Notes on post-secular society', *New Perspectives Quarterly*, 25, no. 4 (2008): 17–29.

Haghagenghi, Medrdad, *Islam and Politics in Central Asia* (New York: St. Martin's Press, 1996).

Hale, William, 'The Turkish Republic and its army, 1923–1960', *Turkish Studies*, 12, no. 2 (2011): 191–201.

Hanioğlu, M. Şükrü, *The Young Turks in Opposition* (Oxford: Oxford University Press, 1995).

Hatzopoulos, Pavlos, and Fabio Petito (eds), *Religion in International Relations: The Return from Exile* (New York: Palgrave Macmillan, 2003).

Haynes, Jeffrey, 'Politics, identity and religious nationalism in Turkey: From Atatürk to the AKP', *Australian Journal of International Affairs*, 64, no. 3 (2010): 312–27.

Haynes, Jeffrey, *Faith-Based Organizations at the United Nations* (New York: Palgrave Macmillan, 2014).

Haynes, Jeffrey, *Religious Transnational Actors and Soft Power* (London: Routledge, 2016).

Haynes, Jeffrey, 'Causes and consequences of transnational religious soft power', in *Political Studies Conference Proceedings*, 2010. Available at https://indiachinain-stitute.org/wp-content/uploads/group-documents/6/1342882510-cause-and-consequences-of-transnational-religious-soft-power.pdf, accessed 5 June 2020.

Henig, David and Karolina Bielenin-Lenczowska, 'Recasting anthropological per-spectives on vernacular Islam in Southeast Europe: An introduction', *Anthro-pological Journal of European Cultures*, 22, no. 2 (2013): 1–11.

Heper, Metin and E. Fuat Keyman, 'Double-faced state: Political patronage and the consolidation of democracy in Turkey', *Middle Eastern Studies*, 34, no. 4 (1998): 259–77.

Heper, Metin and Şule Toktaş, 'Islam, modernity, and democracy in contemporary Turkey: The case of Recep Tayyip Erdoğan', *The Muslim World*, 93, no. 2 (2003): 157–85.

Hirschon, Renée (ed.), *Crossing the Aegean: An Appraisal of the 1923 Compulsory Pop-ulation Exchange between Greece and Turkey* (New York and Oxford: Berghahn Books, 2003).

Hoffmann, Clemens, 'Neo-Ottomanism, Eurasianism or securing the region? A longer view on Turkey's interventionism', *Conflict, Security & Development*, 19, no. 3 (2019): 301–7.

Hopf, Ted, 'The promise of constructivism in international relations theory', *Interna-tional Security*, 23, no. 1 (1998): 171–200.

Howell, Julia D., 'Muslims, the new age and marginal religions in Indonesia: Changing meanings of religious pluralism', *Social Compass*, 52, no. 4 (2005): 473–93.

Hudson, Valerie M., 'Foreign policy analysis: Actor-specific theory and the ground of international relations', *Foreign Policy Analysis*, 1, no. 1 (2005): 1–30.

Humphreys, Stephen, 'Legalizing lawlessness: On Giorgio Agamben's state of exception', *European Journal of International Law*, 17, no. 3 (2006): 677–87.

Huntington, Samuel P., *The Third Wave: Democratization in the Late Twentieth Century* (Norman: University of Oklahoma Press, 1993).

Hurd, Elizabeth Shakman, 'The political authority of secularism in international relations', *European Journal of International Relations*, 10, no. 2 (2004): 235–62.

Ibrahim, Kalin, 'Soft power and public diplomacy in Turkey', *Perceptions*, 16, no. 3 (2011): 5–23.

İlber, Ortaylı, *İmparatorluğun en uzun yüzyılı* (Istanbul: Timaş Yayınları, 2008).

Ilievski, Zoran and Dane Talesk, 'Was the EU's role in conflict management in Macedonia a success?' *Ethnopolitics*, 8, no. 3–4 (2009): 355–67.

İnalcık, Halil, *The Ottoman Empire: 1300–1600* (London: Phoenix, 2003).

Insel, Ahmet, 'The AKP and normalizing democracy in Turkey', *South Atlantic Quarterly*, 102, no. 2 (2003): 293–308.

Ipek, Pinar, 'Ideas and change in foreign policy instruments: soft power and the case of the Turkish International Cooperation and Development Agency', *Foreign Policy Analysis*, 11, no. 2 (2015): 173–93.

Irak, Dağhan, and Ahmet Erdi Öztürk, 'Redefinition of state apparatuses: AKP's Formal–Informal Networks in the online realm', *Journal of Balkan and Near Eastern Studies*, 20, no. 5 (2018): 439–58.

Jazexhi, Olsi, 'Albania', in Oliver Scharbrodt, Samim Akgönül, Ahmet Alibasic, Jorgen S. Nielsen and Egdünas Racious (eds), *Yearbook of Muslims in Europe, Volume 9* (Leiden: Brill, 2017): 19–20.

Kadioğlu, Ayşe, 'The paradox of Turkish nationalism and the construction of official identity', *Middle Eastern Studies*, 32, no. 2 (1996): 177–93.

Karanfil, Gökçen and Eğilmez Burcu, 'Politics, culture and media: Neo-Ottomanism as a transnational cultural policy on TRT El Arabia and TRT Avaz', *Markets, Globalization & Development Review*, 2, no. 2 (2017): 1–24.

Kaya, Ayhan and Ayşe Tecmen, 'The role of common cultural heritage in external promotion of modern Turkey: Yunus Emre Cultural Centres', Istanbul Bilgi University Working Paper, 2011.

Keddie, Nikki R., 'Secularism & its discontents', *Daedalus*, 132, no. 3 (2003): 14–30.

Keyman, Demet, 'Creating a pious generation: Youth and education policies of the AKP in Turkey', *Southeast European and Black Sea Studies*, 16, no. 4 (2016): 637–49.

Keyman, E. Fuat, 'Modernization, globalization and democratization in Turkey: The AKP experience and its limits', *Constellations*, 17, no. 2 (2010): 312–27.

Kirişçi, Kemal, 'Post Second World War immigration from Balkan countries to Turkey', *New Perspectives on Turkey*, 12 (Spring 1995): 61–77.

Klotz, Audie and Cecelia Lynch, *Strategies for Research in Constructivist International Relations* (New York: M. E. Sharpe, 2007).

Koesel, Karrie J., *Religion and Authoritarianism: Cooperation, Conflict, and the Consequences* (New York: Cambridge University Press, 2014).

Kösebalaban, Hasan, *Turkish Foreign Policy* (New York: Palgrave Macmillan, 2011).

Kostanick, Huey Louis, 'Turkish resettlement of refugees from Bulgaria, 1950–1953', *Middle East Journal*, 9, no. 1 (1955): 41–52.

Kreisberg, Seth, *Transforming Power* (Albany: State University of New York Press, 1992).

Kubálková, Vendulka, 'Towards an international political theology', *Millennium*, 29, no. 3 (2000): 675–704.

Kuru, Ahmet T., *Secularism and State Policies toward Religion: The United States, France, and Turkey* (Cambridge: Cambridge University Press, 2009).

Lam, Peng Er, 'Japan's quest for "soft power": attraction and limitation', *East Asia*, 24, no. 4 (2007): 349–63.

Lapid, Yosef and Friedrich V. Kratochwil (eds), *The Return of Culture and Identity in IR Theory* (Boulder: Rienner, 1996).

Levitsky, Steven and Lucan A. Way, *Competitive Authoritarianism: Hybrid Regimes After the Cold War* (Cambridge Cambridge University Press, 2010).

Lewis, Bernard, 'Some reflections on the decline of the Ottoman Empire', *Studia Islamica*, no. 9 (1958): 111–27.

Lim, Chaeyoon and Robert D. Putnam, 'Religion, social networks and life satisfaction', *American Sociological Review*, 75, no. 6 (2010): 914–33.

Lynch, Marc, 'Abandoning Iraq: Jordan's alliances and the politics of state identity', *Security Studies*, 8, no. 2–3 (1998): 347–88.

Malici, Akan, 'Germans as Venutians: The culture of German foreign policy behavior', *Foreign Policy Analysis*, 2, no. 1 (2006): 37–62.

Mandaville, Peter. *Global Political Islam* (Abingdon: Routledge, 2010).

Mandaville, Peter and Shadi Hamid, 'Islam as statecraft: How governments use religion in foreign policy', *Middle East* (November 2018).

Mansour, Imad, *Statecraft in the Middle East: Foreign Policy, Domestic Politics and Security* (London: I. B. Tauris, 2016).

Mardin, Şerif, *Religion and Social Change in Modern Turkey: The Case of Bediuzzaman Said Nursi* (Albany: State University of New York Press, 1989).

Mardin, Serif, *Religion, Society, and Modernity in Turkey* (New York Syracuse University Press, 2006).

Matsumura, Masahiro, 'The Japanese state identity as a grand strategic imperative', *St Andrews University Law Review*, 12 (2008): 53–6.

Mazower, Mark, *The Balkans: A Short History* (London: Phoenix, 2002).

Mead, Walter Russell, 'God's country?' *Dialog*, 47, no. 1 (2008): 5–15.

Mencutek, Zeynep Sahin, and Bahar Baser, 'Mobilizing diasporas: Insights from Turkey's attempts to reach Turkish citizens abroad', *Journal of Balkan and Near Eastern Studies*, 20, no. 1 (2018): 86–105.

Merdjanova, Ina, *Rediscovering the Umma: Muslims in the Balkans between Nationalism and Transnationalism* (Oxford: Oxford University Press, 2013).

Milner, Helen V., *Interests, Institutions, and Information: Domestic Politics and International Relations* (Princeton: Princeton University Press, 1997).

Mitzen, Jennifer, 'Ontological security in world politics: State identity and the security dilemma', *European Journal of InternationalRrelations*, 12, no. 3 (2006): 341–70.

Modood, Tariq, 'Moderate secularism, religion as identity and respect for religion', *Political Quarterly*, 81, no. 1 (2010): 8.

Morgenthau, Hans, *Politics Among Nations: The Struggle for Power and Peace* (New York: Knopf, 1960).

Müftüler-Bac, Meltem, *Turkey's Relations with a Changing Europe* (Manchester: Manchester University Press, 1997).

Nasr, Vali, *The Shia Revival: How Conflicts within Islam Will Shape the Future* (New York: W. W. Norton, 2007).

Nuroğlu, Elif and Hüseyin Nuroğlu, 'Balkanlarda Almanya ve Türkiye: İhracat ve Yatırımlar', *SETA Rapor* (2016).

Nye, Joseph S., 'The information revolution and American soft power', *Asia Pacific Review*, 9, no. 1 (2002): 60–76.

Nye, Joseph S., *Power in the Global Information Age: From Realism to Globalization* (London: Routledge, 2004).

Nye, Joseph S., *Soft Power: The Means to Success in World Politics* (New York: Public Affairs, 2004).

Nye, Joseph S., 'Get smart: Combining hard and soft power', *Foreign Affairs*, 88, no. 4 (2009): 160–63.

Oğuzlu, Tarik, 'Soft power in Turkish foreign policy', *Australian Journal of International Affairs*, 61, no. 1 (2007): 81–97.

Okyay, Aslı Selin, *Diaspora-Making as a State-Led Project: Turkey's Expansive Diaspora Strategy and Its Implications for Emigrant and Kin Populations*, Doctoral Dissertation, European University Institute, Florence, 2015.

Öniş, Ziya, 'Beyond the 2001 financial crisis: The political economy of the new phase of neo-liberal restructuring in Turkey', *Review of International Political Economy*, 16, no. 3 (2009): 409–32.

Öniş, Ziya, 'Turgut Özal and his economic legacy: Turkish neo-liberalism in critical perspective', *Middle Eastern Studies*, 40, no. 4 (2004): 113–34.

Önis, Ziya, 'The political economy of Islam and democracy in Turkey: From the Welfare Party to the AKP', in Dietrich Jung (ed.), *Democratization and Development* (New York: Palgrave Macmillan, 2006).

Oran, Baskın (ed.), *Türk Dış Politikası – Cilt 1 (1919–1980)* (Istanbul: İletişim Yayınları, 2002).

Özbudun, Ergun, 'AKP at the crossroads: Erdoğan's majoritarian drift', *South European Society and Politics*, 19, no. 2 (2014): 155–67.

Özel, Soli, 'Turkey at the polls: after the tsunami', *Journal of Democracy*, 14, no. 2 (2003): 80–94.

Ozkan, Behlül, 'Turkey, Davutoğlu and the idea of pan-Islamism', *Survival*, 56, no. 4 (2014): 119–40.

Özpek, Burak Bilgehan and Yelda Demirağ, 'The Davutoğlu effect in Turkish foreign policy: What if the bowstring is broken?' *Iran and the Caucasus*, 16, no. 1 (2012): 117–28.

Öztürk, Ahmet Erdi, 'The presidential election in Turkey: History and future expectations', *Contemporary Southeastern Europe*, 1, no. 2 (2014): 110–18.

Öztürk, Ahmet Erdi, 'Turkey's Diyanet under AKP rule: From protector to imposer of state ideology?' *Southeast European and Black Sea Studies*, 16, no. 4 (2016): 619–35.

Öztürk, Ahmet Erdi, 'Delectation or hegemony: Turkey's religious actors in South Eastern Europe and Central Asia', *Euxeinos*, 23 (2017): 15–24.

Öztürk, Ahmet Erdi, 'Transformation of the Turkish Diyanet both at home and abroad: Three stages', *European Journal of Turkish Studies. Social Sciences on Contemporary Turkey*, 27 (2018).

Öztürk, Ahmet Erdi, 'Lack of self-confidence of the authoritarian regimes and academic freedom: The case of İştar Gözaydın from Turkey', *European Political Science* (2018): 1–10.

Öztürk, Ahmet Erdi, 'An alternative reading of religion and authoritarianism: the new logic between religion and state in the AKP's New Turkey', *Southeast European and Black Sea Studies*, 19, no. 1 (2019): 79–98.

Öztürk, Ahmet Erdi. 'The ambivalent nature of the relations between Bulgaria and Turkey in the new millennium', in Mete Hatay and Zenonas Tziarras (eds), *Kinship and Diasporas in Turkish Foreign Policy* (Nicosia, Cyprus: PRIO, 2019), pp. 11–28.

Öztürk, Ahmet Erdi, and Samim Akgönül, 'Forced marriage or marriage of convenience with the Western Balkans?' In Florian Bieber and Nikolaos Tzifakis (eds), *The Western Balkans in the World: Linkages and Relations with Non-Western Countries* (Abingdon: Routledge, 2019).

Öztürk, Ahmet Erdi and İştar Gözaydın, 'Turkey's constitutional amendments: A critical perspective', *Research and Policy on Turkey*, 2, no. 2 (2017): 210–24.

Öztürk, Ahmet Erdi, and Istar Gözaydın, 'Turkey's draft constitutional amendments: A critical perspective', *Research and Policy on Turkey*, 2, no. 2 (2017): 210–24.

Öztürk, Ahmet Erdi, and İştar Gözaydın, 'A frame for Turkey's foreign policy via the Diyanet in the Balkans', *Journal of Muslims in Europe*, 7, no. 3 (2018): 331–50.

Öztürk, Ahmet Erdi, and Semiha Sözeri, 'Diyanet as a Turkish foreign policy tool: Evidence from the Netherlands and Bulgaria', *Politics and Religion*, 11, no. 3 (2018): 624–48.

Öztürk, Ahmet Erdi, and Hakkı Taş, 'The repertoire of extraterritorial repression: Diasporas and home states', *Migration Letters*, 17, no. 1 (2020): 59–69.

Öztürk, Bahar Baser, and Ahmet Erdi Öztürk, 'Turkey's diaspora governance policies and diasporas from Turkey in Germany: A critical reading of the changing dynamics', in Mete Hatay and Zenonas Tziarras (eds), *Kinship and Diasporas in Turkish Foreign Policy* (Nicosia, Cyprus: PRIO, 2019), pp. 29–45.

Paechter, Carrie, 'Researching sensitive issues online: implications of a hybrid insider/outsider position in a retrospective ethnographic study', *Qualitative Research*, 13, no. 1 (2013): 71–86.

Petkoff, Peter, 'Church–state relations under the Bulgarian Denominations Act 2002: Religious pluralism and established church and the impact of other models of law on religion', *Religion, State & Society*, 33, no. 4 (2005): 315–37.

Petrovic, Zarko and Dusan Reljic, 'Turkish interests and involvement in the Western Balkans: A score-card', *Insight Turkey*, 13, no. 3 (2011): 159–72.

Philpott, Anthony and Arang Keshavarzian, 'State building and religious resources: An institutional theory of church-state relations in Iran and Mexico', *Politics & Society*, 27, no. 3 (1999): 431–65.

Philpott, Daniel, 'The religious roots of modern international relations', *World Politics*, 52, no. 2 (2000): 206–45.

Philpott, Daniel, 'The challenge of September 11 to secularism in international relations', *World Politics*, 55, no. 2 (2002): 66–95.

Philpott, Daniel, 'Explaining the political ambivalence of religion', *American Political Science Review*, no. 101 (2007): 518.

Putnam, Robert D., 'Diplomacy and domestic politics: The logic of two-level games', *International Organization*, 42, no. 3 (1988): 427–60.

Quataert, Donald, *The Ottoman Empire, 1700–1922* (Cambridge: Cambridge University Press, 2005).

Rakel, Eva Patricia, 'Iranian foreign policy since the Iranian Islamic Revolution: 1979–2006', *Perspectives on Global Development and Technology*, 6, no. 1–3 (2007): 159–87.

Rodrik, Dani, 'Premature liberalization, incomplete stabilization: The Ozal decade in Turkey', *National Bureau of Economic Research Working Paper* no. 3300 (1990).

Rodrik, Dani, 'Ergenekon and Sledgehammer: Building or undermining the rule of law', *Turkish Political Quarterly*, 10, no. 1 (2011): 99–109.

Rumelili, Bahar and Jennifer Todd, 'Paradoxes of identity change: Integrating macro, meso, and micro research on identity in conflict processes', *Politics*, 38, no. 1 (2018): 3–18.

Saatçioğlu, Beken, 'De-Europeanisation in Turkey: The case of the rule of law', *South European Society and Politics*, 21, no. 1 (2016): 133–46.

Sakallioğlu, Ümit Cizre, 'Parameters and strategies of Islam–state interaction in Republican Turkey', *International Journal of Middle East Studies*, 28, no. 2 (1996): 231–51.

Sandal, Nukhet Ahu, 'Religious actors as epistemic communities in conflict transformation: The cases of South Africa and Northern Ireland', *Review of International Studies*, 37, no. 3 (2011): 929–49.

Sandal, Nukhet Ahu, *Religious Leaders and Conflict Transformation: Northern Ireland and Beyond* (Cambridge: Cambridge University Press, 2017).

Sandal, Nukhet Ahu and Jonathan Fox, *Religion in International Relations Theory: Interactions and Possibilities* (Oxfordshire: Routledge, 2015).

Schmitt, Carl, *Political Theology: Four Chapters on the Concept of Sovereignty* (Chicago: University of Chicago Press, 1985).

Seldin, Jeff, 'US official accuses Turkey of pushing extreme Islamist ideology', *Voanews*, 13 December 2017.

Shakir, Aziz Nazmi, 'Bulgaria', in Oliver Scharbrodt, Samim Akgönül, Ahmet Alibasic, Jorgen S. Nielsen and Egdünas Racious (eds), *Yearbook of Muslims in Europe*, Volume 9 (Leiden: Brill, 2017): 142–62.

Smart, Ninian, *The World's Religions: Old Traditions and Modern Transformations* (Cambridge: Cambridge University Press, 1989).

Somer, Murat and Evangelos G. Liaras, 'Turkey's new Kurdish opening: Religious versus secular values', *Middle East Policy*, 17, no. 2 (2010): 152–65.

Spasenovski, Aleksandar, 'Religious diversity and the Macedonian model of secularism', *Occasional Papers on Religion in Eastern Europe*, 35, no. 5 (2015): 2–8.

Stark, Rodney, 'Secularization R.I.P.', *Sociology of Religion*, 60, no. 3 (1999): 249–73.

Tachau, Frank and Metin Heper, 'The state, politics, and the military in Turkey', *Comparative Politics*, 16, no. 1 (1983): 17–33.

Tanasković, Darko, *Neoosmanizam-Povratak Turske na Balkan* (Belgrade: Službeni Glasnik, 2010).

Taylor, Charles, *A Secular Age* (Cambridge, MA: Harvard University Press, 2007).

Thomas, Scott, *The Global Resurgence of Religion and the Transformation of International Relations: The Struggle for the Soul of the Twenty-first Century* (New York: Palgrave Macmillan, 2005).

Todd, Jennifer, 'The politics of identity change and conflict: An agenda for research', *Politics*, 38, no. 1 (2018): 84–93.

Todorova, Maria, 'The Balkans: From discovery to invention', *Slavic Review*, 53, no. 2 (1994): 453–82.

Tsygankov, Andrei P., 'If not by tanks, then by banks? The role of soft power in Putin's foreign policy', *Europe-Asia Studies*, 58, no. 7 (2006): 1079–99.

Tugal, Cihan, *Passive Revolution: Absorbing the Islamic Challenge to Capitalism* (Stanford: Stanford University Press, 2009).

Tugal, Cihan, *The Fall of the Turkish Model: How the Arab Uprisings Brought Down Islamic Liberalism* (London: Verso Books, 2016).

Türbedar, Erhan, 'Turkey's new activism in the Western Balkans: Ambitions and obstacles', *Insight Turkey*, 13, no. 3 (2011), 139–58.

Türkeş, Ali Yaşar, 'The Democratic Party, 1946–1960', in Metin Heper and Micheal Landau (eds), *Political Parties and Democracy in Turkey* (London, I. B. Tauris, 1991).

Türkeş, Mustafa, 'The Balkan pact and its immediate implications for the Balkan states, 1930–34', *Middle Eastern Studies*, 30, no. 1 (1994): 123–44.

Turner, Bryan S., *The Religious and the Political: A Comparative Sociology of Religion* (Cambridge: Cambridge University Press, 2013).

Ünver, O. Can, 'Changing diaspora politics of Turkey and public diplomacy', *Turkish Policy Quarterly*, 12, no. 1 (2013): 181–9.

Vössing, Konstantin, 'Transforming public opinion about European integration: Elite influence and its limits', European Union *Politics*, 16, no. 2 (2015): 157–75.

Waltz, Kenneth N., *Theory of International Politics* (Reading: Waveland Press, 2010).

Watmough, Simon P., and Ahmet Erdi Öztürk, 'From "diaspora by design" to transnational political exile: The Gülen Movement in transition', *Politics, Religion & Ideology*, 19, no. 1 (2018): 33–52.

Watmough, Simon P., and Ahmet Erdi Öztürk, 'The future of the Gülen Movement in transnational political exile: Introduction to the special issue', *Politics, Religion & Ideology*, 19, no. 1 (2018): 1–10.

Wendt, Alexander, 'Collective identity formation and the international state', *American Political Science Review*, 88, no. 2 (1994): 384–96.

Wendt, Alexander, *Social Theory of International Politics* (Cambridge: Cambridge University Press, 1999).

Yavuz, Ahmet, 'The AKP and normalizing democracy in Turkey', *South Atlantic Quarterly*, 102, no. 2–3 (2003): 293–308.

Yavuz, M. Hakan, 'Turkish identity and foreign policy in flux: The rise of neo-Ottomanism', *Critique: Journal for Critical Studies of the Middle East*, 7, no. 12 (1998): 19–41.

Yavuz, M. Hakan, *Islamic Political Identity in Turkey* (Oxford University Press, 2003).

Yavuz, M. Hakan, and Ahmet Erdi Öztürk, 'Turkish secularism and Islam under the reign of Erdoğan', *Southeast European and Black Sea Studies*, 19, no.1 (2019): 1–9.

Yesilada, Birol and Barry Rubin (eds), *Islamization of Turkey under the AKP Rule* (London: Routledge, 2013).

Yıldız, Ahmet, 'Politico-religious discourse of political Islam in Turkey: The parties of national outlook', *The Muslim World*, 93, no. 2 (2003): 187–209.

Young, Antonia, 'Religion and society in present-day Albania', *Journal of Contemporary Religion*, 14, no. 1 (1999): 5–16.

Zürcher, Eric J., *Modern Turkey* (London: I. B. Tauris, 1993).

Zürcher, Eric, 'The Balkan wars and the refugee leadership of the early Turkish Republic', in M. Hakan Yauvuz and Isa Blimi İsa (eds), *War and Nationalism: The Balkan Wars, 1912–1913* (Salt Lake City: University of Utah Press, 2013).

INDEX